T4-AVF-604

POPE PIUS XII LIBRARY, ST. JOSEPH COL.

3 2528 09127 3435

EXPLORING VALUES
Through Literature, Multimedia, and Literacy Events

Making Connections

Patricia Ruggiano Schmidt
Le Moyne College
Syracuse, New York, USA

Ann Watts Pailliotet
Whitman College
Walla Walla, Washington, USA

Editors

INTERNATIONAL
Reading
Association

800 Barksdale Road, PO Box 8139
Newark, Delaware 19714-8139, USA
www.reading.org

IRA BOARD OF DIRECTORS

Donna M. Ogle, National-Louis University, Evanston, Illinois, *President* • Jerry L. Johns, Northern Illinois University, DeKalb, Illinois, *President-Elect* • Lesley Mandel Morrow, Rutgers University, New Brunswick, New Jersey, *Vice President* • Gregg M. Kurek, Bridgman Public Schools, Bridgman, Michigan • Jeanne R. Paratore, Boston University, Boston, Massachusetts • Lori L. Rog, Regina Public Schools, Regina, Saskatchewan • Susan B. Neuman, University of Michigan, Ann Arbor, Michigan • Rebecca L. Olness, Kent Public Schools, Kent, Washington • Doris Walker-Dalhouse, Minnesota State University Moorhead, Moorhead, Minnesota • Patricia L. Anders, University of Arizona, Tucson, Arizona • Timothy V. Rasinski, Kent State University, Kent, Ohio • Ann-Sofie Selin, Cygnaeus School, Åbo, Finland • Alan E. Farstrup, Executive Director

The International Reading Association attempts, through its publications, to provide a forum for a wide spectrum of opinions on reading. This policy permits divergent viewpoints without implying the endorsement of the Association.

Director of Publications   Joan M. Irwin
Editorial Director, Books and Special Projects   Matthew W. Baker
Senior Editor, Books and Special Projects   Tori Mello Bachman
Permissions Editor   Janet S. Parrack
Production Editor   Shannon Benner
Editorial Assistant   Tyanna L. Collins
Publications Manager   Beth Doughty
Production Department Manager   Iona Sauscermen
Supervisor, Electronic Publishing   Anette Schütz-Ruff
Senior Electronic Publishing Specialist   Cheryl J. Strum
Electronic Publishing Specialist   Lynn Harrison
Proofreader   Charlene M. Nichols

Project Editor   Shannon Benner

Art Credits   Cover Design, Linda Steere
                 Cover Photography (student images), Image Productions

Copyright 2001 by the International Reading Association, Inc.
All rights reserved. No part of this publication may be reproduced or transmitted in any form or by any means, electronic or mechanical, including photocopy, or any information storage and retrieval system, without permission from the publisher.

Library of Congress Cataloging-in-Publication Data
Exploring values through literature, multimedia, and literacy events : making connections / Patricia Ruggiano Schmidt, Ann Watts Pailliotet, editors.
    p.   cm.
Includes bibliographical references and index.
ISBN 0-87207-297-5
1. Moral education—United States.   2. Language Arts—United States.   I. Schmidt, Patricia Ruggiano, 1944–   II. Pailliotet, Ann Watts.   III. International Reading Association.
LC311 .E96   2001
370.11'4—dc21   2001002885

Dedication

Le Moyne College Values Program, Syracuse, New York
Rev. Donald J. Kirby, S.J., Director

The Values Program at Le Moyne College encourages the exploration of values
by inspiring the learning community to ask difficult questions and
search for complex answers.

Contents

Foreword

When Patricia Ruggiano Schmidt and Ann Watts Pailliotet first talked with me about this book, our discussion quickened my heart! It reaffirmed and rekindled my hope that within this supercharged, high-tech era of standards and benchmarks and state and national testing, there are still compelling voices for values in literacy education. Indeed, it often seems that our educational system is driven by calls for academic achievement at all costs, and that teachers often are challenged by parents and community when they encourage and assist students in the identification of core values that are held by individuals and communities.

It was only recently, as I vacationed in Belize—a small, beautiful, economically poor country in Central America—that I found myself wondering about the educational system in the United States. This reflection was sparked by a tour a few days after my arrival. I and my fellow travelers visited Hopkins, a village in southern Belize that is inhabited by the Garifuna people, who trace their ancestry back to the Caribs and Africans in the mid-1600s. During our visit to this community, we were welcomed with exuberance by both children and adults and later by the children's compelling performance of original poetry, essays, song, and dance. As they spoke, the children demonstrated precise articulation in two languages—English and Garifuna. They were eager to share their stories with us. We were impressed with their knowledge of their history, values, and culture. The teachers described the strong family and community ties that have drawn the people together both historically and in present times. Interestingly, the literacy rate in this country is about 85%. Many of the children go on to college, either in their country or the United States, and become teachers, physicians, and business leaders. During our visit, a physician who grew up in this village but now lives in the United States proudly interacted with the children and joined in the singing of their national anthem.

I began to understand much about the education system in this village and more broadly, perhaps, in Belize. It is not underwritten by personal or collective wealth from within the country or the community. Nor are there many computers or other electronic tools to enhance and support students' learning. Even so, the students are readers and writers, they are knowledgeable about their history and traditions, and they value personal interactions, family, and community. My conversation with some of the teachers, the physician, and our Belizian tour guide supported and affirmed this observation. At the end of our visit, it was quite clear that the values and traditions that the children demonstrated are an integral part of their education and a part of their common wealth.

Of course, the social, political, cultural, and economic differences between the United States and Belize are enormous. My experience in Belize, however, kindled in me a desire to see U.S. classrooms become alive with learning experiences that touch the lives of students and create a sense of community. *Exploring Values Through Literature, Multimedia, and Literacy Events: Making Connections* contains many treasures—practices that hold promises for these types of classrooms to exist.

Schmidt and Pailliotet are to be commended for raising critical questions about the directions in which our schools are taking our children. For example, How do we sort out what we value and care about in our school and home communities? What responsibility does the school have in facilitating the acquisition of values necessary to live in our communities and the ever-changing world? I firmly believe that all citizens must be able to answer these questions, but it is educators—researchers, teacher educators, classroom teachers, and teacher assistants—who must be proactive in providing the answers and assuming the responsibility for the return of values to our school community. In other words, educators must not be neutral. They must lead, not follow, and make the connection between values and education. Schmidt and Pailliotet underscore this point and argue against teacher neutrality. As they note in the Introduction, "When people take the neutral or objective stance, they distance themselves from knowing."

Most educators acknowledge that a set of core values is common to all citizens of the United States. Few would argue, for example, that courage, honesty, peace, and justice are core values to which most of these citizens ascribe. But we are a multicultural society with diverse backgrounds and histories both within the United States and in foreign lands. Where one group holds communal sharing and interaction as a core value, another might value individual introspection and reflection above all else. Therefore, educators must first help students recognize that others may hold values both similar to and different from their own, and then guide them to respect the right of others to hold these values, even when a conflict in values exists.

As noted in several chapters in this book, literature serves an important function in our society and in schools. Children share their reality about themselves and others based on much of what they read. Students' attitudes, values, and beliefs are influenced by children's literature, and it is the means by which all children come to understand the stories of others. The authors in this text impart information that helps educators effectively use literature as a catalyst for teaching values and character education. Moreover, the chapters highlight a range of specific approaches that have proved successful in the classroom and schoolwide to offer teachers realistic and workable examples.

As we begin our journey into the 21st century, children have access to mass media, technology, and software in their schools and homes. Although there is some degree of inequality of access, these tools can facilitate academic learning for many students. They also transmit values with their implicit and explicit messages. The technology and their tools provide literacy educators and their students the opportunity to become critical analysts— to engage in meaningful dialogue about the values that are transmitted and how and if they can and should be incorporated into the curriculum. Significantly, several authors in this text call for the need to view the new technology and visual/digital literacy with a critical eye.

Unlike Belize, the United States is an economically wealthy country. This wealth has provided unparalleled educational opportunities for most of our citizens. But have we created the level of success that produces a caring community of learners who have the tools to be successful both cognitively and affectively? The wonderful editors and authors in this book respond in chorus with a resounding NOT YET! When we experience drive-by shootings and violence in our schools, all citizens know that we are not yet there. The small country of Belize and the village of Hopkins seem to understand the importance of the deeper values that impact our lives—values that should become an integral part of our educational system. Literacy educators are in a strategic position to lead this return to values. Patricia Ruggiano Schmidt and Ann Watts Pailliotet and the other contributors to *Exploring Values Through Literature, Multimedia, and Literacy Events: Making Connections* have provided an invaluable tool that can serve as a catalyst to lead the way.

Barbara J. Diamond
Eastern Michigan University
Ypsilanti, Michigan, USA

Acknowledgments

We cannot forget to be grateful to all those who helped us with the creation and development of this project during the last 4 years. We must thank our colleagues at Le Moyne College and Whitman College who encouraged us to go forward with this work. We must thank our dear families and friends who commented constructively along the way. And finally, we must thank Joan Irwin, Matt Baker, and Shannon Benner of the International Reading Association for their professional critiques and enthusiastic guidance.

Contributors

Elizabeth A. Baker
Assistant Professor
Literacy Education
University of Missouri
Columbia, Missouri, USA

Matthew L. Davidson
Research Associate
Mendelson Center for Sport,
    Character & Culture
University of Notre Dame
Notre Dame, Indiana, USA

Cynthia Benton DeCorse
Associate Professor and Chair
Department of Education
State University of New York,
    College at Cortland
Cortland, New York, USA

Patricia A. Edwards
Professor of Language and
    Literacy/Principal Investigator for the
    Center for the Improvement of Early
    Reading Achievement (CIERA)
Michigan State University
East Lansing, Michigan, USA

Deborah Hopkinson
Children's Author/Director of Grants
    and Advancement Services
Whitman College
Walla Walla, Washington, USA

Jane Kurtz
Children's Author/Senior Lecturer
University of North Dakota
Grand Forks, North Dakota, USA

Brigette B. Laier
Doctoral Student in Teacher Education
Michigan State University
East Lansing, Michigan, USA

Cathy Leogrande
Assistant Professor of Education
Le Moyne College
Syracuse, New York, USA

Gwendolyn T. McMillon
Assistant Professor of Literacy
Oakland University
Rochester, Michigan, USA

Ann Watts Pailliotet
Associate Professor of Education
Whitman College
Walla Walla, Washington, USA

Patricia Ruggiano Schmidt
Associate Professor of Literacy
    and Elementary Education
Le Moyne College
Syracuse, New York, USA

Ladislaus M. Semali
Associate Professor of Education
The Pennsylvania State University
University Park, Pennsylvania, USA

Michelle Refvik Shaul
Library Media Specialist
Berney Elementary School
Walla Walla School District
Walla Walla, Washington, USA

Jennifer D. Turner
Spencer Research Training Grant Fellow
Center for the Improvement of Early
    Reading Achievement (CIERA)
Michigan State University
East Lansing, Michigan, USA

Shelley Hong Xu
Assistant Professor
College of Education
Texas Tech University
Lubbock, Texas, USA

Introduction

Patricia Ruggiano Schmidt and Ann Watts Pailliotet

Now you know that in every enterprise the beginning is the main thing, especially in dealing with the young and tender nature. For at that time it is most plastic, and the stamp sinks in the deepest.... Shall we then quite lightly give license for our children to hear any chance fables imagined by any chance people, and receive in their souls impressions opposed to those which, when they have come to maturity, we shall think they ought to possess? (Plato, trans. 1968, pp. 54–55)

As we consider Plato's question from *The Republic*, we wonder about the effects of the information explosion on our children's hearts, minds, and behaviors. The daily bombardment from the media connects us with people and places around the world that were never imagined in previous times. We hear and see words and images that invade our lives, we electronically join people like us who are attempting to make meaning from extraordinary events, and we think about personal values and family values. We consider the violence committed by alienated children and merciless adults, and we wonder if these national and international events influence our own behaviors. Consequently, we find ourselves raising questions whose answers seemed clear to previous generations:

What do we care about?

What do we value personally?

Do we have guiding principles that help us assess what we see, hear, and feel?

How do we make ethical decisions?

What do we value in our community?

What do we value on a national level?

What do we value internationally?

Where do we learn—and how do we learn—the values necessary to live in our world?

Those who study these questions present data that increase our concerns about children's exposure to various kinds of values. For instance, the recent Annenberg Report finds that U.S. children spend 5.5 hours a day engaged with

1

various mass media outside of classrooms, including watching films and videos, working with computers, surfing the Web, communicating through networks, and playing video games (see PBS Adult Learning Service, 1999). This also includes children's exposure to magazines, billboards, books, comics, music, the radio, and cultural events of daily life.

The Center for Media Literacy (see http://www.medialit.org) estimates that the average person in the United States is exposed to more than 400 commercial images every day. Interactions with mass media make up, by far, the largest leisure activity in the United States (Buckingham, 1993). Although scholars disagree about the designs of large-scale media impact studies, recent findings link media exposure to profound social outcomes, including eating disorders, obesity, violence, limited attention spans, materialism, body image, sexual identity, risk-taking behaviors, substance abuse, and even epileptic seizures. Despite differences among interpretations of media studies, there is general agreement that television and other media forms are powerful sources of social learning that shape attitudes, social and consumer behaviors, and people's world views (Luke, 1999).

This information and recurring news stories related particularly to school violence startled us, the contributors to this book. We are literacy teachers, teacher educators, and authors of literature for children and young adults, and we believe there is a need to bring the explicit study of values into classrooms and schools to help our young people function more effectively in their communities, the nation, and the world. Our question before writing our chapters was, "Can we have a cohesive community that espouses common values in a pluralistic democratic society?" Our answer now is, "Yes, it is possible." We believe we are all connected in this world and that people need only to agree on basic human values, such as caring about others, respecting individual differences, sharing ideas and possessions, and acting in responsible ways. These are the ingredients necessary for building cooperation and collaboration in the formation of a cohesive community. Furthermore, we believe that the very act of exploring different values will help us understand each other, and therefore will enable us to begin to develop a community that shares and cares in responsible and respectful ways.

From Explicit Instruction to Clarification

We understand that values education is a controversial topic. The mere mention of "values" can create instant debate in almost any public forum. This section includes a brief history of values instruction in public schools to help readers appreciate the authors' ideas about the exploration of values.

Traditionally, U.S. schools have served as places to teach values that build strong moral individuals who contribute to the "common good." Teachers were expected to plan lessons and instruct children about the Ten Commandments; these values were accepted as truth in the dominant white culture until recent history (Ayers, 1998; Dewey, 1909/1975; Lickona, 1991; Miller, 1995). It was believed that these teachings would prepare citizens for a democratic society.

During the last 40 years, the Civil Rights movement— as well as the continuous flow of refugees who have escaped social, economic, and political upheaval around the world—made teachers aware of pluralism in the United States (Diamond & Moore, 1995; Noddings, 1992). Teachers realized the need to understand the diverse ethnic and cultural backgrounds of the students and their families. They began the study of "values clarification," a method that facilitated student discussions about values while the teacher maintained an objective or neutral stance (Simon, Howe, & Kirschenbaum, 1972). Students had opportunities to express their ideas, but particular values were neither praised nor condemned. Consequently, this method led to a key question: Whose values are the accepted norms of society?

Rather than answer this question, educators simply began to ignore the study of values. This appeared to be a logical direction that prevented treading on the family values of children from minority backgrounds (Schmidt, 1998). However, this strategy ignored Plato's warning. Teachers who maintained a neutral stance or neglected the study of values were leaving children's learning to chance.

Since the 1960s, neutrality or objectivity about values has spread to publishers of education materials. To ensure that no reader is offended, books have been designed to report only known facts. There is little or no interpretation related to human consequences. For instance, in some texts, The Holocaust is presented as an event in human history with little discussion about its impact on those involved and the rest of the world. In other texts, the destruction of rainforests is reported, but with little explanation of the potential repercussions. In fact, those who study this textbook phenomenon explain that when schools, classrooms, and educational materials maintain neutrality or objectivity, they are implicitly teaching values (Ayers, 1998; Hakim & Blake, 1996).

We believe that when people take the neutral or objective stance, they distance themselves from knowing. As Parker Palmer states in his book *The Courage to Teach* (1998), "Objectivism is morally deforming and often untrue...the shape of great knowing is intimacy and compassion...great teachers attempt to draw their students into passionate engagement" (p. 54).

Connecting Values for Classroom Community

The authors of this collection believe that students should have opportunities to explore values through reading, writing, listening, speaking, and viewing. Students should learn about compassion, human decency, caring, sharing, cooperation, respect, responsibility, and an appreciation for cultural differences. We believe these are values that can be explored and learned through literature, multimedia, and literacy events and will facilitate the building of classroom and school communities that connect home and school for literacy learning (Kilpatrick, 1993; Myers & Myers, 1999).

Through literature, children can discover diverse populations and learn about the moral power of stories (Diamond & Moore, 1995; Kilpatrick 1993; Myers & Myers, 1999). Through critical analysis of multimedia, children can discover the values portrayed and interpret significance (Pailliotet, Semali, Rodenberg, Giles, & Macaul, 2000). Through literacy events that incorporate democratic classroom procedures, children can learn about cooperative and collaborative learning (Ayers, 1998; Berkowitz, 1998; Lickona, 1991; Watson, Solomon, Dasho, Schwartz, & Kendzior, 1994). They will see firsthand what it means to care and share, and to be respectful and responsible. Finally, through all these experiences, we hope children will learn that human decency is not optional, but an essential ingredient in society (White, 1996).

The authors in this book also believe that global learning should be a major emphasis in the exploration of values. This is a complex process because of shifting populations and global concerns. We believe that one's cultural values do not provide the only truths, and that respect for others does not mean agreement. Therefore, controversial issues need to be discussed openly across content areas, and decision-making skills should be practiced (Noddings, 1994).

Educators around the United States are beginning to introduce values in classrooms and schools through programs that explore global values related to caring for humanity and our planet (Coles & Genevie, 1990; Noddings, 1994). They are promoting classroom and school communities through an appreciation of diversity (Diamond & Moore, 1995; Schmidt, 1998). They realize that they have the power to help children learn to care, share, take responsibility, and respect others through the modeling process (Greene, 1995; Noddings, 1994). We understand that this is not an easy assignment, but that the exploration of literature and multimedia, as well as participation in literacy events, are important ingredients for developing a cohesive community that not only promotes the language arts, but also promotes students' choice, cooperative learning, inquiry, and critical thinking.

Making Connections

This book describes the work of educators and children, and the materials and strategies they use in classrooms, to explore values. We believe that the exploration of values is not a mysterious process that should be left to chance. We also realize that many educators are already helping their children explore values; for those, this book will be affirming and add many useful ideas. For teachers who want to learn more about the process of exploring values, this book will explain activities to bring to classrooms and schools right away.

The book is divided into five sections, each focused on a context in which we may explore our own values and make connections with others: Student-Teacher Connections, Home-School Connections, Content Area Connections, Schoolwide Connections, and Global Connections. The first two sections reflect our belief that the successful exploration of values depends on teachers' abilities to connect with students, families, and communities. Next, the text examines connections with values and content area teaching and learning in classrooms and schools. We believe that the methods and strategies used to teach academics across the curriculum clearly demonstrate the promotion of certain values. Additionally, the text presents ways of connecting with people and their values around the world. We believe that teachers must prepare our students for the global village and the diverse groups of people they will be living and working with during their lifetimes. Our young people need to learn about differing values—ones that we question, ones that divide us, and ones that unite us.

Barbara J. Diamond, teacher educator and coauthor of *Multicultural Literacy: Mirroring the Reality of the Classroom* (1995), has set the stage for this text with her questions concerning the education system in the United States. Her reflections about a recent visit to Belize emphasize the important connection between education and children's moral development.

In Chapter 1, Cynthia Benton DeCorse, teacher educator, lays the foundation for the text by connecting theory and practice related to children's moral development. She explains the use of literature and literacy events at various stages of moral development.

In Chapter 2, Ann Watts Pailliotet, literacy teacher educator, presents the 5 Ws of media literacy to help teachers and students become critical viewers who can explicate the values promoted in literature, multimedia, and literacy events.

In Chapter 3, Shelley Hong Xu, literacy teacher educator, describes classrooms in which teaching assistants make a significant contribution to the exploration of family values by connecting home and school with the model known as the ABCs of Cultural Understanding and Communication.

In Chapter 4, Brigette B. Laier, Patricia A. Edwards, Gwendolyn T. McMillon, and Jennifer D. Turner, reading teachers and literacy teacher educators, connect family values with school values through multicultural literacy and literacy events.

In Chapter 5, Cathy Leogrande, teacher educator, analyzes literacy software and warns readers about the problems and possibilities of using these materials at home and school.

In Chapter 6, Deborah Hopkinson, author of literature for children and young adults, presents literature and literacy events that can be used effectively across the curriculum to teach children about the moral power of stories.

In Chapter 7, Elizabeth A. Baker, literacy teacher educator, studies a classroom in which technology promoted classroom community through caring, sharing, respect, and responsibility.

In Chapter 8, Patricia Ruggiano Schmidt, reading teacher and literacy teacher educator, describes the responses of six children in a classroom in which inquiry learning resulted in numerous opportunities for literacy learning while promoting caring, sharing, respect, and responsibility.

In Chapter 9, Matthew L. Davidson, teacher educator, presents successful schoolwide programs based on the exploration of values through literature, multimedia, and literacy events.

In Chapter 10, Jane Kurtz, author of literature for children and young adults, shows that literature from around the world can promote the study of diversity and an appreciation for universal values.

In Chapter 11, Ann Watts Pailliotet, literacy teacher educator, and Michelle Refvik Shaul, elementary school media specialist, present magical tales from around the world and literacy events that demonstrate the moral power of stories.

The Conclusion, written by Ladislaus M. Semali, cultural studies and media literacy teacher educator, provides a summary of the book's exploration of values, an analysis of ideas from the chapters, and thoughtful questions for present and future teachers to consider as their students respond to literature, multimedia, and literacy events.

Many of the chapters end with annotated bibliographies, lists of resources and references, and Web sites related to the contents. These will provide readers with information for extending and applying ideas from the text.

Conclusion

Like Plato, we think that teaching and learning about values is not an endeavor that we should "lightly give license" to in our own democratic republic and increasingly global world. Plato notes, "the beginning is the main thing," and we hope that this text may enable educational participants to connect with each other and explore values through literature, multimedia, and literacy events.

References

Ayers, W. (Ed.). (1998). *Teaching for social justice: A democracy and education reader.* New York: New Press.

Berkowitz, M.W. (1998). Finding common ground to study and implement character education: Integrating structure and content in moral education. *Journal of Research in Education, 8*(1), 3–8.

Buckingham, D. (1993). Introduction: Young people and the media. In D. Buckingham (Ed.), *Reading audiences: Young people and the media* (pp. 1–23). Manchester, UK: Manchester University Press.

Coles, R., & Genevie, L. (1990). The moral life of America's schoolchildren. *Teacher Magazine, 1*(6), 42–49.

Dewey, J. (1975). *Moral principles in education.* Carbondale, IL: Southern Illinois University Press. (Original work published 1909)

Diamond, B.J., & Moore, M.A. (1995). *Multicultural literacy: Mirroring the reality of the classroom.* White Plains, NY: Longman.

Greene, M. (1995). *Releasing the imagination: Essays on education, the arts, and social change.* San Francisco: Jossey-Bass.

Hakim, J., & Blake, R.F. (1996). Should textbooks be trashed? *Learning, 25*(1), 38–39.

Kilpatrick, W. (1993). The moral power of good stories. *American Educator, 17*(2), 24–30.

Lickona, T. (1991). *Educating for character: How our schools teach respect and responsibility.* New York: Bantam.

Luke, C. (1999). Media and cultural studies in Australia. *Journal of Adolescent & Adult Literacy, 42,* 622–626.

Miller, R. (Ed.). (1995). *Educational freedom for a democratic society: A critique of national standards, goals, and curriculum.* Brandon, VT: Resource Center for Redesigning Education.

Myers, B.K., & Myers, M.E. (1999). Engaging children's spirit and spirituality through literature. *Childhood Education, 76*(1), 28–32.

Noddings, N. (1992). *The challenge to care in schools: An alternative approach to education.* New York: Teachers College Press.

Noddings, N. (1994). Conversation as moral education. *Journal of Moral Education, 23,* 107–118.

Pailliotet, A.W., Semali, L.M., Rodenberg, R.K., Giles, J.K., & Macaul, S.L. (2000). Intermediality: Bridge to critical media literacy. *The Reading Teacher, 54,* 208–219.

Palmer, P. (1998). *The courage to teach: Exploring the inner landscape of a teacher's life.* San Francisco: Jossey-Bass.

Plato. (1968). The republic. In A. Bloom (Trans.), *The republic of Plato* (Translated with notes and an interpretive essay). New York: Basic Books.

PBS Adult Learning Service. (1999). *Scanning television* [video]. Alexandria, VA: Face to Face Media Ltd.

Schmidt, P.R. (1998). *Cultural conflict and struggle: Literacy learning in a kindergarten program.* New York: Peter Lang.

Simon, S., Howe, L.W., & Kirschenbaum, H. (1972). *Values clarification: A handbook of practical strategies for teachers and students.* New York: Hart Publishing.

Watson, M.S., Solomon, D., Dasho, S., Schwartz, P., & Kendzior, S. (1994). Child development project cooperative learning: Working together to construct social, ethical, and intellectual understanding. In S. Sharan (Ed.), *Handbook of cooperative learning methods* (pp. 137–156). Westport, CT: Greenwood.

White, P. (1996). *Civic virtues and public schooling.* New York: Teachers College Press.

Student-Teacher Connections

This section highlights student-teacher connections as the basis for an exploration of values through literature, multimedia, and literacy events. First, teachers must understand child development and cognitive theories in order to use literacy learning to explore values. Furthermore, students tend to make connections with teachers who take the time to know their individual strengths and needs. These caring teachers demonstrate a respect for differences and make opportunities for teaching and learning. They also help their students become critical readers, writers, listeners, speakers, and viewers.

Chapter 1

Children Reading Meaning in Their Stories and Lives: Connecting With Student Response

Cynthia Benton DeCorse

S tudents' ability to process, absorb, and express meaning is determined by their unique ways of assigning value—to objects, or ideas, or stories. It is important for teachers to understand ways to help students make meaning in the contexts of their lives. We must understand what they are capable of achieving and the values they hold, and based on that understanding, we must help them establish a common core of values for decision making. Instruction in values can be controversial, but knowing the accepted range of ways that students process meaning (including values) has become commonly accepted as a desirable goal of basic education (Black, 1996; Ellenwood & McLaren, 1994). How this might be accomplished in the context of diverse educational theories and literacy learning in the classroom is the purpose of this chapter.

Making Meaning: Cognitive Theories and Child Development

What can children understand? How do children at different ages comprehend values, especially those related to literacy comprehension? Robert Coles (1989) recounts a conversation with a dying child who asked a deep question about the meaning of life. Coles responded by asking the student what *he* thought. The boy replied, "If you would tell me what you think, then I could answer better" (p. 32). In other words, if the child could understand the teacher's view of the world, it would be easier to define the struggle of thinking and constructing meaning in his own life. To build knowledge, a child must have building blocks—an understanding of the way things might be, or the way they are for others. Perhaps most important, children need to see models.

Providing models, according to William Kilpatrick (1992), is simple—read stories to children that help them understand life. Seeing heroes as models through stories gives children a sense of something higher than themselves. These models become a desired goal, an example of what to do (moral behavior) and why we do it (moral reasoning). Stories are a way to transmit values and meaning to a generation that may have too few chances to experience or witness such values. Kilpatrick's writing defines the value of good stories. We can identify with courage and virtue; they create a desire to do good. They transmit values and wisdom. One of our concerns is how children interpret these stories and how they make sense of events.

To understand children's ability to process stories, we need to understand how they reason. Part of John Dewey's (1910) contribution to education was explaining why children learn best by doing. Jean Piaget (1963) expanded on Dewey's ideas, and together their theories defined *constructivist* thinking. Constructivism assumes an innate desire to find order, structure, and pre-dictability in life. Children need to actively construct meaning to learn. They interpret new ideas in the context of existing knowledge, and understanding is acquired when students act on learning—elaborating, questioning, recon-structing what they know in light of what is being presented to them. Students create meaning from stories by applying their own ideas to them. Piaget defines this as *schema*, or personal patterns of meaning making.

According to constructivism and other developmental theories, all humans at certain ages progress through predictable changes in their way of thinking. Piaget defined the stages of growth as follows: *sensorimotor* (infancy), in which learning is achieved through touch and movement; *preoperations* (ages 2–7), in which children use speech but logical reasoning is impeded because children are egocentric in their approach, center on single perceptions at a time, and cannot reverse their construction of events; *concrete operations* (ages 7–11), in which children can do logical reasoning tasks but need concrete objects and exam-ples to develop this reasoning; and finally, *formal operations* (ages 12–adult), in which children are able to do hypothetical-deductive reasoning ("if...then..." thinking).

The implications of developmental theory are critical for literacy learning. If children are preoperational, they will understand an event by the perceptual characteristics it represents. For concrete operational children, understanding events means applying concrete experiences students have had in the past. If they have had little or no experience with concepts, they will be superficial or incorrect in interpreting story events. For children capable of formal operations, their abilities in reading can include projection, metaphor, and hypothetical concepts.

Piaget also described a moral reasoning model. For children under the age of 10 or so, he used the term *morality of constraint*, or *moral realism*. In this stage, children perceive that rules are imposed by authority figures, are unchange-able, and must be obeyed. The seriousness of an infraction determines the level of punishment the children feel is just. After age 10 or so, the *morality of coop-*

eration is applied, in which children perceive that rules are determined by consensus and are changeable. In this phase, children consider both the intent and the seriousness of an infraction to determine the appropriateness of the punishment.

Meaning and moral judgment are interpreted differently by children at different stages. A younger child may feel that wrongdoing should simply be punished, as opposed to an older child who believes it is necessary to know the circumstances surrounding an event to understand the necessary outcome. For younger children, what happens is of most importance. For older children, explaining *why* something occurred carries greater weight than simply the incident's details.

A child's analysis of characters in a story may reveal both moral and intellectual development. The definition of character may be a person or a story, a value (a characteristic), or a personal attribute that can be developed or changed. As children gain in intellectual abilities, their analysis of character turns from a simple description of who the person is and what the person did to how and why the individual and events emerge.

Wittrock (1982) provides another analysis of the different ways children approach and interpret characters, events, and each other. His research shows that the transfer of information learned in school is not always used in actual tasks. Teachers can encourage students to apply information from their reasoning by encouraging them to partake in a more thorough investigation of character and plot, to practice, and to project about when and where their reasoning should be used. Teachers exercise this ability when they use participatory discussion and integration of different kinds of reading materials to illustrate challenges to characters and their development.

Recent studies have shown that understanding is limited by students' developmental differences, in addition to their reading comprehension (Narvaez, Gleason, Mitchell, & Bentley, 1999). To understand the importance of recognizing a child's developmental level and reading comprehension, and how these two factors combine to determine comprehension and moral reasoning, try the exercise described in Figure 1.

Social Development and Moral Reasoning

According to Piaget and Vygotsky (1962), social interaction with adults and peers is an important factor in a child's development. Vygotsky's social cognition theory places social interaction in a critically central position to learning. He considers social interaction a major component of cognition, with language development determined essentially by the social context of the

FIGURE 1   Assessing Developmental Levels Using a Fable

Activity: Children at different ages interpret a story uniquely. For instance, to assess children's thinking, read Aesop's fable *The Lion and the Mouse* (below). After reading the story, ask children, "What do you think this story means?" For each of the stages—preoperational (kindergarten through second grade), concrete operational (second grade through seventh grade), formal operational (high school age)—different responses can be expected. Note the differences in responses based on the age/development of your students.

The Lion and the Mouse

One day a great lion lay asleep in the sunshine. A little mouse ran across his paw and wakened him. The great lion was just going to eat him up when the little mouse cried, "Oh, please, let me go, sir. Some day I may help you." The lion laughed at the thought that the little mouse could be of any use to him. But he was a good-natured lion, and he set the mouse free.

Not long after, the lion was caught in a net. He tugged and pulled with all his might, but the ropes were too strong. Then he roared loudly. The little mouse heard him, and ran to the spot.

"Be still, dear Lion, and I will set you free. I will gnaw the ropes." With his sharp little teeth, the mouse cut the ropes, and the lion came out of the net.

"You laughed at me once," said the mouse. "You thought I was too little to do you a good turn. But see, you owe your life to a poor little mouse."

Moral of the Story: Compassion lies within the power of both the mighty and the meek. Kindness is not a feeble virtue. (cited in Bennett, 1993)

The student's level of interpretation is important to processing the story. Is the child focused on literal or egocentric interpretations of the story, or can the child project moral implications that are hypothetical and applicable to his or her own life? For instance, a young child might respond, "The lion didn't like the mouse, because he was small, like me." Higher levels of reasoning are demonstrated in this response: "This is like taking care of the environment; we should plant and take care of trees, because trees make clean air for us."

child. Children's culture determines learning experience; because language is a critical part of culture, it has a great influence on learning. To Vygotsky, the act of reading and using stories as models is a defining event for children's growth, both in spoken language and in cognitive growth. For instance, a teacher might introduce a fable or story in a reading lesson and then ask children to discuss the story, draw a picture, or tell an original story to each other, indicating how they would act in such a situation. Cognitive growth, in combination with moral reasoning, is critical to understanding children's processing of literacy learning.

Research in moral development has provided differing views of children's understanding of moral judgment (Gilligan & Attanucci, 1988; Kohlberg, 1981). Lawrence Kohlberg's theory of moral development provides us with a way to think about individual decision making and meaning making. His method was to introduce a moral dilemma and then study the choices children made in their actions, noting their justification of right and wrong. In addition to noting the decisions children made in choosing right or wrong, Kohlberg was especially interested in how they reasoned about their actions. For instance, in Figure 2, Eddy's dilemma may demonstrate the reasons for actions.

Kohlberg classified the ways we reason into six stages, each with two divisions. First, *preconventional morality* (until about age 10) is described as the ethics of egocentricity—a child interprets right and wrong to be about what would or should happen to him or her. In the first part of this level, children are most concerned about avoiding punishment, and the consequences of an act determine if it is good or bad. The second part of preconventional morality is defined by seeking rewards—a child wants to know what the consequences are for him- or herself.

The next level, *conventional morality*, or the ethics of others, can be expected of adolescents. In the early part of this level, the adolescent seeks approval and avoids disapproval; the goal is to be a nice boy or girl. The later part emphasizes conformity to society's rules; the law is the central focus of determining what is right and wrong.

The highest level of moral reasoning, what Kohlberg called *postconventional morality*, is most typically expected of adults; it is an ethic of principle. The first part of this level consists of the social contract—principles accepted by the community determine the right course to take. The second level is personal ethics or equity, in which decisions of right and wrong are based on individual conscience. It is important to note that in this theory anyone is ca-

FIGURE 2   A Moral Dilemma and Sample Student Responses

Eddy is walking to the store. It is his mother's birthday on Saturday. He is feeling bad because he has not been able to save up enough money to get her the present he would like to give her. Then, on the sidewalk, he finds a wallet with $10 in it—just what he needs to buy the present. But there is an identification card in the wallet telling the name and address of the owner.

What should Eddy do?

1. Return the money because that would be a good deed, and then he would not have a guilty conscience.

2. Return the wallet because the owner would miss the money. If I lost some money I would want someone to return it to me.

3. Return the money because stealing is against the law.

4. Return it because if anyone found out that he kept the money, he would get in trouble. His mother would punish him for lying. Anyway, keeping money that did not belong to him would be like stealing. Someone might tell the police.

Source: Kohlberg (1963)

pable of any level of moral reasoning. Adults do not necessarily reason at higher levels, and children can reason using a social contract perspective.

An alternative to Kohlberg's theory was proposed by Gilligan and Attanucci (1988). They believed Kohlberg's model was focused on concepts of justice and did not accurately reflect the way moral reasoning develops for girls and women. They introduced an *ethics of care*, in which the individual considers the feelings and outcomes for others before her own benefits or consequences. The individual progresses from self-interest toward principles of responsibility and care for all people.

Both an ethics of care theory and justice theory appear to be applied in recent studies that show boys and girls alike adopt a care orientation in addition to a justice orientation in relation to situations of moral reasoning (Garrod, Beal, & Shin, 1990). One implication of the 1990 study is the capacity of using moral attributes of stories such as "The Boy Who Cried Wolf" or "How Many Days to America?" to illustrate the choices and consequences of life decisions.

Like Gilligan and Attanucci's emphasis on the other rather than the self, Selman's (1981) research establishes perspective taking as a critical element in literacy learning. He documents children's development in the ability to imagine what other people are thinking and feeling. Stages in perspective taking are similar to cognitive and moral development: a gradual move from concern about the self to concern about others. Children's perspective progresses from undifferentiated understanding of others' views to knowing that others may have access to different information. In the middle elementary grades, children become self-reflective, developing the ability to "walk a mile in another's shoes." Then they begin to see situations from a third-party view. Finally, older children are able to judge the greatest social value in a situation. Generally, this process is accomplished over the course of elementary and middle grades. It is critically important to provide a wide variety of stories and examples so children can both be monitored and encouraged toward more mature valuative judgments (see Figure 3).

FIGURE 3   Classroom Applications of Moral Dilemmas

Construct a moral dilemma centered on a problem in your classroom (cheating, not attending, belittling others), and give students time to analyze and discuss the problem. Begin with a hypothetical dilemma, and then focus on students' own behavior. Find ways to encourage affective judgment (valuing others, committing to a plan of action to improve), and review cognitive aspects of the problem (why something happened, to whom it is harmful).

Connections to Learning

Benjamin Bloom and his colleagues (1956) explained the domains for learning (cognitive, affective, and psychomotor) that we understand today. His taxonomy is familiar to prospective teachers who learn how to task analyze and construct lessons. The familiar progression from simplest to most complex cognitive learning tasks (knowledge, comprehension, application, analysis, synthesis, and evaluation) is an important one. But other implications of his theory, ones that are especially important for literacy learning, are often overlooked. For instance, it is necessary to have children experience learning at the higher levels of the cognitive taxonomy so they may explore their own and others' values. At the highest levels of the cognitive taxonomy, students create and evaluate using information they have learned. This level of thinking makes it more likely that they can operate at the higher levels of the affective domain, which require personal long-range commitment (valuing) to a behavior or choice. Students need information with which to exercise affective valuing. Literacy activities provide one way for students to gain this information.

A further assumption of Bloom's theories is that students must be connected to curriculum to want to learn more or exercise choice in their own reading and learning. When students reach the higher levels of reasoning, no matter what their age, they are better equipped to understand the moral choices they are making. Students' moral reasoning and judgment about events are at higher levels when they understand and are able to apply critical thinking and creativity. If we want students to be able to apply values to learning and life, we must help them reach the higher levels of both cognitive and affective learning. Refer to the example of Bloom's Taxonomy applied to a learning task (Figure 4). Define how you would use this task or a similar task to draw students to a higher level of the cognitive taxonomy and then connect with the affective taxonomy.

Gardner's (1993) theory of multiple intelligences has given us another view of how to reach all students. Rather than consider a general intelligence level often measured in the past with IQ scores, Gardner defined seven modes of intelligence—linguistic, mathematical-logical, spatial, musical, bodily-kinesthetic, intrapersonal, interpersonal—that all individuals have to a greater or lesser extent. He stressed that there may be more types of intelligences (he added naturalist as an eighth category), but that our focus should be on all learners being encouraged to develop all intelligences. In order to accomplish broad development, teachers must provide appropriate experiences. Teachers should plan for a variety of modalities so all intelligences can be used to optimize student connections to thinking in different ways. Because multiple in-

FIGURE 4 Example of Bloom's Taxonomy Applied to a Learning Task
(Robert Frost's poem "The Road Not Taken")

Bloom's Taxonomy Level	The Student Will Be Able to
Knowledge Level:	Recite from memory Frost's poem "The Road Not Taken."
Comprehension Level:	Explain the meaning of the poem.
Application Level:	Describe a situation in his or her life that is the same or similar to the meaning of the poem.
Analysis Level:	Compare the meaning of "The Road Not Taken" with Frost's "Mending Wall."
Synthesis Level:	Create at least one additional verse for the poem that would communicate a message that students feel is important.
Evaluation Level:	Decide to accept or reject the following statement, with evidence to support the decision: "This poem is no longer relevant. In today's fast-paced, multifaceted, technical, computerized society, there are no 'roads not taken.' People not only have a better understanding of options available to them, but they often have opportunities to revise their previous decisions."

telligences are culturally sensitive and culture bound, we are free to interpret the appropriate and desired level of proficiency for our own lives.

Finally, a way that moral reasoning and cognitive development and learning are connected also may be illustrated by attribution theory. The way children explain success or failure is critical to understanding why behavior occurs and motivation to learn is sustained or not sustained. The attribution theory research of Weiner and Graham (1989) and Stipek (1993) addresses ways children develop achievement motivation. Achievement motivation is a result of appropriate self-attributions for success, and external attributions for failure. That is, students must understand the actions for which they are and are not responsible. In addition, students may learn from vicarious experience, from their peers, or from the examples they read in stories. Whether real or imaginary, such experiences are powerful examples of the results of effort and work, and may explain success or failure, especially in school.

The teacher is important in developing students' abilities to accurately attribute success or failure, and the responsibility for actions toward those events. Leading students to understand motives, rationale, and reasons behind the characters and plots in stories and events helps them reason about consequences of actions in their own and others' lives. Such connections enable students to make choices, and the discussion of their choices cements understanding and attitudes about right and wrong, and about judgments across all areas of their personal and social learning and development. Ultimately, their judgments extend to their willingness to pursue reading and learning, thus determining their future success in schooling.

FIGURE 5   Examining Values in Literacy Learning

For each of your language arts units, examine the taxonomic level of cognitive reasoning, the affective outcomes you expect, and the issues of moral reasoning you might or do incorporate. Create a plan to define how you might more closely address the concepts of values in literacy learning.

Conclusions for Learning—Finding Meaning and Connections

Teachers have always communicated values. "Every teacher teaches values, whether they intend to or not," is a common rationale for the conscious teaching of values. But recognizing appropriate ways to exercise and apply values in the classroom requires effort. Kohn (1991) defined the school's role in creating caring students. A caring community at school includes activities that practice and develop both the knowledge base and the affective responses that create a better society. One way to improve our community is to spend time expanding on the messages of literacy experiences in our classroom (see Figure 5). We need to purposefully address values as they are so richly portrayed in our legacy of literary works.

References

Bennett, W.J. (Ed.). (1993). *The book of virtues: A treasury of great moral stories*. New York: Simon & Schuster.

Black, S. (1996). The character conundrum. *The American School Board Journal, 183*(12), 29–31.

Bloom, S., Engelhart, M.D., Frost, E.J., Hill, W.H., & Krathwohl, D.R. (1956). *Taxonomy of educational objectives. Handbook I: Cognitive domain*. New York: David McKay.

Coles, R. (1989). *The call of stories: Teaching and the moral imagination*. Boston: Houghton Mifflin.

Dewey, J. (1910). *How we think*. Boston: D.C. Heath.

Ellenwood, S., & McLaren, N. (1994). Literature-based character education. *Middle School Journal, 26*(2), 42–47.

Gardner, H. (1993). *Multiple intelligences: The theory in practice*. New York: Basic Books.

Garrod, A., Beal, C., & Shin, P. (1990). The development of moral orientation in elementary school children. *Sex Roles, 22*, 13–27.

Gilligan, C., & Attanucci, J. (1988). Two moral orientations: Gender differences and similarities. *Merrill-Palmer Quarterly, 34*(3), 223–237.

Kilpatrick, W. (1992). *Why Johnny can't tell right from wrong*. New York: Simon & Schuster.

Kohlberg, L. (1963). The development of children's orientations toward moral order, Part 1: Sequence in the development of moral thought. *Vita Humana, 6*, 11–33.

Kohlberg, L. (1981). *The philosophy of moral development: Moral stages and the idea of justice*. New York: Harper & Row.

Kohn, A. (1991). Caring kids: The role of the school. *Phi Delta Kappan, 72*, 496–506.

Narvaez, D., Gleason, T., Mitchell, C., & Bentley, J. (1999). Moral theme comprehension in children. *Journal of Educational Psychology, 91*(3), 477–487.

Piaget, J. (1963). *Origins of intelligence in children*. New York: Norton.

Piaget, J. (1965). *The moral judgment of the child*. New York: Free Press.

Selman, R.L. (1981). *The child as a friendship philosopher*. New York: Cambridge University Press.

Stipek, D.J. (1993). *Motivation to learn: From theory to practice* (2nd ed.). Boston: Allyn & Bacon.

Vygotsky, L.S. (1962). *Thought and language* (E. Haufmann & G. Vakar, Eds. & Trans.). Cambridge, MA: MIT Press.

Weiner, B., & Graham, S. (1989). Understanding the motivational role of affect. *Cognition and Emotion, 4*, 401–419.

Wittrock, M.C. (1982). *Educational implications of recent research on learning and memory*. Paper presented at the annual meeting of the American Educational Research Association, New York.

Recommended Web Sites for Literacy and Values Education

American Association of University Women, Gender Equity
> http://www.aauw.org/index.html

Children's Literature
> http://www.childrenslit.com

Classics for Young People
> http://www.ucalgary.ca/~dkbrown/storclas.html

Cognitive and Psychological Sciences on the Internet (Index)
> http://www-psych.stanford.edu/cogsci

Internet School Library Media Center (ISLMC) Children's Literature and Language Arts
> http://falcon.jmu.edu/~ramseyil/childlit.htm

Kindred Spirits
> http://www.upei.ca/~lmmi/listserv.html

Museum of Tolerance
> http://www.wiesenthal.com/mot

The Newbery Award Winners
> http://www.ala.org/alsc/newbery.html

WWW Schools Registry (to contact other schools for information)
> http://hillside.coled.umn.edu/others.html

Chapter 2

Critical Media Literacy and Values: Connecting With the 5 Ws

Ann Watts Pailliotet

W ho, what, where, when, why, and how might teachers explore values through critical media literacy? This chapter addresses the 5 Ws of media literacy: What is media literacy? Who teaches media literacy? Why and when should teachers employ media literacy to promote values instruction and literacy learning? How might educators teach critical media literacy? Where can readers learn more about media literacy?

What Is Media Literacy?

Like *whole language, authentic assessment,* or *constructivism, media literacy* is a rather tenuous umbrella term. Ask 10 media educators what media literacy is and you will most likely get 10 definitions. Despite differences, however, in 1993 various media experts gathered in Aspen, Colorado, USA, and formulated a definition of media literacy as "the ability to access, analyze, evaluate and communicate messages in a variety of forms" (Firestone, in Hobbs, 1997, p. 7). Most media educators ascribe to this definition in some way, although their emphases may differ.

Examples of Media Literacy Practices

A more traditional or print-based literacy teacher might instruct students how to access visual information when she or he teaches with graphic organizers, maps, Web-based resources, textual illustrations, or a video version of a literary work. A beginning media educator might focus on accessing and analytic skills, using mass media texts such as newspapers and newscasts as references or supplements for a research project, and examining Internet sites for facts versus opinions. Those individuals who ascribe to a protectionist or innoculationist stance—that the media have negative impacts on children—might focus on analysis and evaluation of persuasive devices and inaccuracies in tobacco and alcohol advertisements or violence in cartoons. Other instructors employ the pleasurable traits of popular media as a "hook" to create student interest and motivation for more traditional print texts or content. In a more experienced media educator's classroom, students might access information through varied print and electronic media; analyze them for facts, bias, devices, levels of meaning, omissions, and values; evaluate their relevance, effectiveness, and veracity; then communicate and assess their learning and views by generating a new media text such as a class newspaper, video, advertisement campaign, public service announcement, or Web page. Whenever educators employ visual, popular, or electronic texts in their classrooms, they are tacitly or explicitly teaching forms of media literacy.

Critical Media Literacy and Values Instruction

Despite their diverse approaches, media educators do agree that popular culture and mass media convey many messages. Some information is explicit, urging viewers to buy new products, be entertained, gain information, or acquire services. But powerful, implicit value messages are also conveyed through media. A television situation comedy, for instance—by nature of its characters, plot, setting, dialogue, editing, camera angles, and even laugh track—communicates many tacit judgments about the relative status of people's race, class, gender, age, religion, sexual orientation, profession, or exceptionality. We can all identify media stereotypes and the value messages they send: the boring teacher; the geeky, egghead male adolescent; the airhead blonde; the welfare mother; the clueless father; the minority criminal; the crime victim; the incompetent boss; the corrupt government official; the desperate woman looking for a man.

Television programs teach viewers about desirable family roles and behaviors, the nature of problem solving, social relations, materialism, sexuality, work, rewards, honesty, appearance, gender roles, race, neighbors, success, and how to think about social institutions like schools and government. Values are also conveyed in other media: the selection, sequence, and slant in newscasts; the placement or omission of stories in newspapers; who is interviewed and left out in radio or television talk shows and news programs; the advertisements generated on Web pages, television, magazines, and radio shows targeted toward specific audiences (while excluding others); in the lyrics and images of commercials and music videos; the goals, procedures, and rules in video games; in toys and media tie-ins; and in film characters and their actions.

Recently, there has been a growing interest among literacy educators in critical media literacy that stresses both analytic (or receptive) and generative (or production) communications processes as ways to identify, analyze, and evaluate values and ideologies in all kinds of popular texts. Through careful inquiry into media content and process, critical media literacy aims to empower students and teachers, promote self-reflection and positive identity, critique textual authority, encourage restructuring of inequitable educational and social conditions, further social justice, and foster democratic values. These goals foster the kinds of values education we are proposing in this book—to develop critical consumers, informed voters, and literate, compassionate citizens in a democratic society.

Critical media literacy invites participants to ask vital questions about their own and others' values. Luke (1999) asserted that the teaching of analytic skills through critical media literacy enables students and teachers

> to develop new strategies for thinking about the meanings media transmit and the meanings viewers construct for themselves. Core analytic questions in any media studies program usually include the following: How are society, culture, and persons portrayed? What attitudes and values do images promote? What technical, symbolic and semiotic features are used to generate meanings? How does what we see and read influence our opinions of others, our world views, our social relations, and behaviors? How might others, reading from different sociocultural positions, view a certain text, and what might it mean to them? (p. 623)

There are certain practices that are essential for true critical media literacy to occur, including teacher-based research and development of innovative instruction (Buckingham, 1998); critical analysis of popular culture texts (Alvermann, Moon, & Hagood, 1999); extended notions of "reading" and "writing" to include many analytic and communicative literacy processes across texts and contexts (Semali & Pailliotet, 1999); inquiry into and critique of power relations and injustices reflected and perpetuated by and through mass media (Giroux & Simon, 1989; McLaren, Hammer, Sholle, & Reilly, 1995); sustained, systematic study of media through critical frameworks and questions (Pailliotet, Semali, Rodenberg, Giles, & Macaul, 2000); reflective habits of mind (Semali, 1999); and an outcome of praxis, or positive transformation of self, others, and the world around us (Sholle & Denski, 1993). Engaging in these processes empowers students and teachers to connect and critique values conveyed through myriad literacy contexts.

Examples of Critical Media Literacy Practices

A series of critical media literacy lessons might involve careful analysis of print or television advertisements. Students would examine explicit content and production devices such as spoken or print text, camera shots, use of space, colors, and objects, and then interpret these media messages by graphing elements and connecting them to deeper meanings and values. For instance, advertisers often use the color red to capture viewers' attention, but also to convey feelings of danger, excitement, or sexuality. Students may identify how the ad creators are addressing them, constructing a target audience, and shaping their opinions and feelings through language and imagery. They note information and groups left out of the advertisement. They identify contradictions, facts, opinions, rhetorical devices, and missing information in the advertisement. They might record these observations on an intersected list, or conduct a survey to determine how often they, peers, or their family use these products. Based on observations, their teachers could research related scholarship, share future lesson ideas, and perhaps invite community experts to build on what students discover. Students then could use reflective, individual journaling and group discussion to assess and evaluate how accurate the advertisements' representations are and if the values in the advertisement are really those they hold. A simple candy advertisement might convey deeper value judgments about appearance and gender; alcohol and tobacco ads often contain powerful contradictions and tacit messages about health, race, sexuality, and class status. Next, students may create print, video, or Web-based advertisement parodies using devices they have discovered, or public service announcements that convey more positive values, to be posted in classrooms or shared in their school. They might take further action by conducting teach-in sessions with other students and siblings, or writing to the corporations who produced the advertisement. Teachers might tie the study of advertisements to units on health, science, the environment, or the community.

Who Teaches Media Literacy?

Media literacy is interdisciplinary and multicontextual in nature. Teachers of all educational levels and subjects, librarians and media specialists, school administrators, university researchers from diverse fields, members of nonprofit advocacy groups, physicians and health professionals, media production personnel, artists, psychologists, counselors, cultural and media critics, social workers, computer software developers, technological aficionados, students, community leaders, politicians, business persons, and parents might meet at a typical media literacy conference.

Given the diversity of its proponents, it is no wonder that many debates about media literacy's focus and aims occur. Hobbs (1998) listed several: how and if teachers should protect children from negative media influences, proper uses of media production and popular culture texts in classrooms, explicitness of political and ideological agendas, the focus of media literacy in K–12 school-based environments and whether it should be taught as a distinct subject or integrated throughout the curriculum, and issues of financial support. Additionally, media educators wrestle with issues of time, national and state media literacy standards, assessment of media processes and products, institutional resistance, who should create media literacy materials and what form they should take, issues of access and equity, funding, training, using new technological innovations, interpreting results of media studies, identifying types of needed media research, political and social events that impact public opinion and support, commercial influences in the classroom, the ethics of corporate underwriting for media literacy resources, and future directions the movement should take.

Hobbs (1998) called for "a pedagogy of inquiry" through which participants cultivate "an open, questioning, reflective and critical stance" using varied media texts (p. 27). This "pedagogy of inquiry" is well suited to teaching values and furthering literacy, because it is grounded in certain guiding principles that build on what many teachers already know and do. In the next sections, I first explain these principles and their relations to literacy learning and values instruction. I then provide additional rationales for teaching critical media literacy to promote literacy learning and values instruction.

Why Critical Media Literacy Helps Us Teach Values and Develop Literacy

Guiding Principles of Media Literacy

During the 1993 Media Literacy National Leadership Conference, media educators also established guiding principles for media literacy instruction. The following is a compilation from several sources (Ferrington & Anderson-Inman, 1996; Hobbs, 1998; Thoman, 1999):

1. Media messages are constructed.

2. Media messages are produced within economic, social, political, historical, and aesthetic contexts.

3. Each form of media is constructed with unique creative language. Understanding the characteristics of each form—genres, grammar, syntax, symbols, devices, and metaphor systems of media languages— increases our appreciation and lessens our susceptibility to manipulation.

4. Audiences actively negotiate meaning. Different people experience the same media message differently; the interpretive meaning-making processes involved consist of interactions among readers, texts, and cultures.

5. Media are primarily business-driven by a profit motive.

6. Media representations play a role in people's understandings of social reality.

7. Media have embedded values and points of view.

Literacy educators will most likely see many parallels between their own instructional philosophies and this list. For example, the notion that audiences actively negotiate meaning is similar to reader response theory (Rosenblatt, 1978), in which readers construct multiple meanings through transactions with texts. Each form of media, just like print, has specific styles, grammars, genres, and languages that can be studied, learned, and used to generate new texts. Specific, teacher-directed instruction about media conventions, elements, and skills to understand them are not unlike comprehension and decoding strategies taught in content area reading (Pailliotet, 1997). Media messages are constructed texts, just as authors' points of view are conveyed through writing and reflect the economic, social, political, historical, and aesthetic contexts in which they arise. Mass media, like textbooks and trade books, are produced by large corporations; their content, format, and availability are largely determined by marketing and profit motives. All must be scrutinized carefully for content, bias, relevance, timeliness, accuracy, and omissions.

Many educators already teach with varied literature and print texts to shape students' understandings of themselves, others, values, and social reality. Both print and mass media texts convey specific values through plot, character development, symbolism, point of view, textual devices, and omissions. For instance, the happy, white, middle-class children portrayed in the Dick and Jane series taught a generation of students much more than just how to read; they presented a narrow and distorted image of social norms, appropriate lifestyle, proper behaviors, family structure, gender roles, and desirable values, as well as powerful messages about racial identity and class status. The popular "Find the Amway Products" advertisement campaign depicting families in home settings surrounded by every consumer product imaginable uncannily recalls the messages and values conveyed by the adventures of Dick, Jane, Father, Mother, and Spot a generation ago.

Parallels Between Print Literacy and Media Literacy

There are additional ways that critical media literacy promotes print literacy learning and exploration of values. Critical media literacy extends and complements many teachers' instructional frameworks and favored methods, including critical thinking (Considine, Haley, & Lacy, 1994); inquiry learning (Hobbs, 1997; Macaul, Giles, & Rodenberg, 1999); whole language (Fehlman, 1996); multicultural curricula (Kincheloe & Steinberg, 1997); cooperative learning (Pailliotet, 1998); content area reading (Pailliotet, 1997); constructivism (Alvermann, Moon, & Hagood, 1999); existing values programs (Considine & Haley, 1999); interdisciplinary teaching (Leveranz & Tyner, 1996) or thematic teaching (Considine, 1987); literature appreciation and study (Considine, Haley, & Lacy, 1994); and skills-based literacy programs (Moline, 1995; Thoman, 1999).

Practical Examples

Careful, guided analysis of print and visual information, whether in a content area textbook or television program, fosters student awareness of, competence in, and critical thinking about such textual elements as point of view, organization, production devices, fact versus opinion, bias, omission, argument, and rhetorical devices. Such analysis also invites students to think deeply about the veracity and personal relevance of values conveyed though texts. Graphic aids and supporting media texts such as film and comics have long been staples of educators who want to promote literacy skills in reluctant or struggling readers and writers. Comparing multiple media texts with similar or contrasting themes or characters furthers student understanding and clarification of values conveyed in these works. The range of personal response and interpretative activities through multiple texts afforded by critical media literacy furthers practices of constructivism, whole language, and literature response.

Because students often generate topics, questions, and projects for future study within a critical media literacy classroom, it is an essential part of inquiry learning. Because media literacy serves as a bridge between contexts and content, it is well suited to interdisciplinary or thematic teaching. Educators ascribing to a multicultural curriculum may employ critical media literacy practices to expose students to texts from diverse authors and sources; invite them to appreciate multiple viewpoints; encourage students to interrogate their own and others' values about race, power, and class; and inspire them to take action to justify social inequities.

There are other compelling reasons for teaching values and literacy through critical media literacy: its prevalence in and relevance to our students' lives; its impacts on their literacy development and values formation; the changing nature of literacy; the growth of media literacy curricular standards; and the roles of teachers in contemporary classrooms. Each of these reasons is discussed briefly in the following sections.

Connecting Literacy Contexts: Prevalence of Mass Media in Our Students' Lives

Consider these statistics from more than a decade ago:

> By the time 6-year-olds enter first grade, they will have seen over 100,000 ads on television; by the time they graduate from high school, they will have spent 11,000 hours in classrooms and 15,000 hours watching television, during which time they will have seen as many as 350,000 advertisements on television.... [B]y the time we die we will have spent one and one-half years of our lives watching just television commercials. (Lutz, 1989, pp. 73–74)

Today, children engage with mass media in even more ways: watching films and videos, creating texts on computers, surfing the Web, communicating through networks, playing electronic games, as well as interacting with magazines, billboards, books, comics, music, the radio, and daily cultural events. As teachers, we assume the time our students spend in school has impacts—hopefully positive—on their learning and social behaviors. Common sense, as well as recent literacy research, tells us that mass media are also teaching children many lessons about themselves, others, and the world around them.

Relevance of Critical Media Literacy to Classroom Literacy Learning

Experienced educators know that home and school literacy contexts are connected and interdependent (Schmidt, 1993). Literacy development and learning occur across interdependent social systems that transcend classroom barriers (Emig, Goswami, & Butler, 1983; Heath, 1983). Furthermore, individuals utilize interdependent processes when they interact with oral, print, and electronic texts (Neuman, 1991). We also know that for literacy learning to occur, we must activate students' schema or background knowledge by creating lessons that are interesting, relevant, build on prior knowledge, and foster success. Our students enter classrooms with rich knowledge gained from diverse communicational environments; however, some students and teachers see schools and society as distinct, separate worlds. In particular, struggling students may view school learning as hard or irrelevant and home communication experiences as pleasurable, exciting, and "real." Critical media literacy may serve as an important connection between school-based and "real life" literacy learning.

Several studies of elementary children demonstrate how home and school communications environments are deeply interconnected. Weber and Mitchell (1995) studied elementary students' and preservice teachers' drawings of teachers. They found that both students and teachers drew uncannily similar symbols and figures that largely had their genesis in popular media sources like film and television. Their participants constructed stereotypical, simplistic, often negative representations of what teachers do, revealing deep-seated values about gender, power, student and teacher identity, classroom roles, and the process of learning. Robinson (1997) provided in-depth accounts of how television viewing at home influences children's orientations, preferences, and expectations about reading, as well as power relationships in the classroom. In their accounts of lessons involving superheroes and music preferences, Alvermann, Moon, and Hagood (1999) offer further confirmation of media impacts on primary and upper elementary students' conceptions of identity, gender roles, difference, pleasure, school attitudes, and learning in classrooms.

In her study of children's writing and play, Dyson (1997) provided compelling evidence that "the commercial media are central to contemporary childhood. The media—not adult story tellers (or readers)—provide most U.S. children with their common story material" (p. 7). Dyson offered numerous examples of elementary pupils' actions, plot lines, characters, and discussions that revealed how children draw from media texts and construct their social realities, including value systems, in large part from mass media sources.

Dyson asserted, "In forming imagined worlds on both paper and playground, children reveal their sense of the social world; their unfolding stories reflect deeply embedded cultural story lines about human relations" (1997, p. 6). The following anecdote exemplifies Dyson's points about the relevance, prevalence, and impacts of mass media in our students' lives and on the values children form.

An Example of Media Impacts

Several years ago, as the Bill Clinton and Monica Lewinsky scandal was just beginning to emerge, I visited a local school to observe student teachers. One class was constructing valentines. A fifth-grade student approached me and, with obvious delight, shared his work. Several figures were depicted on a large blue heart with cartoon balloons coming from their mouths. Additional text was written on the top and sides. The heading read, "Bill Loves Monica. Or DOES he?" The first male figure had a caption reading, "President of the United States—Busted!" with a large arrow directed at Clinton, who was surrounded by an American flag and a frowning eagle. It read, "Oh no! Oh Monica! Don't tell!" There was an additional arrow pointing to Clinton's necktie with the statement, "Monica gave this to him." Monica (indicated by an arrow noting "the OTHER woman") was drawn with exaggerated female curves, wearing a dark blue dress and sporting a winning smile with oversized lips. Her caption balloon read, "Oh Bill! I love you! Oh No! Here comes Hillary!" The third figure (arrow indicating Hillary Clinton—"She's REALLY mad!!!") showed the first lady striding across the page with a stick in her upraised hand. In jagged letters, her caption read, "Love hurts!!!!!!!" (the title of a popular rock song). At the bottom of the page, in an obvious allusion to the current McDonald's advertisement jingle, was written, "At the white house, we do it all for you!" followed by, "What will happen next? Stay tuned for part 2!"

To construct his valentine, this young student drew from information and images gleaned through multiple media sources—television, newspapers, commercials, and rock music—and from a recent writing lesson on exclamation points. In doing so, he revealed knowledge and values I found both amazing (in terms of their complexity) and disturbing (in terms of sophistication and precociousness). What kind of literate adult, citizen, and media consumer will this child become? The answer may depend on what sorts of media learning experiences and invitations for questioning values he encounters in the future, both in and out of classrooms.

The Changing Nature of Literacy

We live in a "post typographic world" (Reinking, McKenna, Labbo, & Kieffer, 1998) in which many contemporary media—including software, video, games, television, Hypertext, Internet sites, commercial advertising, and CD-ROMs—are rapidly evolving into dynamic, sophisticated blends of audio, print, visual, and even tactile information. We rely increasingly on these new media forms. Prevailing social conditions require us to view and teach literacy through broader, more critical lenses if we want to develop citizens who hold democratic values and act in just, thoughtful, and productive ways.

Many current literacy teaching methods now identify diverse literacy modalities, including reading, writing, speaking, listening, viewing, moving, and representing (e.g., Pike, Compain, & Mumper, 1997). To be literate today means actively engaging with multiple sign systems and constructing critical meanings through them (Semali & Pailliotet, 1999). Modern literacy is now becoming media literacy: the ability to "read" (deconstruct, understand, interpret, evaluate) and "write" (synthesize ideas and elements to create new texts) all modern communications media, as they exist in and out of the classroom.

Curriculum Standards

Recognizing the need to prepare students for contemporary literacy environments, Canada and Australia have implemented provincial or nationwide media literacy programs, curricula, and standards. Educators in the United States are also beginning to formulate media literacy standards and curriculum. The International Reading Association/National Council of Teachers of English *Standards for the English Language Arts* (1996) include the following media and values education competencies:

Students read a wide range of print and nonprint texts to build an understanding of texts, of themselves, and of the cultures of the United States and the world.

To respond to the needs and demands of society...apply a wide range of strategies to comprehend, interpret, evaluate and appreciate texts...adjust their use of spoken, written and visual language...to communicate effectively with a variety of audiences and for different purposes.

Conduct research on issues.

Gather, evaluate and synthesize data.

Use a variety of technological and informational resources (libraries, databases, computer networks, video).

Develop an understanding of and respect for diversity.

Use spoken, written, and visual language to accomplish their own purposes.

Participate as knowledgeable, reflective, creative and critical members of a variety of literacy communities. (p. 3)

Additionally, media literacy standards are now mandated in 48 states (Kubey & Baker, 1999), under reading, language arts/ English, communication, and writing competencies, as well as explicit technology, media, viewing, and representing categories. Many of these curricular competencies also tacitly or explicitly involve values education. For instance, in Washington, our State Essential Learnings (1996) are typical of new literacy standards and identify the following goals for students:

Reading
- understands and uses different skills and strategies to read
- uses features of nonfiction text and computer software
- thinks critically about authors' use of language, style, purpose and perspective
- reads different materials for a variety of purposes
- develops interests and shares reading experiences

Writing
- identifies, analyzes, and writes for chosen audiences
- writes in a variety of forms and for a variety of purposes
- publishes using a variety of tools including pen, pencil, and technology

Communications
- identifies and evaluates the techniques and influence of mass media messages
- uses communication strategies and skills to work effectively with others
- uses appropriate sound, action, and image to support presentations

If you are like many teachers and teacher educators I know, you are probably cringing at the thought of adding more to your already packed curricula. I have already discussed how media literacy extends the kinds of literacy learning and teaching that many teachers already do. I also contend that critical media literacy serves as a useful vehicle to teach the sorts of values most teachers already teach.

When Should We Begin to Teach Values Through Critical Media Literacy?

Throughout the day, educators assume many roles, and "teacher" is just one. We are listeners, talkers, sharers, referees, monitors, guides, resource persons, surrogate parents, negotiators, paper pushers, planners, decision makers, and so forth. Through each act, role, and moment, we are already teaching values in some form. Students watch and learn from what we say and do. We convey values through the texts, activities, and subjects we choose and omit; the academic philosophies to which we ascribe; in the structure, in routines, rewards, and interactions that occur daily in our classrooms; in our own behaviors and modeling; and in the academic and personal goals we desire for the students we teach.

Hobbs (1998) lists many media literacy aims that promote the same values many teachers seek to instill in their students and the kinds of values we are proposing in this book. These include

> improving reasoning and communication skills...confronting issues of race, class and gender inequalities...improving attitudes towards democracy, citizenship, and political participation...facilitating personal growth...dealing with youth substance abuse and violence prevention...enhancing career skills...promoting issues of faith and social justice...inspiring awareness of consumerism and the commodification of culture...and improving the quality of education. (p. 18)

Additionally, critical media literacy invites students (and teachers) to question contemporary issues such as the environment and poverty; to forge stronger community and family ties; to develop self-esteem, reflective habits of mind, positive identities, tolerance, compassion, and appreciation for others; and to create sound ethical frameworks.

When should we begin to teach values instruction through critical media literacy? Educators can no longer resist teaching explicit values and critical analysis of mass media. The time is now.

How Do We Explore Values Through Media Literacy?

Before offering a range of critical media literacy activities designed to foster values education and literacy learning, I must offer a few caveats. First, because critical media literacy involves many kinds of texts, the following lessons employ multiple literacy modalities and media sources. Educators looking for lessons in one specific medium, such as newspapers, video, or computers/Internet should refer to the annotated bibliography for some excellent sources. Second, experienced educators, like musical composers, know that there are no real completely original ideas, but only borrowed and adapted ones. The lessons that follow have been chosen and adapted from myriad sources and classroom experiences. They share several common aspects: use of multiple texts; active student learning; a stress on critical, reflective thinking; and objectives that further both literacy learning and values exploration. Third, empowerment and informed decision making are at the core of both critical media literacy and values instruction. I strongly believe that teachers are highly capable decision makers who draw on their own experiences, students' needs, classroom conditions, and knowledge to plan and implement instruction. Therefore, I resist simply presenting ready-made, one-size-fits-all lesson plans here. It is my hope that these ideas will serve as launching points for readers to adapt, create, combine, research, explore, and enjoy!

Practical Examples

Analyzing Visual Images. An excellent opening media activity for learning media analysis and exploring values involves connecting elements in picture books to those in print advertisements. Production elements present in both these media send many tacit and explicit value messages. Begin with analysis of one or more book illustrations and then apply the same elements to a print advertisement.

The following points are summarized from *Imagine That! Developing Critical Thinking and Critical Viewing Through Children's Literature* (Considine, Haley, & Lacy, 1994, pp. 59–83) and serve as a sound basis for future learning:

Posture: Students examine images from several ads or illustrations and identify the characters' emotions depicted in them.

Appearance: Students examine dress, age, physical traits, and other features of people and note what these elements convey about them. Teachers may prompt, "Tell me about the people in this picture based on what you see."

Point of view: Strength and authority—and thus value judgments about gender, character, relative worth, and good or evil—are often conveyed through the posturing of figures.

Position: Positioning of characters within a frame (close-ups vs. long shots) are often used to convey their relative importance. Students can look for patterns of people's relations and thus messages about their importance.

Proportion: Relative size also conveys importance. Who is the biggest? What does this say about the character?

Props: What objects accompany the characters? These elements offer many clues about values. For instance, clothes, artifacts, settings, symbols, and surrounding objects define characters' relative worth and roles. Teachers may show students just a picture of a character and ask them to make predictions about him or her based on props.

Panels, pages, spreads, and vignettes: Layout, use of space, fonts, color, and other design may add tacit but important layers of meaning. Bold print or bright color often connotes importance; white space, boxing, or distance may convey subtle forms of stereotyping through separation and isolation.

Adbusters. Collect print advertisements from popular magazines or download digital print and video from data sites like AdFlip (print; http://www.adflip. com), AdCritic (video; http://www.adcritic.com), or Adbusters (spoofs and parodies of popular advertisements; http://www.adbusters.org). Preview these sites beforehand. Most contain some material that may not be suitable for children.

Using one of the many critical questioning frameworks (see Figure 1), lead students in small- or whole-group guided discussion through examination of content and devices, followed by discussion about the advertisements' value messages.

After analysis, engage in one or more of the following activities:

- What do we buy and why? Discuss or write about the differences between needs and wants. How do advertisements create needs and wants in us, the audience? How real are these needs and wants?

- Relate purchasing patterns or media viewing habits to math lessons by keeping logs of purchases and motivations for them, or graphing the time students spend engaging with media. Many students are astonished by the amount of time or money they spend after engaging in this activity. Develop alternative at-home activities or guidelines for purchasing that reflect more positive and personally relevant values.

- Favorite advertisements: Students identify their favorite advertisements and analyze them for devices, untruths, and values. Through e-mail or written means, students then exchange insights and critiques about advertisements.

- Talk-back ads and parodies: Students generate print, video, radio, or Web pages that utilize devices and messages to present more accurate or positive messages. Post these in your school, classroom, network, or

FIGURE 1   Sampling of Critical Questioning Frameworks

Considine & Haley (1999)

Who?	Source, structure/organization/ownership of the media
Says what?	Statement, content, values, ideology
To whom?	Audiences
In what way?	Form, style, codes, conventions, technologies
With what effect?	Influence and consequences
Why?	Purpose, profit, motivation

Lester (1995)

Personal Perspectives	What do I think or feel about this? What meaning do I create from it?
Historical Perspectives	When was this text produced? How does it reflect values, technologies, events, and understandings from its time?
Technical Perspectives	What artistic and technical devices are used?
Ethical Perspectives	What values does this text convey and reflect? Who constructed it and why? What moral impacts does it have on viewers?
Cultural Perspectives	Whose point of view is represented by the text? Who is left out? How does it reflect information, knowledge, events, and values? What are these?
Critical Perspectives	What ideologies are conveyed through this text? How does it establish and/or maintain power relations and social institutions?

Lloyd-Kolkin & Tyner (1991)

Media Agencies	Who is communicating and why?
Media Categories	What type of text is it?
Media Technologies	How is it produced?
Media Languages	How do we know what it means?
Media Audiences	Who receives it and what sense do they make of it?
Media Representations	How does it present its subject?

Luke (1999)

Coding Practice	What analytic skills can I apply to crack the codes of this text? How does this text work?
Text Meaning Practice	What different cultural readings and meanings does this text enable? How does the combination of language, ideas, and images hold together to produce ideas?
Pragmatic Practice	How does this text work in different contexts? How does context shape its uses? What does this text mean to me and what might it mean for others in different situations and cultural contexts?
Critical Practice	How does this text attempt to position me? Who is the ideal person this text addresses? Whose interests are served in this text? Who is present or absent in this text?

Pailliotet (1995, 1998)

Action/Sequence	What happens? In what order? When and how long?
Semes/Forms	What objects are observed? What are their traits?
Discourse/Actors	What words are used? Who "speaks"? How do we understand them?
Proximity/Movement	What sorts of movements and space use occur (vectorality/relationships, relative sizes)?
Culture/Context	What social knowledge is referred to or assumed? What is implied? What is missing? Where are the authors and actors in this text situated historically and culturally?
Effects/Processes	What technologies, artistic devices, and production processes were used to construct this text?

community. For an example of this process, see the "BadAd" Web site at http://www.nmmlp.org, or go to Reading Online's New Literacies in Action, July 2000 (see http://www.readingonline.org/newliteracies/lit_index.asp for index).

Stereotyping and Representation. Students generate a list of cultural subsets: varied ethnicities and language, women, disabled, age groups, religion, and others. Discuss what lists are the longest and shortest. Why? Over the following week, student groups track the frequency and representations of each subset in one more medium. Teachers may encourage students to ask these types of questions: How do the media construct images and messages about race, age, gender, and ethnicity? What examples can you draw from news, advertising, films, television programming, or textbooks to illustrate missing, biased, simplified, or distorted images? Based on people you know, are these images accurate? fair? positive? negative? Students may then participate in the following activities:

- Create a magazine, news story, video, or advertisement that depicts more positively or accurately an underrepresented group.
- Create a comic book character superhero that reflects more accurately and positively your target population.
- Write a letter to the producer or editor describing findings of your study and asking for more extensive or fair coverage of your target group.

What's the News? Compare and contrast a feature in two or more newspapers or newscasts. This may be done by presenting two or more texts in class or asking that student teams perform the task at home. Begin with issues such as placement and positioning, then move to other devices by highlighting or writing fact versus opinion, action words, captions, and graphics. After discovering aspects of bias, move to discussions of value judgments reflected in the news. Sample charts are provided in Figure 2.

News Story Tracking. Following are some activities based on news media:

- Follow a story's coverage in one or more media throughout a given time. Whose point of view is covered? Whose is left out?
- Collect news magazines over several weeks. Ask students to identify through lists or on world and U.S. maps where most news stories occur. They will see, for example, that certain areas—and thus people—are rarely covered in depth.

FIGURE 2   Comparison and Evaluation of News Media

Newscasts	Broadcast One	Broadcast Two
Location and time or space devoted to coverage:		
Who talks?		
Who is the audience?		
What do you see?		
What language is used?		
What is missing?		
Main point or problem (narrative):		
Details, metaphors, and images evoked:		
Solutions to problem? (How many? What are they?)		
Do we agree with the way the people and issues are presented? Why or why not?		

Daily Newspapers	Paper One	Paper Two
Location and time or space devoted to coverage:		
Who talks?		
Who is the audience?		
What do you see?		
What language is used?		
What is missing?		
What sources are cited? How?		
Main point or problem (narrative):		
Details, metaphors, and images evoked:		
Solutions to problem? (How many? What are they?)		
Do we agree with the way the people and issues are presented? Why or why not?		

- Research facts about a particular issue. Then create more accurate news stories that cover a missing point of view or underrepresented area. Publish in print or electronic form.

Creating Communities. Begin by defining what a community is and types of communities. For instance, the class might list shared beliefs, values, dress, behaviors, rules, or points of view. List these on a graphic organizer. Next, examine varied media to see how they shape and define (or ignore) communities through coverage, language, and point of view. Students may also focus on a certain issue of concern to the global, regional, local, or classroom community. Students should analyze findings for positive or negative values, accurate depictions of communities, and ways that media may help communities through promoting awareness of certain issues or appreciation of people. Last, as a class, students create a scrapbook, bulletin board, Web page, newsletter, newscast, advertising campaign, or letter writing project that reflects their opinions about an issue or beliefs and values as a community.

Substance Abuse: Alcohol and Tobacco. Every day, thousands of school-age children begin smoking or drink alcohol. Prevention begins with critical media analysis to promote student awareness of tobacco and alcohol producers' marketing devices and values used to appeal to young people. Students can participate in the following activities in class in whole or small groups, or at home with parents and siblings:

- Analyze one or more tobacco or alcohol advertisements.
- List instances of smoking, alcohol use, and drug use in popular movies. What devices do the producers use to make these behaviors seem desirable? What purposes do these behaviors serve (e.g., to make the behavior seem glamorous, mature, elite, etc.)?
- Research effects of substance abuse on the Internet.
- Interview peers to determine attitudes about smoking, drinking, or drug use.

Using devices and data gained from research, create parodies of these advertisements, music videos, mock radio announcements, comic strips, scripts, skits, or movie posters that show the true consequences of these behaviors. Share in your classroom or school.

Media Autobiographies: Who Am I? Students collect media representations of people who are like them in terms of age, race, and gender. Use advertisements in magazines that target children or popular television shows such as teen television sitcoms. Through journal entries and discussion, students can explore the following:

- What products are advertised?
- How do these products shape students' beliefs about who they are, what they should have, and how they should act?
- What images dominate?
- Discuss the accuracy of gender roles, body images, dress, and lifestyles. Are these depictions accurate?
- Do students really act this way and believe these messages?
- How do these images impact how students feel about themselves and others?

Next, take film or digital photos of each student. Students construct written or artistic narratives that depict who they really are. Post these on bulletin boards or in a class scrapbook.

Ask students to create collages of media images with captions that "talk back" to them. Ask a guest speaker to address the class about body image, or create a unit about eating disorders and nutrition. Compare these images of teens and children in the United States with ones from other countries.

Supermarket or Toy Aisle Scavenger Hunt/Toy Tie-Ins/Product Placements. Students become field researchers and investigate how products are arranged in stores or depicted subtly in media to target consumers. Elements to observe include placement on shelves and in the store, packaging, labeling, promotions, colors, and language, or uses of products and labels in films, television shows, and Web sites. A second option is to investigate toy tie-ins—promotions for films that involve giveaways of promotional toys at fast food outlets. For both activities, students may note manipulative marketing devices, then compare relative prices and worth of goods with others. These are excellent activities for students to do with their families. Teachers may also give students a list of products targeted at children, including toys, cereal, and junk food. Tie to math lessons when comparing cost, study health and nutrition, or employ a "talk back" advertising strategy, as described previously.

Increasing Personal Awareness. Use one or more of the following to track students' interactions with media: journals, graphs, logs, interviews, surveys, field work, observation in school and community. Ask students to answer the following questions about their interactions with media:

- How often do I interact with media? What kinds? Why?
- What messages do I learn? Do I agree with these messages? Why or why not?

Start a class list of alternative behaviors. Solicit parents' input about media use guidelines. Ask students to set up learning or media use goals.

Who Is My Hero? These activities enable students to explore value differences among celebrities, heroes, and real role models or leaders. Begin by defining a hero or leader. List the traits of a hero. Students then discuss or write about:

- Who are my heroes?
- Brainstorm heroes in particular categories, such as male/female, race, age, occupation. Identify the traits of these heroes. What does the hero look like? Say? Do? Believe?
- What problems does the hero encounter? How does he or she resolve them?
- Do I agree with how he or she resolves problems? Why?

- Would I want this person to be my friend? Why or why not?
- Would I want to be like this person? Why or why not?

After discussing these questions, students begin to realize that media celebrities do not often have values and traits they wish to emulate.

Compile a list of family, community, national, or historic figures who embody more positive values. Students can then create mock research interview questions, generate reports, or create a media text about a more appropriate hero or role model.

You Are the Critic. In a whole- or small-group format, critically watch any media text that appeals to students: a film clip, television show, advertisement, or music video (prescreen for objectionable content). Often, as students examine content, devices, and values in their favorite media, they gain increased awareness of manipulation and negative values, as well as appreciation for well-crafted texts and positive values. After viewing and discussion, students may write a review, create a poster, presentation, Web page, talk show, report card, or mock movie review that critiques content and values.

Saying No to Violence. Videotape one or more cartoons, movies, or television programs containing violence. Students may also identify rules and goals in video or computer games. Be familiar with your district's and school's policy regarding this type of content before you begin the lesson, and gain permission as needed.

Ask students to define violence using dictionaries and examples. After watching the program, make a checklist of the types of violence and outcomes/consequences depicted. Discuss how realistic these outcomes are and the real consequences of violence. Students may also complete the following:

- Develop a list of alternative programs, films, toys, or games.
- Create a public service announcement that urges other viewers to boycott violent shows.
- Interview parents and other children about types of media violence.
- Develop a list of alternative activities for parents and children.
- Write a letter to a television station that airs violent children's shows or to a business that sponsors them. Request more positive programming.
- Rewrite a violent scene in a nonviolent way, or rewrite a character's actions to reflect more positive behaviors.
- Create designs for board games or toys that convey more positive values.

(Re)Writing Popular Media. This activity bridges literacy environments of home and school, as well as print and media texts. Compare and contrast two plot lines, characters, or symbols in print and electronic text. Using Venn diagrams, identify and compare devices and the value messages they send. Some follow-up questions include

- Were the characters believable?
- Whose point of view was represented and whose was left out?
- What decisions do the characters make?
- How are they depicted?
- What alternatives can I identify?
- Rewrite the ending and/or change the setting, character description, or point of view to reflect positive values.

Social Action. Students research a local issue by using the Internet, local newspapers and newscasts, magazines, radio, interviews with community leaders, guest speakers, and other sources. Discuss the ways mass media determine which issues are considered "important" and which are ignored. As a class, choose a relevant issue for action: recycling, a local homeless shelter, registering to vote, or another issue that interests students.

Create an advertising campaign to create public awareness. Posters may be generated for local businesses, media texts for the school. Implement a "make a difference day" in which students enlist parent and community support for a specific action, such as cleaning up trash at a local park or collecting canned food.

Where Do I Find Out More?

At the end of this chapter I have included recommended Web sites for media literacy and a list of media education centers and organizations for educators in North America. There is also an annotated bibliography of media resources, including articles and books that are teacher friendly and loaded with practical ideas for both beginning and experienced media literacy educators.

References
Alvermann, D.E., Moon, J.S., & Hagood, M.C. (1999). *Popular culture in the classroom: Teaching and researching critical media literacy.* Newark, DE: International Reading Association.
Buckingham, D. (1998). Introduction: Fantasies of empowerment? Radical pedagogy and popular culture. In D. Buckingham (Ed.), *Teaching popular culture: Beyond radical pedagogy* (pp. 1–17). London: UCL Press.

Considine, D.M. (1987). Visual literacy and the curriculum: More to it than meets the eye. *Language Arts, 64*(6), 34–40.

Considine, D.M., & Haley, G.E. (1999). *Visual messages: Integrating imagery into instruction.* (2nd ed.). Englewood, CO: Teacher Ideas Press.

Considine, D.M., Haley, G.E., & Lacy, L.E. (1994). *Imagine that! Developing critical thinking and critical viewing through children's literature.* Englewood, CO: Teacher Ideas Press.

Dyson, A.H. (1997). *Writing superheroes: Contemporary childhood, popular culture and classroom literacy.* New York: Teachers College Press.

Emig, J., Goswami, D., & Butler, M. (Eds.). (1983). *The web of meaning.* Upper Montclair, NJ: Boynton/Cook.

Fehlman, R.H. (1996). Viewing film and television as Whole Language instruction. *English Journal, 82*(2), 43–50.

Ferrington, G., & Anderson-Inman, L. (1996). Media literacy: Upfront and on-line. *Journal of Adolescent & Adult Literacy, 39,* 666–670.

Giroux, H., & Simon, R. (1989). *Popular culture, schooling, and everyday life.* New York: Bergin & Garvey.

Heath, S.B. (1983). *Ways with words: Language, life and work in communities and classrooms.* Cambridge, UK: Cambridge University Press.

Hobbs, R. (1997). Literacy for the information age. In J. Flood, S.B. Heath, & D. Lapp (Eds.), *Handbook of research on teaching literacy through the communicative and visual arts* (pp. 7–14). New York: Macmillan.

Hobbs, R. (1998). The seven great debates in the media literacy movement. *Journal of Communication, 48*(1), 16–32.

International Reading Association & National Council of Teachers of English (IRA/NCTE). (1996). *Standards for the English language arts.* Newark, DE, & Urbana, IL: Authors.

Kincheloe, J.L., & Steinberg, S.R. (1997). *Changing multiculturalism.* Philadelphia: Open University Press.

Kubey, R., & Baker, F. (1999, October 27). Has media literacy found a curricular foothold? *Education Week,* 56+.

Lester, P.M. (1995). *Visual communication: Images with messages.* Belmont, CA: Wadsworth.

Leveranz, D., & Tyner, K.R. (1996). What is media literacy? Two leading proponents offer an overview. *Media Spectrum, 23*(1), 10.

Lloyd-Kolkin, D., & Tyner, K.R. (1991). *Media and you: An elementary media literacy curriculum.* Englewood Cliffs, NJ: Educational Technology Publications.

Luke, C. (1999). Media and cultural studies in Australia. *Journal of Adolescent & Adult Literacy, 42,* 622–626.

Lutz, W. (1989). *DoubleSpeak.* New York: HarperPerrenial.

Macaul, S.L., Giles, J.K., & Rodenberg, R.K. (1999). Intermediality in the classroom: Learners constructing meaning through Deep Viewing. In L.M. Semali & A.W. Pailliotet (Eds.), *Intermediality: The teachers' handbook of critical media literacy* (pp. 53–74). Boulder, CO: Westview Press.

McLaren, P., Hammer, R., Sholle, D., & Reilly, S. (Eds.). (1995). *Rethinking media literacy: A critical pedagogy of representation.* New York: Peter Lang.

Moline, S. (1995). *I see what you mean: Children at work with visual information.* York, ME: Stenhouse.

Neuman, S.B. (1991). *Literacy in the television age: The myth of the TV effect.* Norwood, NJ: Ablex.

Pailliotet, A.W. (1995). "I never saw that before." A deeper view of video analysis in teacher education. *The Teacher Educator, 31*(2) 138–156.

Pailliotet, A.W. (1997). Questing toward cohesion: Connecting advertisements and classroom reading through visual literacy. In R.E. Griffin, J.M. Hunter, C.B. Schiffman, & W.J. Gibbs (Eds.), *VisionQuest: Journeys toward visual literacy* (pp. 33–41). State College, PA: International Visual Literacy Association.

Pailliotet, A.W. (1998). Deep viewing: A critical look at texts. In J. Kincheloe & S. Steinberg (Eds.), *Unauthorized methods: Strategies for critical teaching*. New York: Routledge.

Pailliotet, A.W., Semali, L.M., Rodenberg, R.K., Giles, J.K., & Macaul, S.L. (2000). Intermediality: Bridge to critical media literacy. *The Reading Teacher, 54,* 208–221.

Pike, K., Compain, R., & Mumper, J. (1997). *New connections: An integrated approach to literacy* (2nd ed.). New York: Longman.

Reinking, D., McKenna, M.C., Labbo, L.D., & Kieffer, R.D. (Eds.). (1998). *Handbook of literacy and technology: Transformations in a post-typographic world*. Mahwah, NJ: Erlbaum.

Robinson, M. (1997). *Children reading print and television narrative: "It always ends at the exciting bit."* Washington, DC: Falmer.

Rosenblatt, L. (1978). *The reader, the text, the poem: The transactional theory of the literary work*. Carbondale, IL: Southern Illinois University Press.

Schmidt, P.R. (1993). Literacy development of two bilingual ethnic minority children in a kindergarten program. In D.J. Leu & C.K. Kinzer (Eds.), *Examining central issues in literacy research, theory, and practice* (pp. 189–196). Chicago: National Reading Conference.

Semali, L.M. (1999). Critical viewing as response to Intermediality: Implications for media literacy. In L.M. Semali & A.W. Pailliotet (Eds.), *Intermediality: The teachers' handbook of critical media literacy* (pp. 183–205). Boulder, CO: Westview Press.

Semali, L.M., & Pailliotet, A.W. (1999). Introduction: What is Intermediality and why study it in U.S. schools? In L.M. Semali & A.W. Pailliotet (Eds.), *Intermediality: The teachers' handbook of critical media literacy* (pp. 1–30). Boulder, CO: Westview.

Sholle, D., & Denski, S. (1993). Reading and writing the media: Critical media literacy and postmodernism. In C. Lankshear & P.L. McLaren (Eds.), *Critical literacy: Politics, praxis and the postmodern* (pp. 297–321). Albany, NY: State University of New York Press.

Thoman, E. (1999). Skills and strategies for media education. *Educational Leadership, 56*(5), 50–54.

Washington State Commission on Student Learning. (1996). *Revised essential learnings*. Olympia, WA: Author.

Weber, S., & Mitchell, C. (1995). *That's funny, you don't look like a teacher! Interrogating images and identity in popular culture*. London: Falmer Press.

Recommended Web Sites for Media Literacy

Center for Media Education
   http://www.cme.org
Center for Media Literacy
   http://www.medialit.org
Jesuit Communication Project
   http://interact.uoregon.edu/MediaLit/JCP/index.html
Media Awareness Network
   http://www.media-awareness.ca
Media Literacy Clearinghouse
   http://www.med.sc.edu:81/medialit/default.htm

New Mexico Media Literacy Project
   http://www.nmmlp.org
PBS Teacher Source
   http://www.pbs.org/teachersource

Media Education Centers and Organizations for Educators in North America

Association for Media Literacy
40 McArthur Street
Weston, ON M9P 3M7
Canada
416-394-6992

Center for Media Literacy
4727 Wilshire Boulevard, Suite 403
Los Angeles, CA 90010
800-226-9494 (toll free) or 323-931-4177
Fax: 323-931-4474
E-mail: cml@medialit.org
Web site: http://www.medialit.org

Citizens for Media Literacy
38 1/2 Battery Park Avenue, Ste. G
Asheville, NC 28001
704-255-0182

Educational Video Center
55 E. 25th Street, Ste. 407
New York, NY 10010
212-725-3534

International Visual Literacy Association
Contact: Dr. Darrell Beauchamp
Director of Learning Resource Center
Navarro College
3200 W. 7th Avenue
Corsicana, TX 75110
903-874-6501, ext. 320
E-mail: dbeau@nav.cc.tx.us

Media Education Foundation
26 Center Street
Northampton, MA 01060
800-897-0089
E-mail: mediated@igc.org

The Media Foundation
1243 West 7th Avenue
Vancouver, BC V6H 1B7
Canada
604-736-9401

Media Workshop New York
333 W. 17th Street, Rm. 324
New York, NY 10011
212-229-1776
Web site: http://www.mediaworkshop.org

National Telemedia Council
120 E. Wilson Street
Madison, WI 53703
608-257-7712

Newspaper Association of America Newspapers in Education Program
Box 17407, Dulles Airport
Washington, DC 20041
703-648-1051

Annotated Bibliography of Media Resources

Cheyney, A.B. (1992). *Teaching reading skills through the newspaper* (3rd ed.). Newark, DE: International Reading Association.

> I love this little book! My preservice teachers and I have used its many ideas for teaching with newspapers in elementary, secondary, and college classrooms for years. It contains many sound ideas for using newspapers to promote literacy skills as well as ideas to integrate across disciplines and subjects. "Activities for Social Studies and Science" is loaded with ideas for values instruction with headings such as values, different cultures, issues, concepts, social problems, rights and freedoms, and government.

Considine, D.M., Haley, G.E., & Lacy, L.E. (1994). *Imagine that! Developing critical thinking and critical viewing through children's literature.* Englewood, CO: Teacher Ideas Press.

> The subtitle says it all. Beginning media educators will find many relevant reading, writing, speaking, and artistic activities here that connect print literature and mass media. The last chapter, "Windows on the World: Picture Books as Social Construction and Representation," presents excellent teaching ideas and actual classroom examples for values instruction about topics ranging from gender and race to sports mascots and the values they convey. Check out pages 174–175—"Cultural Strategies and Activities for a Multicultural Curriculum." These wonderful booklists, samples of illustration, and art activities can help educators connect print-based literature curriculum to media literacy. This book also contains an excellent chapter chock full of ideas to teach about stereotypes, heroes, gender, and pluralism, among many others.

Considine, D.M., & Haley, G.E. (1999). *Visual messages: Integrating imagery into instruction* (2nd ed.). Englewood, CO: Teacher Ideas Press.

> This is the epitome of media literacy teaching books in its scope, variety of media texts and topics, thoroughness, and usefulness. It offers clearly stated rationales and tons of activities in an accessible and easy-to-read format. Some activities are more appropriate for secondary students, but most are easily adapted for younger pupils. It contains a plethora of ideas for teaching with specific media texts, as well as examining values about gender, race, consumerism stereotyping, substance abuse, and other important issues. No matter what your stance on media literacy issues, you'll find useful teaching activities here.

Educational Leadership, February 1999, 56(5).

> This entire journal is devoted to media literacy and technological topics. Short, easy-to-read articles by many leading authors discuss examples of curricula integration, media literacy,

and video technology, as well as issues of equity, ethics, and access. There are also several firsthand accounts from teachers about uses of technology and media in classrooms and schools.

Leu, D.J., Jr., & Leu, D.D. (1999). *Teaching with the Internet: Lessons from the classroom* (3rd ed.). Norwood, MA: Christopher-Gordon.

    An encompassing, accessible book for teachers about Internet uses and resources. Many sites and lessons are easily adapted to include values lessons.

Lockwood Summers, S. (1999). *Media Alert! 200 activities to create media-savvy kids.* Castle Rock, CO: Hi Willow Research.

    There are so many great things about this book. Each lesson identifies a guiding concept that encourages multiple ways of responding and analyzing diverse media texts. Each lesson also presents age-appropriate ideas for preschool/first grade, elementary school, middle school, and high school, enabling teachers to easily tailor lessons to their students' needs. Many lessons—like "Reflect on the Need to Read," "Relate Democracy to Media Literacy," and "Think for Yourself"—foster print literacy competencies, critical thinking, and values instruction.

Newman, B., & Mara, J. (1995). *Reading, writing & TV: A video handbook for teachers.* Fort Atkinson, WI: Highsmith Press.

    This book contains numerous ready-to-go activities and materials for video analysis and production.

Pailliotet, A.W., Semali, L.M., Rodenberg, R.K., Giles, J.K., & Macaul, S.L. (2000). Intermediality: Bridge to critical media literacy. *The Reading Teacher, 54,* 208–221.

    This article provides premises of critical media literacy, each illustrated by classroom examples and a list of critical viewing frameworks.

Rosen, E.Y., Quesada, A.P., & Lockwood Summers, S. (1998). *Changing the world through media education.* Golden, CO: Just Think Foundation.

    One of the best books. It contains ready-to-go, creative materials and activities that further media literacy and values education throughout.

Thoman, E. (1998). Media literacy: A guided tour of selected resources for teachers. *English Journal, 87*(1), 34–37.

Thoman, E. (1999). Skills and strategies for media education. *Educational Leadership, 56*(5), 50–54.

    Two excellent, pragmatic articles by a leader in media literacy.

Valmont, W.J. (1995). *Creating videos for school use.* Boston: Allyn & Bacon.

    A nuts-and-bolts how-to book about many aspects of video production. Many activities and ideas, particularly in the chapters on "Text, Graphics and Special Effects," "Writing School Videos," and "Suggestions for Making School Videos," which are very relevant to media and values education.

Worsnop, C.M. (1994). *Screening images: Ideas for media education.* Mississauga, Ontario, Canada: Wright.

Worsnop, C.M. (1999). *Assessing media work: Authentic assessment in media education.* Mississauga, Ontario, Canada: Wright.

    Assessing Media Work contains wonderful rubrics for all sorts of media education learning objectives. Many examples of assessment forms and formats for teachers and students are included. Given the current focus on assessment in many schools, a must have. Also check out *Screening Images*, a thin volume worth its weight in gold for the numerous lists of media activities.

Home-School Connections

Knowing family and community values is key to beginning the exploration of values through literature, multimedia, and literacy events. As teachers are forming connections with the students in their classrooms, they are simultaneously reaching out to the families and communities of their children. A recent model known as the ABCs of Cultural Understanding and Communication, developed by Patricia Ruggiano Schmidt, has been used by teachers in urban, rural, and suburban schools to connect home and school for literacy learning. Family values have emerged from these intimate connections and have proven to help teachers and teaching assistants develop culturally sensitive pedagogy as well as promote family participation in classrooms and schools.

Family values can also be connected through the use of multicultural literature and literacy software. Students need to see themselves, their communities, and others from diverse ethnic and cultural backgrounds portrayed in the literature, materials, and software in their homes and schools. Finally, on a cautionary note, families and schools must be aware of stereotypical examples used in literature and multimedia and guide their children in becoming critical viewers.

Chapter 3

The ABCs of Cultural Understanding and Communication: Teacher Assistants Learn to Respect, Appreciate, and Apply Differences in Literacy Instruction

Shelley Hong Xu

The purpose of this chapter is to help present and future teachers understand and value diversity in their classrooms and schools. I describe how teacher assistants used the model of the ABCs of Cultural Understanding and Communication, known as the ABCs Model (Schmidt, 1998a, 1998b, 1999), in their classrooms to promote their own awareness of cultural values and to enhance a connection of their knowledge about students and literacy instruction. While using the ABCs Model in conjunction with case studies of individual students in their classrooms, teacher assistants developed enhanced understandings of their own cultural values and experiences and became more knowledgeable of their students' cultural and academic backgrounds. Teacher assistants made efforts to connect their knowledge about students to literacy instruction, that is, they built literacy lessons on students' prior knowledge and cultural experiences. I provide one example of literacy lesson teaching to illustrate such a connection. At the conclusion of the chapter, I share teacher assistants' reflections on using the ABCs Model. I also offer two additional examples to illustrate how present and future teachers can use the ABCs Model in literacy instruction and literacy across curriculum.

As we enter the 21st century, school-age children continue to become increasingly diverse in linguistic, cultural, and socioeconomic backgrounds. In the past decades, studies of successful teachers of diverse students have informed us of "culturally responsive instruction" (Au, 1993). Teachers build classroom instruction on their knowledge about their students, including the students' cultural backgrounds and personal experiences (Au, 1980, 1993; Au & Jordan, 1981; Au & Mason, 1983; Diamond & Moore, 1995; Edwards & Pleasants, 1998; Ladson-Billings, 1994, 1995). Although knowledge about students is crucial for "culturally responsive instruction," some scholars (Banks, 1994; Florio-Ruane, 1994; Zeichner, 1993) have also pointed out the critical role of teachers' knowledge about themselves before getting to know their students who are culturally and linguistically different from them. Schmidt (1998a, 1998b) further states that teachers' knowledge of their students' life experiences is one means to learn about their students' cultures. Likewise, Spindler and Spindler (1987) view cross-cultural analysis of one's own and others' culture as a way to promote one's awareness of various cultures.

What Is the ABCs Model?

Building on the premises related to the importance of knowing one's and others' cultures and cross-cultural analysis, Schmidt (1998a, 1998b, 1999) developed a model known as the ABCs of Cultural Understanding and Communication that integrates examining oneself into understanding others. The model includes these five components (Schmidt, 1999):

1. An autobiography, written in detail, by each student to include key life events related to education, family, religious tradition, recreation, victories, and defeats.

2. The biography of a person who is culturally different from the student, written from in-depth, unstructured interviews (Spradley, 1979) that include key life events.

3. A cross-cultural analysis of similarities and differences between the life stories is charted (Spindler & Spindler, 1987).

4. An analysis of cultural differences examined in writing with encouragement for students to explain personal discomforts and identify positive affect.

5. Modification for classroom practice and communication plans for literacy development and home/school connections based on the preceding process are designed. (pp. 334–335)

Why Was the ABCs Model Used?

I allowed the teacher assistants to experience the model for two reasons. First, the ABCs Model has proven effective with present and future teachers. In a multicultural education course, Schmidt (1998a) discovered that the model helped the teachers to become more aware of cultural differences and of building classroom instruction on students' cultural experiences. Other studies (Schmidt, 1998b, 1999; Xu, 2000a, 2000b) document the impact of the ABCs Model on present and future teachers and on elementary and secondary students. The present and future teachers learned more about their students through student biography and cross-cultural analysis than through student files. Likewise, while participating in various literacy activities, the students came to understand and appreciate the value of cultural differences.

The second reason for using the ABCs Model with teacher assistants deals with the scarcity of literature that is related to teacher assistants who are working with students in a culturally responsive fashion. Most teacher assistants work individually with students who have difficulty with literacy skills and who are often from homes other than middle-class and European American families (Allington, 1998; Blodgett & Miller, 1997; Hoffman & Pearson, 2000). Therefore, it becomes crucial that teacher assistants learn how to get to know their students well and accommodate literacy instruction to unique needs of individual students. It is my hope that the teacher assistants' experiences with the ABCs Model highlighted here will offer other teacher assistants and teachers of diverse students who struggle with literacy some insights into connecting themselves with diverse students and into modifying literacy instruction to meet their students' needs.

Who Were the Teacher Assistants?

The 17 female teacher assistants worked in several neighboring school districts in a southwestern state in the United States, and had been teaching from 2 to 20 years. They worked daily with students in pre-K classes through Grade 12 in small groups and on a one-on-one basis. The majority of their students were at reading levels below their grade levels. The teacher assistants were enrolled in a teacher education program to become certified teachers. I was the instructor for two integrated literacy methods courses—reading and language arts. The content of both courses included discussions of literacy theories, demonstrations of instructional strategies, discussions of questions arising from their work in classrooms, the sharing of reflective journals, and critiques of videotaped lessons that each of the teacher assistants taught.

How Was the ABCs Model Used?

I used the ABCs Model with teacher assistants in conjunction with case studies of their individual students. Based on my experiences with future teachers (Xu, 2000a, 2000b), I realized that an in-depth study of one student would allow the teacher assistants to become familiar with the ABCs Model and with the process of getting to know individual students and oneself. At the end of the semester, each teacher assistant wrote a case study report in which she wrote her case study student's biography, including the student's cultural background and home and school literacy experiences; described student literacy development; discussed her own reactions to differences; and reflected on her experiences with adapting her teaching to the students.

Autobiography

Two weeks after the semester started, the teacher assistants wrote their autobiography, in which they provided details of their cultural traditions and values, family stories and roots, and important life events, among other things. Additionally, I asked them to describe their literacy experiences at home and at school. I wanted them to acknowledge their own unique experiences with reading and writing and to note how such unique experiences would affect their perceptions of learning and teaching, and ways of teaching.

Biography

I asked the teacher assistants to use multiple means to get to know their students' cultural, linguistic, and life experiences. At the beginning and end of the semester, the teacher assistants conducted unstructured and partially structured interviews with their case study students. Throughout the semester, the teacher assistants had informal talks with their students in instructional and noninstructional settings. At the end of the semester, the teacher assistants wrote about their students' biography based on what they had obtained from formal and informal interactions with students over the semester.

Cross-Cultural Analysis

Each teacher assistant listed in a chart format the similarities and differences in cultural backgrounds and literacy experiences between herself and her case study student. I did not provide the teacher assistants with categories of similarities and differences for the cross-cultural analysis. They came up with the categories that applied to themselves and their students. Because getting to know their students was an ongoing effort throughout the semester, the teacher assistants had revised their charts several times before the charts were included in their case study reports.

Analysis of Cultural Differences

In each class session, the teacher assistants shared their own reactions to cultural differences between themselves and their students that they had gathered through interactions with their students. They also discussed the sources of comfort and discomfort toward differences (e.g., personal experiences with people from diverse backgrounds). Additionally, the teacher assistants talked about how the differences in cultural values and life experiences provided them with insights into culturally responsive teaching. The teacher assistants further discussed, in their case study reports, their attitudes toward differences and about applying such differences in literacy instruction.

Classroom Practices

The teacher assistants documented in their case study reports how they taught their case study student based on their knowledge of the student's cultural background and experiences. Specifically, they wrote reflections on lessons taught to a small group of students or a whole class, including the case study students. They detailed what worked and what did not work as they applied children's literature and literacy instructional strategies with the case study students.

Teacher Assistants' Experiences With the ABCs Model: Learning to Respect, Appreciate, and Apply Differences

Who Am I? Exploring Cultural Self and Literacy Experiences

In their autobiographies, the teacher assistants highlighted their own cultural values that were important to them and made them proud of who they were. The similar values among all teacher assistants were beliefs in God, working ethics, a commitment to respecting and helping others, and prioritizing their family's needs to come first. Identifying their own cultural values provided the teacher assistants with the opportunities to note that cultural values shaped who they were, what they believed, and how they acted. For instance, Kay expressed,

> My cultural background is important to me because it is my roots. I am a product of my ancestors, and I am proud of that. I was raised to work and make an honest living, go to church, be kind to others, and work to make the world a better place.

In addition, an examination of their own literacy experiences allowed the teacher assistants to note the crucial role of parents and teachers in the process of learning to read and write. Kathleen noted that her parents "helped to mold me into the person that I am today." She continued,

> My parents were not wealthy, but they always provided what we needed. We lived in a rural area 30 miles from the nearest library, but my parents took us to the library every two weeks. I would read my books and my sister's books. We discovered that you could travel anywhere in the world and to both real and imaginary places by reading books.

Rosa could not recall any literacy experience at home, but "only early recollections of school." She described her kindergarten teacher as "wonderful," adding,

> I do not remember ever being read to as a child, so when she [the kindergarten teacher] read to us I thought she had the most beautiful voice, and loved listening to her. I only remember learning in a school environment, and I feel that this is probably why I loved reading so much.

Although all teacher assistants were able to recall the level of involvement of their parents and other family members in their learning to read, not all of them shared fond memories of their teachers and learning experiences. Shari, for instance, described that she "was hit a lot by my second grade teacher for not being able to read; she felt I was just being stubborn." She vividly remembered the effect of ability grouping on her self-perception:

> It did not matter what the teacher called the groups each year. I and everyone in my class knew I would never be a member of the blue car group racing down the highway of reading, nor a yellow bike group member whizzing along. I would always be a slow red wagon barely making it.

Teacher assistants' own unpleasant literacy experiences caused them to put themselves in their students' shoes and to view literacy teaching from students' perspectives. Shari reflected on her own literacy experiences that "have influenced my interactions with children." She stated, "I have a duty to teach as many children as possible how to read and for them to enjoy this journey. It is important for those teaching children to expect effort from all children, but not to make them feel stupid."

Who Is My Student? Exploring Students' Cultural and Literacy Experiences

Like most teachers, the teacher assistants in my literacy methods courses had worked with their case study students on a daily basis. However, they seldom had a chance to learn thoroughly about their students' diverse backgrounds due to such reasons as time constraints and teacher assistants' responsibilities. Through interviews, informal talks, and work with case study students, the teacher assistants learned that their students shared many similarities with them and, at the same time, their students were also very different from them.

Figures 1 and 2 show the cross-cultural analyses between the case study students, Mary and BJ, and the teacher assistants, Prudence and Kay. The case study students and teacher assistants were cultural beings with unique life experiences. It is interesting to note that the categories in each figure reflect different emphases on similarities and differences. In Figure 1, Prudence focused the similarities between herself and Mary on literacy experiences (e.g., was read to at night) and personality (e.g., kind of shy, not very outgoing). As to the differences between them, Prudence continued to center on literacy experiences. For example, Mary "reads only what is required or very easy books" while Prudence "read[s] everything [she] can find." Prudence also added the different roles of parents and the family's socioeconomic status: Mary lives in a "single parent family" and "doesn't do much with her family," whereas Prudence is from

FIGURE I   Cross-Cultural Analysis Chart: Mary and Prudence

Mary and Prudence
- were read to at night
- like to read
- like to write stories
- speak English
- went to kindergarten
- kind of shy, not very outgoing
- oldest children in the family

Mary

(case study child)
- from a single parent family with lower income
- five brothers and sisters
- went to pre-K
- responsible for younger siblings
- has learning disabilities
- reads only what is required or very easy books
- does not do much with her family
- cannot get spelling words
- parents show very little affection

Prudence

(teacher assistant)
- from a traditional family with middle income
- one brother and sister
- Anglo American
- has no learning disabilities
- reads everything she can find
- took trips as a family
- has no trouble with spelling
- affection shown by family

FIGURE 2   Cross-Cultural Analysis Chart: BJ and Kay

BJ and Kay
- average income
- writing and reading is important
- same size family
- come from a home based on work ethics
- both mother and father worked together to keep home and marriage successful
- like school but get frustrated with it

BJ

(case study child)
- Hispanic
- has a puppy and likes pets
- likes mystery books
- enjoys art and drawing
- tall and dark-haired
- enjoys socializing
- likes to participate in sports

Kay

(teacher assistant)
- White
- does not care for animals
- likes novels and fiction
- has little to no artistic ability
- short and dark-haired
- prefers sitting and listening
- likes to watch sports activities

a "traditional family" and "took trips as a family." Figure 2 reflects more similarities than differences between Kay and BJ. In the similarities section, Kay included literacy experiences and cultural values. She highlighted that "writing and reading is important" to her and BJ and that "both mother and father [in both of their families] worked together to keep home and marriage successful." For the differences, Kay focused on ethnicity (e.g., White vs. Hispanic), hobbies (e.g., "likes novels and fiction" versus "likes mystery books"), and physical features ("short and dark-haired" versus "tall and dark-haired").

Using the Knowledge of Self and Student in Literacy Instruction

Once the teacher assistants became familiar with their case study students' backgrounds, they made efforts to build literacy instruction on students' home and school literacy and cultural experiences. Specifically, after they realized a crucial need to be more supportive for the students who came to school with little knowledge of print, they accordingly provided the students with varying activities that allowed them to have active interactions with print, such as read-alouds, journal writing, and shared reading and writing. In addition to maximizing students' interactions with print, the literacy activities promoted student engagement and personal connection. The teacher assistants, for example, introduced to case study students multicultural books that dealt with self-esteem, feelings, and cultural experiences, and then built lessons on students' knowledge of their community and environment. The following lesson illustrates how one teacher assistant, Carol, made an effort to promote the value of self-esteem among her students in a literacy lesson. (See Figure 3 for the lesson plan.) The lesson integrated a children's book, engaged the students in sharing their life experiences, and encouraged the students to perceive themselves as unique human beings.

Carol often worked with a small group of second graders who were struggling with literacy skills. Because of negative and unsuccessful literacy experiences in kindergarten, first-, and second-grade classrooms, these four students had low self-esteem. After learning that the second-grade students in their regular classrooms were doing a thematic unit on self-esteem, Carol decided to choose the book *I Like Me!* (Carlson, 1988) for her lesson. *I Like Me!* tells about a little pig who likes how she looks and what she can do, and who continues trying to accomplish something after making mistakes. Carol thought that by using the book, she would reinforce the concept of self-esteem that her students were learning in their regular classrooms. Meanwhile, Carol would provide the students with a sense of consistency in literacy learning. Carol used the book also as a means to get to know her case study student better and as a

FIGURE 3   Carol's Lesson Plan

Grade Level: Second Grade

Content:	Increase the children's awareness of themselves and help them identify characteristics about themselves that are likely to result in improved self-esteem.
Objectives:	1. Students will continue to develop their oral language and communication skills and move to becoming independent readers and writers.
	2. Students will listen and respond to a wide variety of children's literature.
	3. Students will recognize the distinguishing features of stories, poems, and informational texts.
	4. Students will continue to develop their concepts of how print connects with spoken language.
	5. Students will demonstrate their comprehension by asking and answering questions, retelling stories, predicting outcomes, and making and explaining inferences.
	6. Students will relate children's literature to their own life experiences.
Materials:	• *I Like Me!* (Carlson, 1988)
	• chalkboard, chalk, eraser, peach-colored ovals of construction paper, pencils, scissors, glue, craft sticks
	• other books used prior to the lesson to produce schema for this lesson
Teaching Steps:	1. Read aloud the book *I Like Me!*
	2. Discuss the book—all the reasons given why the little pig likes herself.
	3. Have the students do a cluster of ideas of what they like about themselves as I write the ideas on the board.
	4. Have the students draw their own faces on the ovals cut out from construction paper and then glue the "mask" onto the stick. On the back of their faces, the students write down what they like about themselves.
	5. Go over the students' clusters on the chalkboard and ask them to share their "masks" to reaffirm their worth and self-esteem.

springboard to stimulate her students to talk about what they liked about themselves.

After reading aloud *I Like Me!* to the group, Carol shared things that she liked about herself, such as being hard working and enjoying her job teaching and working with students. When asked to share what they liked about themselves, all students in the group talked about things they liked, such as pizza, books, movies, and television shows. After reflecting on this lesson, Carol told our class that her students have probably had little experiences with sharing what they liked about themselves. Carol and her students discussed the difference between what they like and what they like about themselves. At that point, she continued to discover that "some children were not very enthusiastic about telling about themselves." However, she did learn that her case study student liked herself because she "likes funny books and always enjoys jokes."

Carol wrote in her reflection that she had learned "some truth" about her case study student through the lesson that she would otherwise never get from a formal student-teacher interview. Carol also noted the importance of using books in literacy instruction to which students may have varying levels of personal connections. Such personal connections allowed the teacher assistants to prepare additional opportunities to learn about their students' backgrounds and to build corresponding literacy lessons. For example, after this lesson, Carol decided that in subsequent literacy lessons with the students, she should read and discuss more books related to self-esteem and self-worth. She explained,

> I would do a word wall that the students and I would put together and let them choose [words] from [it] as they do their own clusters [on self-esteem].... It might encourage them to have more diversity in the reasons they like themselves.

An annotated list of children's books on self-esteem can be found in Figure 4.

FIGURE 4   Annotated Bibliography of Children's Books on Self-Esteem

Cannon, J. (1997). *Verdi*. San Diego: Harcourt Brace.
Verdi, a young python, is always proud of his bright yellow skin. One day, as he spots a patch of green appearing on his skin, he tries to stop this sign of aging. No matter how hard he tries (he even almost kills himself), his green skin never goes away. Verdi learns not to let his appearance stop him from enjoying himself.

Carlson, N. (1997). *ABC I like me*. New York: Viking.
A little pig tells what she can do from A to Z. The book starts with "Feeling good about me is as easy as ABC." The little pig characterizes herself as "Awesome, Brave, and Cheerful."

Carlson, N. (1988). *I like me!* New York: Viking.
A little pig tells the importance of feeling good about herself and taking good care of herself. She considers herself as her own best friend, good-looking, and able to draw pictures, ride bikes, read books, cheer herself up when she feels sad, and pick herself up when she makes mistakes.

Fox, M. (1997). *Whoever you are*. Ill. L. Staub. San Diego: Harcourt Brace.
The little ones around the world may be different from one another in skin colors, languages, lives, homes, and schools. They, however, share similar joys, laughs, tears, and love. "Smiles are the same, and hearts are just the same—wherever they are, wherever you are, wherever we are, all over the world."

Henkes, K. (1991). *Chrysanthemum*. New York: Greenwillow.
Chrysanthemum thinks that her parents have given her a perfect name, and she loves her name. But when she starts her first day of school in kindergarten, her classmates make fun of her name. Chrysanthemum starts to feel that "school is no place" for her. Chrysanthemum's music teacher, whose name happens to be a flower, makes Chrysanthemum feel special about her own name. She even names her own newborn baby girl Chrysanthemum. What makes Chrysanthemum feel even more special is that her classmates all begin to name themselves after flowers.

(continued)

Hoffman, M. (1991). *Amazing Grace*. Ill. C. Binch. New York: Dial.

 Grace loves stories and acting out her favorite parts of the stories. Grace wants to play the role of
 Peter Pan in a class play, but some classmates tell her that she cannot, because she is a black girl.
 Grace's Ma and Nana encourage her to be anything she wants to be. Grace practices the role of
 Peter Pan all week long and is voted in the auditions by her class as the best person for the role.

Hudson, C.W., & Ford, B.G. (1990). *Bright eyes, brown skin*. Ill. G. Ford. South Orange, NJ: Just Us
Books.

 This book, written in a rhyming text, describes four African American children's daily interactions
 and activities in a kindergarten classroom. The text highlights what makes each of them so special.
 "Bright eyes, brown skin.... A heart-shaped face, a dimpled chin."

Kraus, R. (1994). *Leo the late bloomer*. Ill. J. Aruego. New York: HarperCollins.

 Leo cannot read, write, draw, or even eat with proper manners. But his father believes Leo is a late
 bloomer, and he patiently waits for that moment to come. Leo keeps practicing, and "in his own
 good time, Leo bloomed!"

Walsh, E.S. (1994). *Pip's magic*. San Diego: Harcourt Brace.

 Pip, a salamander, is afraid of darkness. The frogs advise him to find Old Abra, whose magic will help
 him overcome his fear. After traveling through the dark woods, tunnel, and night, Pip finally finds
 Old Abra, who tells Pip he does not need his magic. Pip has found his own magic to overcome his
 fear of darkness through the journey of searching for Old Abra's magic.

Wilhelm, H. (1996). *The royal raven*. New York: Cartwheel Books.

 Crawford, a raven, feels that he is very special inside, but his looks seem to be so ordinary. He
 asks a witch to change him into a beautiful bird with dazzling and shiny feathers. Crawford is so
 happy with his new looks that he shows off to all his friends. But they cannot recognize him at
 all. He flies to a royal garden in which he is first adored by the princess and then feels so deserted
 when the princess stops paying attention to him. She even throws him out after Crawford pulls out
 his dazzling and shiny feathers. Crawford returns to his friends, feeling happy with them and his
 ordinary looks.

What Did the Teacher Assistants Learn From Using the ABCs Model in Their Classrooms?

The ABCs Model provided the teacher assistants with multiple opportunities
to learn about their case study students, to compare and contrast similarities
and differences between themselves and their students, and to build literacy instruction on individual students' cultural and academic backgrounds. They
came to realize that having knowledge of literacy pedagogy did not mean that
they were able to teach diverse students. Teaching literacy meant connecting
lessons to student culture and experiences and constantly self-examining and
reflecting on lessons, among other things. The teacher assistants also became
aware that they should not assume each student shared similarities with themselves in terms of life experiences and self-esteem; nor should they believe

that students from non–middle-class families did not want to learn. Within the context of teaching their students, the teacher assistants had varying opportunities to learn from "what children have to tell us and show us" (Wolf, Carey, & Mieras, 1996) about literacy learning and teaching and witness how culture functions in education (Ladson-Billings, 1995).

As the teacher assistants explored their own lives and their students' experiences through the ABCs Model, they gained an increased understanding of how to teach literacy to students with diverse backgrounds. The power of the ABCs Model lay with its linkage between the teacher assistants and their students. Through self-explorations, the teacher assistants allowed themselves to bring up their deeply rooted beliefs from the subconscious level to the conscious level, to become closer to their students, and to position themselves— including their beliefs and experiences—within the context of teaching and their students. The effectiveness of using the ABCs Model with the teacher assistants echoed Delpit's (1988) assertion, "We do not really see through our eyes or hear through our ears, but through our beliefs" (p. 297). The quotes that follow indicate some of the teacher assistants' reflections on the use of the ABCs Model in conjunction with case studies of individual students:

> Through the work I have done on this case study I have learned the importance of learning a child's cultural and linguistic background. The reflection of my own cultural and linguistic background will help me understand how my background influences my view and approach to helping a child from a different background from myself. (Shari)

> Working with special education students has really opened my eyes. They have just as much of a right to learn, if not more so, as the student who doesn't need "extra" help. In doing this case study, I was forced to pay close attention to what one particular student was doing on a daily basis. It has made me aware of the importance of paying close attention to ALL of the students on a daily basis. (Kerry)

> I never realized all the different learning styles and how beneficial they are to those students who struggle, as well as those who do not. I also knew that students learned differently. This case study showed me how diverse students are, but it also taught me that no matter how a student learns, there are strategies or techniques that will help them. We, as teachers, have the job of finding and implementing it. (Rosa)

> Working individually with students for an extended length of time has helped me look at each student a little differently. I now look to see if there is something in their lives that is affecting their learning. Many of the children we work with have emotions and environmental interruptions on a daily basis. (Leona)

The following list summarizes the benefits the teacher assistants gained as they expanded their knowledge about their students, about literacy teaching and learning, and about teaching students with diverse backgrounds:

1. The teacher assistants developed a firmer belief that students who speak English as a second language (ESL) may have stronger literacy skills in their native language. English literacy instruction needs to be built on such literacy skills.

2. The teacher assistants realized that some parents are more involved in students' school learning than others. They noticed that parental involvement took many different forms, some of which was not always acknowledged by teachers.

3. The teacher assistants acknowledged that students may, according to some narrow-minded teachers, appear to be lazy, unintelligent, and disinterested. These characteristics of barriers to successful learning actually result from teachers' poor classroom instruction and from their failure to engage students in literacy activities that are personally meaningful to them.

4. The teacher assistants understood that individual students can be very different from their teacher and peers in varying ways, but they all have the potential and right to learn to be literate. It is the teacher's responsibility to find ways to build on students' strengths and address their needs as well as to use classroom instruction to make up for what students might have missed in their home literacy experiences.

5. The teacher assistants stressed that the cultural and linguistic diversity that students bring into classrooms can be used in literacy instruction to take teachers and students to places "outside our own little world."

6. The teacher assistants realized that the concept of diversity is not only limited to students' cultural and linguistic differences but also includes multiple levels of literacy skills, varying learning styles, and different types of school and home experiences.

7. The teacher assistants acknowledged that students' opinions and perspectives need to be valued and respected, no matter how different they are from their own. Teachers need to view students' perspectives through their lived experiences.

8. The teacher assistants admitted that misconceptions and stereotypes of students with different backgrounds and experiences are the products of teachers' limited experiences with student culture and perspectives.

What Can Present and Future Teachers Do in Classrooms to Promote Multicultural Values?

In the previous sections, I have described teacher assistants' endeavors to examine their own cultural experiences, to learn about their students' cultural experiences, and to build literacy instruction on their knowledge of their students. I conclude this chapter by providing two examples to illustrate how present and future teachers can use the ABCs Model in classrooms and schools. Specifically, I will demonstrate how the model can be integrated into literacy instruction and how the use of literacy across the curriculum can enhance teachers' and students' awareness and appreciation of diversity and multicultural values.

The ABCs Model can be incorporated into thematic units that focus on creating a classroom community of learners with diverse backgrounds (e.g., "Let's Learn About Each Other" and "Let's Celebrate Multicultural Values"). This would be a great opportunity for a teacher to engage students in meaningful and authentic literacy experiences in conjunction with applications of various literacy strategies. Here is an example of how it might work.

1. The teacher starts by sharing his or her autobiography. Then the teacher models how to write an autobiography by conducting several mini-lessons on elements of autobiography.

2. Each student writes his or her autobiography during writer's workshop.

3. The teacher becomes a member of the community of learners. Each member selects a partner for an interview. The teacher works with the students to create a list of possible interview questions related to elements such as cultural values, family traditions, and school and home literacy experiences. Each interviewer can come up with additional questions based on his or her knowledge of the interviewee by using a K-W-L chart (know, want to know, learned) (Ogle, 1986). The interviewer and interviewee then reverse the roles.

4. Each pair lists the similarities and differences between them in a chart format (e.g., a Venn Diagram). The teacher makes sure that no predetermined categories of similarities and differences are assigned to the students.

5. The teacher models his or her reactions to differences between himself or herself and a student. The teacher encourages students to share their attitudes toward differences.

6. The teacher leads the discussion on student comfort and discomfort toward differences. The teacher may use think-aloud (Pressley & Afflerbach, 1995) to assist the students in examining their own cultural and life experiences to identify the sources of positive and negative feelings. Possible prompts for think-aloud would be, "Tell us why you find it weird that John's mother never read to John." In upper grades, a

teacher and students can participate in a debate on the importance of appreciating and respecting differences in multicultural values.

Another example of using the ABCs Model is to involve teachers and students from all grade levels in a school as well as parents and others from a community. The steps of using the model would be very similar to those in the first example. Teachers and students, however, would have opportunities to grasp the sense of breadth and depth in multicultural values and diversity. For example, tracing family roots through interviewing key informants would be an opportunity for teachers and students to learn about the history of multicultural values and contributions that different generations in a family have made to a multicultural society.

In closing, teaching students of diverse backgrounds to become literate has increasingly been a challenge. By increasing their knowledge of students' cultural and academic backgrounds, teachers can increase their ability to meet the challenge. Teachers constantly need to examine their own culture and experiences, frequently seize "learnable" moments to get to know their students' culture and experiences, and regularly build literacy instruction on students' prior cultural experiences and knowledge. The ABCs Model can serve as a powerful means for teachers to connect to students and to link literacy instruction to students' life experiences and literacy knowledge.

References

Allington, R.L. (Ed.). (1998). *Teaching struggling readers: Articles from* The Reading Teacher. Newark, DE: International Reading Association.

Au, K.H. (1980). Participation structures in a reading lesson with Hawaiian children: Analysis of a culturally appropriate instructional event. *Anthropology and Education Quarterly, 11,* 91–115.

Au, K.H. (1993). *Literacy instruction in multicultural settings.* Fort Worth, TX: Harcourt Brace.

Au, K.H., & Jordan, C. (1981). Teaching reading to Hawaiian children: Finding a culturally appropriate solution. In H. Trueba, G. Guthrie, & K. Au (Eds.), *Culture and the bilingual classroom: Studies in classroom ethnography* (pp. 139–152). Rowley, MA: Newbury House.

Au, K.H., & Mason, J.M. (1983). Cultural congruence in classroom participation structures: Achieving a balance of rights. *Discourse Processes, 6,* 145–167.

Banks, J.A. (1994). *An introduction to multicultural education.* Boston: Allyn & Bacon.

Blodgett, E.G., & Miller, J.M. (1997). Speech-language paraprofessionals working in Kentucky schools. *Journal of Children's Communication Development, 18,* 65–79.

Delpit, L. (1988). The silenced dialogue: Power and pedagogy in educating other people's children. *Harvard Educational Review, 58,* 280–298.

Diamond, B.J., & Moore, M.A. (1995). *Multicultural literacy: Mirroring the reality of the classroom.* White Plains, NY: Longman.

Edwards, P.A., & Pleasants, H.M. (1998). How can we provide for culturally responsive instruction in literacy? In S.B. Neuman & K.A. Roskos (Eds.), *Children achieving: Best practices in early literacy* (pp. 98–120). Newark, DE: International Reading Association.

Florio-Ruane, S. (1994). The future teachers' autobiography club: Preparing educators to support literacy learning in culturally diverse classrooms. *English Education, 26*(1), 52–56.

Hoffman, J., & Pearson, P.D. (2000). Reading teacher education in the next millennium: What your grandmother's teacher didn't know that your granddaughter's teacher should. *Reading Research Quarterly, 35,* 28–44.

Ladson-Billings, G. (1994). *The dreamkeepers: Successful teachers of African-American children.* San Francisco: Jossey-Bass.

Ladson-Billings, G. (1995). Toward a theory of culturally relevant pedagogy. *American Educational Research Journal, 32,* 465–491.

Ogle, D.M. (1986). K-W-L: A teaching model that develops active reading of expository text. *The Reading Teacher, 39,* 564–570.

Pressley, M., & Afflerbach, P. (1995). *Verbal protocols of reading: The nature of constructing responsive reading.* Hillsdale, NJ: Erlbaum.

Schmidt, P.R. (1998a). The ABC's of cultural understanding and communication. *Equity & Excellence in Education, 31*(2), 28–38.

Schmidt, P.R. (1998b). The ABC's Model: Teachers connect home and school. In T. Shanahan & F. Rodriguez-Brown (Eds.), *47th Yearbook of the National Reading Conference* (pp. 194–208). Chicago, IL: National Reading Conference.

Schmidt, P.R. (1999). Know thyself and understand others. *Language Arts, 76,* 332–340.

Spindler, G., & Spindler, L. (1987). *The interpretive ethnography of education: At home and abroad.* Hillsdale, NJ: Erlbaum.

Spradley, J. (1979). *The ethnographic interview.* New York: Holt, Rinehart & Winston.

Wolf, S.A., Carey, A.A., & Mieras, E.L. (1996). "What is this literachurch stuff anyway?" Preservice teachers' growth in understanding children's literary response. *Reading Research Quarterly, 31,* 130–157.

Xu, S.H. (2000a). Preservice teachers integrate understandings of diversity into literacy instruction: An adaptation of the ABC's model. *Journal of Teacher Education, 51,* 135–142.

Xu, S.H. (2000b). Preservice teachers in a literacy methods course consider issues of diversity. *Journal of Literacy Research, 32,* 505–531.

Zeichner, K.M. (1993). *Educating teachers for cultural diversity.* East Lansing, MI: National Center on Teacher Learning.

Children's Literature Cited

Carlson, N. (1988). *I like me!* New York: Scholastic.

Chapter 4

Connecting Home and School Values Through Multicultural Literature and Family Stories

Brigette B. Laier, Patricia A. Edwards, Gwendolyn T. McMillon, and Jennifer D. Turner

> The heart of school beats in the classroom. It is the place where students and teachers interact. (Danridge, 1998, p. 1)

Few would disagree with this statement, but all too often the classroom environment does not reflect the ideas, ethics, attitudes, and values of the people who live in it. These incongruencies make it more difficult for students and teachers to interact with each other (Edwards, Pleasants, & Franklin, 1999). We believe that educators can move closer to achieving the goal of providing a school environment that reflects the home cultures of its students by recognizing and appreciating the family values that students bring to the classroom. We feel that one way to accomplish this goal is by utilizing literature in the classroom, especially multicultural literature, to identify and discuss family values. The purpose of this chapter is to provide a model for using multicultural literature as a means of illuminating the universal values that exist among diverse families and communities.

Why Use Multicultural Literature?

Multicultural literature is a powerful vehicle for teaching children about family and community values. Diamond and Moore (1995) assert, "As students read multicultural books, they gain new insights into the values and beliefs of their own culture and the culture of others" (p. 10). Given the predominance of mainstream literature used in school, we believe it is important for students to be exposed to diversity in texts. To illustrate this point, consider an informal conversation we had with elementary European American teachers working in a district composed of mostly European American students. When we asked the teachers to recommend titles of multicultural literature to use in this chapter, they each responded similarly: "Well, I don't really use a lot of multicultural literature in my classroom." We are concerned about this kind of statement.

At the same time, we understand the reluctance. Some teachers may be hesitant about using multicultural literature in their classrooms because they are concerned about offending students and/or parents with books that "perpetuate stereotypes or present inaccurate cultural information" (Cai, 1995, p. 14). This problem is exacerbated by the fact that inaccurate multicultural books often get positive reviews in the professional literature (Fang, Fu, & Lamme, 1999), making it more challenging for conscientious teachers to make quality selections.

We believe, however, that the absence of exposure to multicultural literature is detrimental to minority and nonminority students alike. Nonminority students need opportunities to understand both the differences and similarities that exist between their own families and the multicultural families they encounter through literature. At the same time, the cultures of minority students are respected when they see themselves reflected in some of the stories that are read. We believe that multicultural literature must be regularly incorporated into classroom practice.

We also believe it is critical that multicultural literature be chosen carefully. The literature should meet the following criteria identified by Diamond and Moore (1995):

1. Characters who authentically reflect the distinct cultural experiences, realities, and world view of a specific group.
2. Character representations portrayed in a true-to-life and balanced manner.
3. Settings representative of an environment consistent with a historical/contemporary time, place, or situation of the specific culture.
4. Themes developed within the story or selection that are consistent with the values and beliefs, customs and traditions, needs, and conflicts of the specific culture.
5. Informational literature presented in a detailed and accurate manner.
6. Language characteristic of the distinctive vocabulary, style, patterns, and rhythm of speech of the specific cultural group.
7. Literature that is free of stereotypes in language, illustrations, behavior, and character traits.
8. Language that reflects a sensibility to the people of the culture; offensive, negative, or degrading vocabulary in descriptions of characters, their customs, and lifestyles is absent.
9. Gender roles within the culture portrayed accurately and authentically reflecting the changing status and roles of women and men in many cultures. (pp. 44–46)

Although the process of selecting appropriate multicultural literature is beyond the scope of this chapter, we strongly suggest that teachers familiarize themselves with criteria for judging the quality of this literature.

Using Multicultural Literature to Uncover Family Values

Once appropriate multicultural texts have been selected, how can they be used in lessons that center on family values? To answer this question, we provide a brief summary of relevant theoretical and empirical research that provides a landscape for issues around values, literacy development, and cultural diversity.

Culture is defined as a "social system that represents an accumulation of beliefs, attitudes, habits, values, and practices that serve as a filter through which a group of people view and respond to the world in which they live" (Shade, Kelly, & Oberg, 1997, p. 12). Values are an integral part of culture because they represent the shared ways of thinking, believing, and acting that members respect and legitimize. As such, one of the most significant social "groups" for teaching and learning cultural values is the family.

Family values incorporate systems of values on multiple levels. For example, many families teach "national" values such as equality, freedom, and justice by celebrating national holidays and discussing national historical events (Gay, 1994). But families can also teach "culturally specific" values that are rooted in their ethnic and cultural heritages. For example, Hidalgo (1993) contends that values are located within family systems in several aspects, including (1) languages and dialects spoken in the home; (2) family traditions; (3) family composition (who makes up the family?); (4) family religious traditions; and (5) family literacy experiences and practices. Consequently, family values can have representations on multiple levels.

For teachers who want to emphasize family values in their classrooms, multicultural literature can accomplish two important goals. First, multicultural literature can guard against inadvertently reinforcing cultural stereotypes. Teachers can explicitly discuss with their students how each multicultural text represents or does not represent the family values of a particular culture. In doing so, both teachers and students move away from monolithic views of culture. Multicultural texts can uncover some of the "intercultural differences" that are often ignored or misrepresented, and in effect, empower teachers to foster multiple levels of meanings and understandings of cultural diversity.

Second, multicultural literature uncovers some of the "hidden" family values that are deeply interwoven into the fabric of family life. Because values are most often taught and learned in families in implicit ways, they seem invisible to family members. However, multicultural literature makes these family values more explicit by contextualizing them within a narrative. Consequently, readers of multicultural texts can engage with and make sense of the family values within the story by connecting to their own family's practices and stories (Diamond & Moore, 1995).

Family Values Lesson Framework

In the following section, we describe a lesson sequence for using children's multicultural literature to teach students about family values. We draw heavily from Holdaway's (1986) developmental model for language learning, which involves the following components:

1. Observation of "demonstrations"—According to Holdaway (1986), "the learner at this stage acts as a fascinated 'spectator' while the skilled person is active, not as a 'performer,' but as a genuine user of the skill" (p. 59).

2. Participation—"In this phase of the natural learning cycle, the learner is active as a participant, while the skilled person—the 'teacher figure'—facilitates the social interaction, making a place within the flow of the action for the unskilled collaborator, and often slowing down the action to accommodate the new member" (Holdaway, 1986, p. 59).

3. Role-playing or practice—"The learner is given the opportunity to practice the skill without direction or observation by the demonstrator or teacher" (Routman, 1994, p. 9).

4. Performance—"Now it is possible for roles to be reversed from what they were at the beginning of the cycle in demonstration/observation. The 'teacher figure' becomes the significant audience, while the learner becomes performer" (Holdaway, 1986, p. 60).

It is important to note that we have adapted Holdaway's model to frame our family values lessons. Adaptation was necessary because the model was designed to explain visible literacy processes rather than invisible, "in-the-head" processes that cannot be directly observed by learners. Thus, we found it necessary to modify the first phase of Holdaway's model, observation of "demonstrations," to include the teacher thinking aloud to make his or her invisible thoughts known to the students. In other words, we utilize direct teacher modeling rather than indirect modeling described by Holdaway. Further, although Holdaway's model was originally intended to describe "natural" language-learning processes, we believe it can be applied to specific strategy instruction. In particular, we believe that the model can be utilized in the process of teaching children the comprehension strategy of identifying family values in literature.

The following is an overview of the sample lesson format we use to teach children about family values through multicultural literature. First, the teacher demonstrates for the class how he or she thinks about the family values represented in multicultural literature. Second, the teacher invites student participation in a shared discussion of family values gleaned from a common text. Next, students practice uncovering family values in literature in small groups. The final phase, performance, involves the publishing of stories from the students' own families. We draw from Holdaway's developmental model as a way to frame language arts lessons that emphasize values from students' homes.

Teaching Students to Recognize Family Values

Phase 1: Observation of Demonstrations

The first component of Holdaway's model, observation of "demonstrations," involves teacher modeling of the desired literacy practices. In this case, the literacy practice is recognizing the family values represented in literature.

To demonstrate the process of recognizing values in literature, the teacher reads several different multicultural literature selections to the class over time. While reading aloud, the teacher explicitly demonstrates the ways in which he or she thinks about the family values present in the literature. Using the think-aloud format (Pressley & Afflerbach, 1995), the teacher models the thought processes used to infer the family values depicted. For example, while reading *Dreamcatcher* (Osofsky, 1992), the teacher thinks aloud about the values revealed in the story:

> Sometimes when I read, I think about what the story is teaching me about the family values of the characters in the story. Family values are the ways of behaving or acting that are important to members of a family. Thinking about the family values helps me understand stories better. There are many clues in stories that help me decide what is valued by the characters in the story. When I read, I act as a detective and try to find these clues. As I read *Dreamcatcher*, I will show you some of the clues that I use to figure out the family values in the story.
>
> To help me decide what is important to the characters in stories, I often ask myself, "What do the pictures show me?" On this page, the illustration shows the characters acting lovingly toward the baby. The mother is tucking the baby in his cradle, while the sister and grandmother are making gifts for the baby. Tucking in children and making gifts for them are ways of showing love. Based on the picture clues, I think that love could be a family value for this family. Let's keep track of the clues that I use on a class chart. [The teacher writes the clue "What is shown in the pictures?" on a chart for later reference. See Figure 1.] I'll keep reading and see if there are other clues.

FIGURE 1   Clues for Understanding Family Values in Literature

What is shown in the pictures?
What do the characters say?
What do the characters do?
What happens in the story (plot sequence)?
What is the title?

Paying attention to what the characters say is another clue about what is important to them. In this part of the story, the big sister says "Good dreams" to the baby as she hangs the dreamcatcher up near the baby. The sister is showing love toward the baby by wishing him good dreams. Love seems to be an important theme in this book. Let's add the clue "What do the characters say?" to our chart. I'll keep reading to see if there are additional clues.

"Way-ba-ba-way," croons mother, rocking baby in a hammock slowly singing, "way-ba-ba-way"

> sleep baby sleep
> sleep baby sleep
> your dream net will protect you
> sleep baby sleep
> sleep baby sleep
> and dream...

As I read, I also ask myself, "What do the characters do?" to show me what their values are. In this part of the story, the mother rocks her baby and sings a song to him. By rocking and singing to her baby, the mother is showing that she loves him. In this story, the mother's actions show that love is a family value. I'll add the clue, "What do the characters do?" to our chart.

Love seems to be a theme found across many kinds of clues: what is shown in the pictures, what the characters say, and what they do. Because there are many clues that suggest that love is important to this family, I can be pretty sure that love is a family value in the story.

After reading the story, the teacher engages the children in the development of a concept map to keep track of the family/community values present in the multicultural literature read by the class. A concept map is drawn on a large chalkboard, bulletin board, or large piece of butcher paper. See Figure 2 for a model concept map.

The teacher introduces the concept map to the class:

Let's keep track of the family values that we find in books over the next few weeks. We can use a concept map to keep track of the values we find. It will help us see how family values are similar and different.

We'll start with the concept we are looking for in the center of our map. [The teacher draws a circle in the middle of the board.] What do you think I should write here? Right. I'll write the word *values*. And what kind of values will we be looking for in the stories we read? Okay. Let's add *family* to *values* because that's the concept we'll be studying. Let's draw a line and a box and write the name of the value we found in the story. I'll write *love* in the box because that was the family value in the story. Now I'll write the title of our story, *Dreamcatcher*, on the sticky note and put it underneath the value of love. This will help us remember that love was a family value in the story *Dreamcatcher*.

As the teacher reads various multicultural texts over the next few weeks, she repeats the process of thinking aloud about the family and community

FIGURE 2   Family Values Concept Map

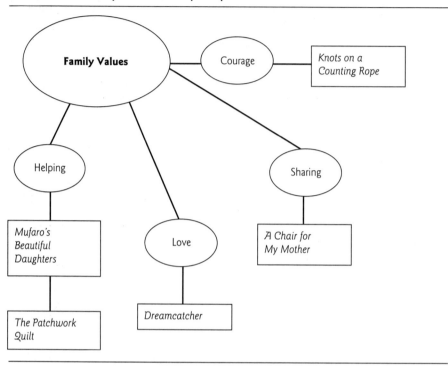

values present in the stories, making explicit the clues used to determine the values. As the teacher identifies new clues (e.g., what happens in the story and the title), she adds theses clues to the chart (see Figure 1, p. 68). The teacher explicitly shares with students the aspects of the story that are helpful in determining the characters' family values. In so doing, the teacher enables the children to observe the demonstrations of discovering family values through literature.

After each book is read, the teacher adds the title and appropriate value to the concept map (see Figure 2). After the teacher has demonstrated several books over the course of a few weeks, she encourages the children to participate more actively in the process of using clues to uncover the family values in texts. This brings us to the second phase of Holdaway's model.

Phase 2: Participation

In the second phase of Holdaway's model, participation, "the child is invited to participate and collaborate" with the teacher (Routman, 1994, p. 9). The

teacher invites the students to participate in the process of analyzing literature for the family values present within it.

We have selected *A Chair for My Mother* (Williams, 1982) as the focus
book for this lesson because the values are easily accessible to elementary
school children. It is the story of a Hispanic family that works together to
save money to buy a special chair after their furniture is destroyed in a fire.

Before reading the story, the teacher engages the class in a brief discussion about family values. The discussion will establish the purpose for reading. The teacher may begin the discussion in the following way:

> We have been learning about the ways that stories can teach us about family values.
> Remember that family values are ways of living that are important to families. Turn to
> your neighbor and name one of the family values we have found in the books we've
> read so far. [After a minute or two of sharing with a partner, the teacher asks volun-
> teers to share the family value they remembered with the whole class. The teacher asks
> everyone who named the same value to stand up, and continues calling on volun-
> teers until everyone is standing up.] Let's read to see what we can learn about family
> values in today's story. Look and listen for clues about what is valued by the family in
> *A Chair for My Mother*.

After reading the story, the teacher will encourage the students to collaborate in identifying the values present in the text. Begin the discussion by
saying, "Let's share ideas about what was valued by the family in the story."
Allow children to make suggestions of family values depicted in the story,
such as working together, cooperating, sharing, or helping. When children
share their ideas, encourage them to find support in the text by asking, "What
kinds of clues did you use to tell that _____ was a family value in the story?"
Help children explicitly state their evidence by referring them to the "Clue
Chart" (see Figure 1, p. 68) as needed. Keep in mind that children may uncover additional values in the story. Encourage diverse interpretations that can
be substantiated.

Because the children may not mention some of the evidence available in
the story, be prepared to lead them through the process of discovering missing
clues. In the following example, the teacher helps the students discover several
clues in the story:

> Let's think about the clue "What is shown in the pictures?" I'm going to slowly turn
> the pages of the book without reading it so you can look for clues about the family val-
> ues that are in the pictures. Stop me if you find a clue…. Look at this picture. What
> is happening? Yes, they are putting more money into their savings jar. Who is giving
> them money? Uh-huh, it looks like Grandma is taking money out of her wallet to
> add to the money jar. This picture seems to be showing that sharing is a family value
> in this story. Who would like to read the part of the story that tells us what the char-
> acters are doing here? [A student reads the following.]

Often she has money in her old leather wallet for us. Whenever she gets a good bargain on tomatoes or bananas or something she buys, she puts by the savings and they go into the jar.

The text gives us another clue. It tells us what the characters are doing. We find out that the Grandma is sharing the money she has saved. When we think about what the characters are doing, we find out that they are sharing with one another.

As you can see, the teacher in the lesson invites student participation, but she supports them in the process. After children have had opportunities to participate in the process of determining the family values in multicultural literature, give them time to practice and refine their newly acquired skill.

Phase 3: Role-Playing or Practice

In the third phase of Holdaway's model, role-playing or practice, the student "independently engages in the literacy act and attempts to self-regulate, self-correct, and self-direct his own learning" (Routman, 1994, p. 9). We have used the instructional framework of Book Club (McMahon & Raphael, 1997) to provide an avenue for students to practice uncovering values in literature. Book Club is an appropriate strategy because it can be used with students from diverse backgrounds and reading abilities. It also involves group work. As such, it is a particularly appropriate strategy in light of research cited by Diamond and Moore (1995): "Recent studies further suggest that reading and writing instruction that permits students to collaborate in discussing and interpreting texts results in dramatic improvements in both reading and verbal intellectual abilities (Au, 1979; Mason & Au, 1990)" (p. 8).

Book Club consists of four components: "reading, writing, book club, and community share" (Raphael & Hiebert, 1996, p. 29). We will discuss how each of these components of Book Club is incorporated into our family values unit.

Reading. Students will begin the Book Club cycle by selecting a multicultural book to read from those provided by the teacher. Multiple copies of the texts are needed so that small groups of four to six students will be reading the same text. Figure 3 provides a list of some possible titles of multicultural literature appropriate for elementary children. This list is meant to be a starting point. Each teacher will undoubtedly have other appropriate selections that may be used.

Various configurations of reading may take place that will enable students of varying reading ability to comprehend the texts. Books may be read independently or in pairs. They may be listened to on tape or read with a parent or cross-aged tutor.

FIGURE 3   Multicultural Literature That Depicts Family Values

Courage
Coles, R. (1995). *The story of Ruby Bridges*. New York: Scholastic.
Martin, B. Jr., & Archambault, J. (1987). *Knots on a counting rope*. New York: Henry Holt.
Polacco, P. (1990). *Thunder cake*. New York: Scholastic.

Helping
Falwell, C. (1993). *Feast for 10*. New York: Scholastic.
Flournoy, V. (1985). *The patchwork quilt*. New York: Scholastic.
Steptoe, J. (1987). *Mufaro's beautiful daughters: An African tale*. New York: Scholastic.

Imagination
Dorros, A. (1991). *Abuela*. New York: The Trumpet Club.
Ringgold, F. (1991). *Tar Beach*. New York: Scholastic.

Love
Cowen-Fletcher, J. (1993). *Mama zooms*. New York: Scholastic.
Greenfield, E. (1993). *Grandpa's face*. New York: The Trumpet Club.
Joosse, B.M. (1991). *Mama, do you love me?* San Francisco: Chronicle Books.
Rylant, C. (1987). *Birthday presents*. New York: The Trumpet Club.

Respect for Nature
Bunting, E. (1991). *Night tree*. New York: The Trumpet Club.
Yolen, J. (1987). *Owl moon*. New York: Scholastic.

Sharing
Havill, J. (1989). *Jamaica tag-along*. New York: Houghton Mifflin.
Scott, A.H. (1993). *On mother's lap*. New York: Scholastic.
Williams, V.B. (1986). *Cherries and cherry pits*. New York: Scholastic.

Writing. Once students have read their books, they are ready to participate in the writing phase of Book Club. Students provide a written response to the story in their literature logs. For the purposes of this lesson, the response is structured specifically to reflect the students' understandings of the family values present in the story. In particular, the teacher asks the children to write about the family values in the story and the clues used to determine what those values are. It should be noted that because the literature logs are meant to promote reflection, the children's main concern in writing is to record their thoughts and ideas about text. As such, the children need not be overly concerned with print conventions, such as spelling, punctuation, or grammar.

Book Clubs. The task of writing a response to the story prepares the children for participation in "book clubs," or small-group discussions. Students who read the same book will engage in a small-group discussion. In these student-led discussions, the children should talk about their ideas of the values present in the story and find evidence to support their ideas. The teacher asks each group to reach some agreement about the values present in the story for sharing with the large group in "community share."

Community Share. In "community share," the findings of the individual small groups are reported to the entire class. The small groups also add their findings to the values concept map (see Figure 2, p. 70). Based on the results, the teacher leads the class in noticing similarities and differences among the family values portrayed in the texts.

Phase 4: Performance

In the final phase of Holdaway's model, performance, the learner takes on the role of demonstrator, displaying his or her proficiency with the learning. In the study of values in literature, the student completes the performance stage by sharing and analyzing his or her own family stories. This serves as a final step in helping students appreciate the similarities and differences that exist among the values of diverse families.

As a homework assignment, the children prepare family story presentations. To facilitate this process, the teacher outlines three major steps. First, students interview family members about values they hold. Second, the children ask family members to think of a story about their family or told by their family that conveys these values. Finally, students prepare to present their family stories to the class. The presentations should include puppets, posters, overheads, video, or other props to support engaging storytelling.

After each student presents his or her family story to the class, the teacher asks, "What family values were represented in this story? How do you know?" Children are asked to support their ideas with evidence using clues from the story. Each child then adds the family values represented in his or her story to the values concept map (see Figure 2, p. 70). As a class, the students compare and contrast the values of different families.

Finally, as a way to celebrate learning, students publish their family stories using the writing process. The personal stories are bound together in a class book, with separate chapters representing different family values such as helping, trust, and courage. Copies of the book are shared with each family.

Conclusion

In this chapter, we have shared practical ways that elementary school teachers can use multicultural literature and students' personal stories to teach universal values and strengthen the students' home-school connections. It is important that multicultural literature be used in every classroom. There are universal values that most people agree on regardless of race, ethnicity, religious background, or other differing factors. We have listed a few of these values as a starting point and invite you to add to the list as you implement the ideas suggested in this chapter.

As we stated earlier, each classroom environment should reflect the ideas, beliefs, attitudes, and values of the students and teacher in the classroom. More broadly, it should also reflect the values of the wider society. Students need to understand the similarities and differences between themselves and others, and they must be taught to value the home cultures of all people. Multicultural literature is an important vehicle for accomplishing this goal, one that we hope will lead to a world of greater peace and harmony for our children.

References

Cai, M. (1995). Can we fly across cultural gaps on the wings of imagination? Ethnicity, experience, and cultural authenticity. *The New Advocate*, 8(1), 1–16.

Danridge, J. (1998). *Culturally responsive literacy pedagogy and student motivation.* Unpublished paper, East Lansing, MI: Michigan State University.

Diamond, B.J., & Moore, M.A. (1995). *Multicultural literacy: Mirroring the reality of the classroom.* White Plains, NY: Longman.

Edwards, P.A., Pleasants, H.M., & Franklin, S.H. (1999). *A path to follow: Learning to listen to parents.* Portsmouth, NH: Heinemann.

Fang, Z., Fu, D., & Lamme, L.L. (1999). Rethinking the role of multicultural literature in literacy instruction: Problems, paradox, and possibilities. *The New Advocate*, 12(3), 259–276.

Gay, G. (1994). *At the essence of learning: Multicultural education.* West Lafayette, IN: Kappa Delta Pi.

Hidalgo, N.M. (1993). Multicultural teacher introspection. In T. Perry & J. Fraser (Eds.), *Freedom's plow: Teaching in the multicultural classroom* (pp. 99–108). New York: Routledge.

Holdaway, D. (1986). The structure of natural learning as a basis for literacy instruction. In M.R. Sampson (Ed.), *The pursuit of literacy: Early reading and writing* (pp. 56–72). Dubuque, IA: Kendall/Hunt.

McMahon, S.I., & Raphael, T.E. (1997). *The Book Club connection: Literacy learning and classroom talk.* New York: Teachers College Press; Newark, DE: International Reading Association.

Pressley, M., & Afflerbach, P. (1995). *Verbal protocols of reading: The nature of constructively responsive reading.* Mahwah, NJ: Erlbaum.

Raphael, T.E., & Hiebert, E.H. (1996). *Creating an integrated approach to literacy instruction.* Austin, TX: Holt, Rinehart & Winston.

Routman, R. (1994). *Invitations.* Portsmouth, NH: Heinemann.

Shade, B.J., Kelly, C., & Oberg, M. (1997). *Creating culturally responsive classrooms.* Washington, DC: American Psychological Association.

Children's Literature Cited

Osofsky, A. (1992). *Dreamcatcher.* New York: Orchard.

Williams, V.B. (1982). *A chair for my mother.* New York: Scholastic.

Chapter 5

Beware of Literacy Software:
Connecting With Home and School Values

Cathy Leogrande

Personal computers are becoming more and more accessible to children, at home and in school. Many would say that they have become a tool as commonplace and frequently used as a pen or pencil (Jonassen, 2000). With the amount of time and multiple purposes for computer use increasing, teachers and parents must take a careful and critical look at what is on the monitor screen. As with television programming, subtle as well as overt values are being transmitted along with educational skills. What are these values? Are the messages perceived by children those that promote caring, sharing, compassion, respect, and other positive values that are discussed throughout this book?

My son and daughter began to use the computer before they could read. At first, I sought programs based on factors such as educational value, match with future school curriculum, reviews in family and teacher journals, cost, and compatibility with our computer. I was happy if my children liked using the software, and I focused on the learning that took place relative to school skills. As time went on, my children began to request certain programs that they had seen advertised or that they had used at friends' homes. As long as the software seemed to have educational merit, I purchased these programs and encouraged their use.

After a while, I began to notice the subtle but obvious values within some of these programs. Why were so many of the characters robots, space creatures, and aliens? Where were the people? When human characters did appear, they were often male and almost always white. My children are Asian. Why didn't they see themselves mirrored in the monitor? Also, how did the characters treat each other? With cooperation and collaboration, or rudeness and lack of caring?

As a former special education teacher, I began to question aspects of the learning process. Why was everything done so quickly? Why wasn't slower but more thoughtful thinking rewarded with points like the fast response rewarded in most computer and video games? Where was the place of deliberation and accuracy? Why did every program have a competitive context, a goal of "winning" and "beating" the computer? I was concerned about how children with diverse learning strengths and weaknesses—often the very children who are placed in front of the drill and practice programs—might perceive themselves when gauged against such software.

My questions led me to this study. Parents and teachers seeking literacy software to reinforce and extend skills have a wide variety of choices. Typical evaluation procedures focus on aspects such as ease of use and curriculum alignment. Other authors in this volume have raised similar issues with regard to curricula, teaching strategies, and classroom materials. However, these computer programs constitute a new type of instructional material that must be viewed with a critical eye in terms of the "text" itself. This chapter describes the results of an analysis of literacy software programs using the technique of "deep viewing" to identify and analyze values that are promoted and ignored within these programs.

Background of Technology in Education

In the past 10 years, studies have addressed various issues regarding technology availability and use in schools. As the amount and variety of literacy software has increased, related research has addressed areas such as appropriate evaluation and equity issues (Caftori, 1994; National Association for the Education of Young Children, 1996). This research served as a springboard for my study. In addition, my study is based on the concept of intermediality, which Semali and Pailliotet (1999) define as "the ability to work with diverse symbol systems in an active way where meanings are both received and produced" (p. vii). This was used as a vehicle for critical analysis of electronic texts.

Media Literacy and Intermediality

With the growing use of mass media and technology in education, teachers and parents are questioning and extending the traditional definition of reading and literacy. Macaul, Giles, and Rodenberg (1999) provide a portrait of the changes in the concepts of literacy. The definition has moved away from the traditional constructive process of making meaning from print to the idea of multiple literacies, including "digital literacy," the ability to understand and integrate information delivered by the computer in various formats.

This study is based on the assumption that "readers" today must be able to construct meaning from visual texts, and that this requires new application of literacy skills. In addition, the assumption is made that teachers and parents must first employ critical skills themselves before helping students use these skills to analyze what they view. This leads to the use of the concept of intermediality as a way of thinking about electronic texts. Intermediality involves making meaning and connections across various media forms based on one's prior experiences with media, including songs, graphics, mass media, and other forms of representation.

Most parents and teachers recognize that students, no matter how young, are knowledgeable regarding media. By the time they encounter literacy software in the classrooms, they have already watched thousands of hours of television, much of it animated in the same fashion as the software in terms of setting, characters, and language. Intermediality builds on the connections between the student receivers and the larger societal context in which media messages are produced. It forces students, teachers, and parents to examine the social, political, economic, and cultural forces that have shaped their lives in order to understand them and change them if warranted. Kincheloe and Steinberg (1999) describe the intermedial process as one in which

> individuals step back from the world as they have been conditioned to see it. In the process, they uncover power-driven representations, linguistic codes, cultural signs, and embedded ideologies—a central dynamic in the critical process of remaking their lives and renaming their worlds. (p. viii)

Children are never too young to become critical viewers. It is the responsibility of the adults around them to assist them in deconstructing the elements presented and questioning them.

Software Evaluation

Many articles suggest criteria by which to evaluate educational software (Comer & Geissler, 1998; Ellsworth & Headley, 1993; Heyboer & Mayo, 1993). These tend to use criteria such as educational content, grade level, motivation, and ease of use. There are also Web sites devoted to popular and useful programs. For example, the Superkids Web site (http://www.superkids.com) provides feedback forms so teachers, parents, and children can give varying feedback and reviews to software they use. Included in the review form are questions related to age appropriateness, degree to which the program is interactive, and difficulty levels. In terms of content bias, only one question on the teachers' product evaluation asks if the software is gender neutral.

Others have focused on the evaluation of software for bias. Areas of bias that are identified include gender, race, setting, culture, and economic deprivation (Houston, 1998; Singer, 1997; Taylor & Napier, 1992). Agalionos and Cope (1994) found that content-specific educational software is far from neutral when it comes to issues of bias. The software they examined perpetuated values, beliefs, assumptions, and ideologies presented by the dominant groups in society. They saw the software as a product of cultural politics and a potential vehicle for social control.

Bias in Technology

Many educators have examined and discussed bias and equity in technology. The National Association for the Education of Young Children (NAEYC) (1996) published a position paper that encouraged educators to address equitable access, especially for children with special needs, and stereotyping and violence in software when planning for technology use with children ages 3 through 8. Gender bias in software content received particular attention. Chappell (1996) found that violence and competition increase across grade level while female characters decrease. Hodes (1995) found a majority of main characters to be male; when female characters were included, they all represented traditional female roles. Another study found that when androgynous humanoid figures are presented in software, primary students of both genders tend to assign male gender to the figures (Bender, 1987).

Other authors examined the impact of gender on children's computer use and selection of programs. Valenza (1997) found male-oriented software was a possible reason for the limited use of computers by females. Collins and Ollila (1990) found that computer use was seen as a masculine activity by all children, although the first graders studied did not perceive reading or writing as a gendered activity. Although previous studies have focused on bias issues in other visual mediums, such as television and movies, values in software remain a relatively unexamined issue. The detailed analysis presented in this chapter, along with the suggestions for assessing values in software, can serve as a springboard for parents and teachers.

Looking Below the Surface

When I decided to examine values in literacy software, I wanted to find a method that was more than merely a tallying of the number of males versus females and other analyses that relied on counting examples in different categories. In "deep viewing" (Pailliotet, 1998), I found a process that not only allowed me to critically view many aspects of the software, but also served as a method that I could share with other parents, teachers, and my children to help them explore the nuances in software programs.

Deep Viewing

Deep viewing is a structured process through which elements of the "text" are identified, interpreted, and responded to through various levels (Pailliotet, 1998). A brief description of the process is provided here; more complete explanations with examples are available from other sources (Semali & Pailliotet, 1999).

Deep viewing is a three-leveled process. First, the viewer completes a thorough observation and description of aspects of the text (in this case, software) that fit the six codes of analysis described in Figure 1. Simple recording of data for each code is done, and the viewer attempts to describe text evidence without interpretation. At the second level, the viewer questions, responds to, and interprets what he or she has seen. At this point, the viewer makes inferences. Finally, at the third level, the viewer synthesizes concepts and ideas across data sets and categories. At this level, the viewer evaluates observations and inferences and applies prior knowledge. The viewer may question the developer's purpose and whether or not the inferences are intended or chance. This level causes the viewer to critically analyze what has been seen. Although deep viewing can be done in groups, my study is based on an individual analysis of the software programs.

Pailliotet (1998) originally identified the codes of analysis used in deep viewing. Macaul, Giles, and Rodenberg modified these codes in their work with elementary and middle-level students (1999). I used these modifications

FIGURE 1   Coding Categories for Deep Viewing

Category	What Is Included	Questions to Ask
Action/Sequence (time relationships)	order, content, and duration of events	What happens? What order? When and for how long?
Semes/Forms (visual meaning units)	characteristics of objects, icons, graphics, visual content	Who/what is pictured? What are the characteristics of people and objects?
Actors/Discourse (words and phrases)	how written and spoken language convey content: actual message, tone, pitch, rate	What is said and by whom? How is it said and heard?
Proximity/Movement (directionality and relationship of movement)	use of space and all movements, including gestures, relative size	How is space used? What types of movements occur?
Culture/Context (references to cultural knowledge)	point of view, assumptions related to understanding based on "common" knowledge, stereotypes	To whom might this video be targeted? What symbols do you notice? What is implied? What is missing?
Effects/Processes (production devices, visual and audio)	how production elements and quality affect meaning	What is seen? What is missing? What is the quality?

Source: Pailliotet, 1999

also so that the analysis process described here could serve as a framework for future use by teachers, students, and parents.

I used these coding categories to view all selected software programs. The process was particularly valuable as a method for analyzing visual, interactive electronic text, because it included examination of the more subtle aspects.

Software Selection

First, I selected software for analysis according to several criteria. I conducted an informal survey of five area elementary computer labs to compile an extensive list of literacy software. I then consulted online sources that provide prices and cite marketing statistics. I narrowed the list to include titles that are available to a wide population in terms of a reasonable price and that appeared to be widely used in terms of sales figures. Finally, I obtained software reviews for these titles from venues that are available to teachers and parents, such as journals, magazines, and online sites. This was done in order to determine that the actual focus of each title was traditional literacy (reading, writing, speaking, and listening). The final list included more than 50 titles (see Figure 2). These are all available on CD-ROM and are all priced for individual purchase within a $10 to $50 range. In addition, all programs examined in this study run on both Windows and Macintosh operating systems and are accessible to most parents, students, and teachers.

FIGURE 2   List of Software Titles Reviewed

Title	Date Produced	Publisher
Amazing Writing Machine	1995	Learning Company
American Girls Premiere	1997	Broderbund
Arthur's Birthday	1994	Broderbund
Arthur's Teacher Trouble	1993	Broderbund
Babysitters Club Friendship Kit	1996	Scholastic
Babysitters Club 4th Grade Learning Adventures	1998	Scholastic
Babysitters Club 3rd Grade Learning Adventures	1998	Scholastic
Bailey's Book House	1995	Edmark
Barbie Fashion Designer	1997	Mattel
Carmen Sandiego, Junior Detective	1995	Broderbund
Carmen Sandiego, Word Detective	1997	Broderbund
Casper Animated Early Reader	1998	Sound Source Interactive
Clue Finders 4th Grade Adventures	1998	Learning Company
Clue Finders 5th Grade Adventures	1999	Learning Company
Disney's Reading Quest With Aladdin	1998	Disney
First Ladies Costume Maker	1998	IBM/Crayola
Fractured Fairy Tales: The Frog Prince	1996	SegaSoft
Get Ready for School, Charlie Brown!	1995	Virgin
Green Eggs and Ham	1996	Broderbund

(continued)

FIGURE 2   List of Software Titles Reviewed (continued)

Title	Date Produced	Publisher
Hercules: Disney's Animated Storybook	1997	Disney
Imagination Express–Destination: Castle	1995	Edmark
Imagination Express–Destination: Neighborhood	1995	Edmark
I Saw a Strange Little Man	1994	Essex Interactive Media
JumpStart 1st Grade Reading	1997	Knowledge Adventure
JumpStart 2nd Grade	1996	Knowledge Adventure
JumpStart 3rd Grade Adventures: Mystery Mountain	1996	Knowledge Adventure
JumpStart 4th Grade Adventures: Haunted Island	1996	Knowledge Adventure
JumpStart 5th Grade Adventures: Jo Hammett, Kid Detective	1997	Knowledge Adventure
Let's Go Read 2: Ocean Adventure	1998	Edmark
Lion King: Disney Animated Storybook	1995	Disney
Magic Princess Paper Doll Maker	1998	IBM/Crayola
Mike Mulligan and His Steam Shovel	1996	Houghton Mifflin
Mission Masters: Freezing Frenzy (Language Arts Grade 3)	1999	McGraw-Hill
Mulan: Disney Animated Storybook	1998	Disney
New Kid on the Block	1993	Broderbund
NFL Reading	1996	Sanctuary Woods
Paint 'n Play Pony	1998	IBM/Crayola
Paper Bag Princess	1994	Discis
Read, Write and Type!	1996	Learning Company
Reader Rabbit 3	1996	Learning Company
Reader Rabbit's 2nd Grade	1998	Learning Company
Reading Blaster (Ages 6–9)	1997	Davidson
Reading Blaster (Ages 9–12)	1997	Davidson
Reading Blaster Junior	1996	Davidson
Reading Blaster Vocabulary	1997	Davidson
Reading Galaxy	1996	Broderbund
Rockett's Adventure Maker	1998	Purple Moon
Rockett's Camp Adventure	2000	Purple Moon
Rockett's First Dance (Episode 4)	1999	Purple Moon
Rockett's New School (Episode 1)	1997	Purple Moon
Rockett's Secret Invitation (Episode 3)	1998	Purple Moon
Rockett's Tricky Decision (Episode 2)	1998	Purple Moon
Saban's Power Rangers Zeo Power Active Words	1996	Saban Interactive
Sabrina the Teenage Witch	1997	Purple Moon
Secret Paths to the Forest	1997	Purple Moon
Secret Paths to the Sea	1998	Purple Moon
Selfish Giant	1992	Sanctuary Woods
Sesame Street Let's Make a Word!	1995	Creative Wonders
Starfire Soccer Challenge	2000	Purple Moon
Storybook Weaver Deluxe	1998	Learning Company
Super Solvers: Midnight Rescue!	1997	Learning Company
Tortoise and the Hare	1993	Broderbund
Toy Story: Disney Animated Storybook	1996	Disney
Treasure Cove!	1994	Learning Company
Treasure Mountain!	1995	Learning Company
Word Munchers	1995	Softkey
Your Notebook (With Help From Amelia)	1999	Mattel

What's in There Besides Literacy?

Next, I followed the deep-viewing process. I viewed each program repeatedly. The first step asks for concrete examples of the elements observed. Selected examples from each of the six categories are listed in Figure 3. In the second step, I noted my responses and interpretations for each category in the various software programs. In the third step, I looked at my observations and interpretations across all programs and attempted to make some generalizations based on the data. I tried to look beyond what was included to consider what was

FIGURE 3   Specific Examples for Each Category From Literacy Software

Category	Findings	Implicit Values
Action/Sequence	quick pace pause-related prompt ("Hey, are you still there?")	Speed is important. Think time means you're too slow.
Semes/Forms	little texture or shadowing simple icons cartoon-like art/animation	Cartoons are good. Realism is not important.

Actors/Words
 (Female)
	Mrs. Grunkle, [evil]
	  substitute teacher
	Jo Hammett, skateboard-
	  riding detective
		Stereotypes generally
		  perpetuated.
		Men are smarter and
		  better looking

(Male)	Chase Devereaux [handsome] Evil mad scientists	than women. Heroes and heroines are generally young.

(Mixed Gender Teams)	Mission Masters: Pauline, Mia,
	  Rakeem, T.J.
	Clue Finders: Joni, Santiago,
	  Leslie, Owen
		Multicultural characters
		  have stereotyped
		  names but middle-
		  class appearance.

(Animals)	Frankie, circus dog [male]
	Will Chill and sinister sister
	Reader Rabbit, Sir Drayson
	  Dragon, Sam the Lion
		Robots and animals
		  are generally male.

(Nongendered)	MC (Mostly Chrome) Botley the Robot	

Proximity/Movement	space filled with objects
	viewer must discriminate
	  among moving figures
		Busy environments are
		  good and exciting;
		  if you are confused,
		  it's your problem.

Culture/Context	circus, haunted house, mad
	scientist's lab, rainforest
	magic spells, message in bottle
		Fantasy and cultural
		  stereotypic icons
		  are better than reality.

Effects/Process	little use of realistic video
	primarily soft pop-type music
	sound effects (bells, whistles)
		More is better. If you
		  are distracted, that's
		  your problem.

omitted or missing. I made hypotheses based on broader inferences. I examined the programs again to make sure that these were the result of actual evidence and not my prior experiences and beliefs. I attempted to articulate the values and join the findings into broader themes. Several themes emerged as I compared and contrasted the deep-viewing categories across software programs.

Caveat Emptor: Silent Values Included

It was clear on closer examination that no literacy software is completely neutral. Parents and teachers may be unpleasantly surprised with some of the messages that are subtly—and sometimes not so subtly—transmitted to children via supposedly sound educational materials.

What's Really Real? Blurring of Fantasy and Reality

Literacy software contains a large amount of fantasy elements. Characters are generally talking animals, science fiction beings, or humans who possess atypical features and traits. Of particular note is the use of science fiction. Space creatures, spaceships, robots, and unusual, unrealistic machines and devices abound in these programs. When seemingly realistic settings are presented, they include fantasy elements. Although this may increase motivational aspects for children, it may also limit the crossover to real-world situations.

The JumpStart software series by Knowledge Adventure includes programs for infants and children through the elementary school grades. Until Grade 3, the characters are generally talking animals, including dogs, frogs, and a cricket helper. There is a mix of fantasy and reality. At Grade 1, Frankie, a talking dog, is the main character at the circus. Other characters include Madame Tigre, a gypsy-like character with a crystal ball whose focus activity is storytelling, with additional activities related to listening skills and word recognition. Samson is a weight-lifting dog who makes correct words on barbells with rhyming words, synonyms, and antonyms. When human characters appear, they do so in unrealistic ways. The premise of the program is that The Amazing Mel, a mean magician, has turned all the big top performers into puzzle pieces. In Spatter-the-Batter, the player helps the wacky chef splatter his dinner guests with cake batter by building sentences with the words they are holding, focusing on nouns, adjectives, and verbs. Young children may be amused, but the link to similar characters in their own environments is nonexistent. Is throwing cake batter at guests really behavior we want children to emulate? The values of cruel, unkind, and even physically violent behavior, although a staple of slapstick humor throughout history, are troubling in materials carrying the approval for children implicit in educationally beneficial activities.

At third grade and above, programs include literacy skills across the language arts, math, history, science, art, and music. The programs are called JumpStart Adventures. The settings appear to be more realistic, with human characters. However, they are remarkable worlds, with many unusual aspects. In the third-grade program, Mystery Mountain, a main character is a girl named Polly. She is the daughter of Professor Spark, and she is attempting to program robots to go back in time to change her poor performance on a test. The machines in the game run on electricity, a seemingly realistic aspect. However, the electricity is generated in the Jumbo Electro Generator, which runs on batteries. The player must return to the basement of the mansion to complete a series of operations quickly in order to run the machines and complete the mission. For third-grade students who do not have a complete understanding of the actual workings of electricity and power, this may unintentionally confuse and misinform. In addition to the erroneous application of scientific knowledge, the message seems clear: "Be fast and perfect." Think time gets the player in trouble; for punishment the player has to answer knowledge questions. Is play more important than work? Is learning work? Is learning punishment?

In the fourth-grade level program Haunted Island, Mrs. Grunkle, the mean substitute teacher, has turned the students in one class into monsters. The player's task is to find each student's prized possessions and visit Madame Pomreeda, a fortune teller, who will then transform the monsters back into children and put their photos in the yearbook. This could be upsetting and negative for some children, whether or not they understand that it is not really possible. Settings for the various games include a labyrinth, a cemetery, an enchanted forest, a pirate's map, and a mummy's tomb. This mix of fantasy elements combines settings based on science and history with fictional ones. For fourth-grade students, the lines may be blurred between what is real and what is merely a mechanism of the program.

A similar pattern exists in the Reading Blaster series. Developed by the Davidson Company, Reading Blaster Junior (ages 4–7) features space-oriented characters such as Galactic Commander (female), Blasternaut (male), and Spot (robot). The human-like characters throughout the programs are cartoon-like in appearance and vocal quality. In Reading Blaster (ages 9–12), characters are the human-like but fantastic residents of Bizzaroville who have disappeared in the mansion of the evil Dr. Dabble, who appears to be human but is an evil mad scientist. Characters are stereotypic (an aging movie star, an over-the-hill man-about-town) and are all drawn with exaggerated features. It seems that children are being taught that adults are all ridiculous, incapable of taking care of themselves, and at the mercy of any individual with a bit more knowledge. People in the program are one dimensional, giving children the idea that it is appropriate to judge others quickly by looks and occupation, the very foundation of prejudice.

Several programs have settings and characters that are more realistic and positive. The more recent Clue Finders series by The Learning Company includes a multicultural team of children: Joni Savage, Santiago Rivera, and their friends Owen and Leslie. The settings are modern-day places such as the rainforest and Egypt. However, in The Clue Finders Reading Adventure (ages 9–12), the team is transported to a faraway galaxy and fantasy again reigns. In Feeding Frenzy, a Mission Masters series by McGraw Hill, young agents working for a fictional global agency called Intelliforce are the main characters. The multiethnic team consists of Pauline, Mia, Rakeem, and T.J. Although the young characters are realistic, their agency and their mission (to stop villains Will and Anita Chill, a pair of sinister penguins, from freezing the entire planet) are grounded in fantasy.

Parents and teachers have to ask why there is an overabundance of wild and unusual settings and characters. It appears that literacy-focused software has a tendency to incorporate fantasy and fictional elements as the basis for cohesive plots and motivation. The software is geared to a story or mission format that often has a rescue goal. This is positive in that it promotes the values of cooperation, altruism, assistance, kindness, and caring. The fantasy elements may serve to motivate students, but at what cost? The message seems to be that reality is boring. In order to be interesting, things must be constantly exciting, moving, full of conflict and crises. Also, there are elements that may cause children to question what is real and what is fantasy. Are all substitute teachers mean and skilled enough to change children into monsters? Can little girls who have done poorly on a test resort to sending people back in time? Although children may know this is not really possible, it still may cause them to form negative stereotypes or impressions. Where are the plots set in a more typical neighborhood or school? Are the events and problems of daily life so boring and unimportant that they are not worthwhile as settings?

When I asked my children some of these questions, I was surprised that they had noticed some of these issues and wondered about them, but had not raised any questions with me. This is the danger of subtle values. When left unexamined, children may form opinions and ideas that are unintended. I do not believe we can just hope they will not notice. That itself may be a problem.

Boys Rule and Girls Drool! Bias and Stereotypes

For the most part, the actors or characters in literacy software perpetuate stereotypes, especially gender, race, and class. I found that even when the characters were supposedly nongendered or neutral, they often contained aspects of gender stereotypes. There is little doubt that traditional dominant male characters are the main focus of most programs. When female characters are found, they are often ancillary, negative, or superfluous.

An overwhelming amount of characters are white and male. Even when multiethnic characters are presented, they appear dressed in the preppie style of the middle class and are well spoken with traditional English. I found no software in which the nonwhite character was the primary main character, although in the Clue Finders and Mission Masters programs, the nonwhite characters seem to have equal status. Furthermore, in the Clue Finders, Leslie and Santiago are the main sources of knowledge and they are an equal pair in terms of status. Overall, the Clue Finders team is the most balanced, including an African American female, an Asian male (with glasses), a Hispanic male, and a red-headed white female (with glasses).

Stereotypes exist on several levels. There is a lack of presence of appropriate adult characters, both in appearance and function. There are very few adult women included at all, and those that do appear are often ancillary or evil, such as Mrs. Grunkle, the substitute teacher. In JumpStart Third Grade: Mystery Mountain, Polly has a father but no mother. Male characters who are fathers or uncles do not have spouses; they are related to the child characters, but no mention is made of adult female relatives. Men often appear as the evil mad scientists. This raises several questions. Are all scientists male? Are all scientists evil? Does scientific knowledge only lead to destructive ends?

Characters who are androgynous are often male-oriented. For example, in Reading Blaster (ages 9–12), the main character is a gender-neutral being named Rave, who is listed as the "hero," a male term. However, other characters appear female in orientation in stereotypic fashion. Long curled eyelashes, curvaceous figures, and full red lips are often used for female fantasy characters such as aliens or ghosts. Stereotypes are also present in ancillary human characters. In The Clue Finders 4th Grade Adventure, Egyptians are present in scenes with the team. The females have a very feminine appearance, while the male is a giant with a wrestler's build. Older persons are rarely present; when they are present, their physical appearance is generally wizened and almost frightening.

Cultural references are made to people, places, and things that require a certain amount and type of prior knowledge. For example, The Clue Finders 4th Grade Adventure contains a subgame called The Nile Kingdom. In this subgame, two of the activities are called Columns 'R' Us and Rolling Stone Builders. The dog that assists the team is named Socrates. The cafe owner is a Sydney Greenstreet look alike, complete with fez. One questions whether any student at this level perceives these references with meaning, let alone students from diverse backgrounds. Perhaps the adult developers were inserting humor to attract and entertain parents and teachers who have the necessary background to "get" the joke. Why include references that seem outside the understanding of the intended audience? Would this cause confusion or would the references just be ignored and the humor missed?

The examples that seemed the most obvious were found in Reading Galaxy, a program that uses classic stories to encourage reading comprehension. At first glance, this is a positive package. Comprehension is rarely emphasized in software, and the selections of classic literature here include a wide variety such as *Dragonwings* (Yep, 1975), *...And Now Miguel* (Krumgold, 1984), and *Julie of the Wolves* (George, 1974). However, the premise of the software is a competitive alien game show, including games such as Stump the Human, Beat the Krok, and To Tale the Truth. The alien celebrity panelists include the following: Bodom of Dabarle, Brekphust of Shampeonz, Duhvoyd of Braynes (whose hobbies are listed as "grasping at straws" and "whine tasting"), Fahdir of Dabryde, and Yer Yout of Yer Mynd (whose claim to fame is a close encounter with Dean Martin and Jerry Lewis). The "insider" jokes seem based on schema that are possibly lacking in many students, particularly those from diverse cultures or with limited English proficiency. This unnecessarily limits the potential use of this software to students whose experiences allow them to understand the multiple meanings and subtle humor.

Several programs are available that feature characters from popular movies and television shows. The Casper Early Reader program is based on the video movie *Casper and Wendy* (Macnamara, 1998). Programs that use characters from Sesame Street and the Peanuts comic strip are available. The Random House/Broderbund Living Books series includes popular children's books by authors such as Marc Brown, Dr. Seuss, Jack Prelutsky, and Mercer Meyer. Disney has marketed a series of animated storybook software programs that are based on each of its children's movies, including *Toy Story*, *Lion King*, *Pocahontas*, *Mulan*, *Hercules*, and *Tarzan*. More drill-type programs such as Disney's Reading Quest with Aladdin have followed these.

These programs raise troubling issues regarding values. Disney films have been criticized for their lack of sensitivity to multicultural issues and authenticity (Christiansen, 1997). The issues of false depiction of characters of color and the overemphasis on female sensuality in appearance and manner are areas of concern. In addition, the plethora of computer software connected to mass media advertising is worrisome. Will children see the computer software as a "must have" in the same vein as a stuffed animal or a toy from a Happy Meal? Parents are already concerned with manufacturers and advertisers who target our youngest members of society in hopes of turning them into consumers as early as possible. Also, it appears that the line between computer software that resembles video games and those programs with real educational value is being blurred. Deals between school districts and companies such as Coca Cola are becoming more commonplace despite the concerns that are raised. Materialism and mainstream middle-class values of what is necessary and important for children to "fit in" have been compromised in recent years. These problems are perpetuated in software that reinforces those concerns.

In addition, parents and teachers of females must be vigilant in seeking out literacy software with positive and strong female characters. At the same time, we must help both our sons and daughters question what they see on the computer screen in response to what they see around them. My daughter raised this issue herself. She asked why all the characters who were named "doctor" (usually scientists) were men. Her pediatrician is a female of color, her mother is a female academic, and she knows many females who carry that title. She had enough personal experience to question the disparity between her reality and the multiple programs she saw. But will other children with more limited contacts do the same? My son did not.

Although analysis of the development teams listed by the manufacturers in the accompanying manuals was not part of the design of the study, I examined it in light of the findings. All design teams included females and at least one person who appeared (by name only) to be a person of diverse ethnic background. Yet the programs do not, for the most part, address the multicultural makeup of the global community. One is left to question issues of power and control. Is it intentional that the dominant white middle-class culture is perpetuated on the computer screen? Is it because the money behind the development and marketing is in the hands of traditional power brokers in this society—white men? Why are some of the very people whose skills allow these programs to be successful invisible or secondary in their own work? These are difficult questions, and ones that must be examined more directly in future research.

What Are We Teaching Besides Reading? Tacit Values

Literacy software is laden with implicit values regarding qualities such as competition, perseverance, intrinsic versus extrinsic motivation, mistakes as a positive part of learning, risk taking, and cooperation. If we ignore that these values are part of these programs, our children may perceive that we agree and approve.

Cool Is Better Than Smart

There is a relatively narrow view of intelligence. Characters who appear to be intelligent are presented in a questionable light. In JumpStart Third Grade, a smart character is named Egbert (sic), the resident egghead. The player is advised to hand the analyzer, a tool in the program, back to Egbert when done because "he's kind of a neat freak." In Mission Masters' Feeding Frenzy, an undercover meteorologist is named Ignatius Corduroy Pantz (I.C. Pantz, for short), making him a source of humor.

The characters that are smart are not "too" smart. In many cases, the "nerdy" character serves as the help function; the players go to him or her when they are stuck, but the smart character basically waits around until needed rather than being a vital part of the game. In most cases, smart characters are not as physically appealing as the "cool" or popular characters. They often wear glasses, and their hair and clothing styles are not trendy. Also, in many cases the smart character is evil and serves as the source of the conflict that the popular hero must resolve. This sends an antiintellectualism message that is unfortunately found in many areas of society, such as television situation comedies.

Parents and teachers must be concerned about this mixed message. Although intelligence is valued in terms of problem solving, it seems that too much of it or book smarts (and therefore school smarts) are not as valued as cleverness and quickness. On the one hand, we are encouraging our children to improve their academic skills and problem-solving abilities by gaining skills through the use of software. At the same time, there is a message that being too smart is not a good idea or carries with it many problems.

Fast Is Good, Slow Is Punished

Software differs in terms of speed of processing. In some packages, quickness is the only way to move ahead; rate is a critical component of the task. A slower rate in terms of thinking and responding can even have a negative impact on success. For example, in JumpStart Fourth Grade: Haunted Island, there is a game called What's Caught in the Spider Web? Students control a spider, which has to eat bugs attached to letters in the right order to spell a word spoken by the computer. The spider has three lives, and the student has a limited time to move the spider. Not only is correct spelling being tested, but the student must rely on fine motor dexterity and spatial directionality. If the student does not complete the task within the allotted time, the spider dies. At higher levels, the words become more difficult, and another threatening spider appears on the web as a threat to the student-controlled creature.

In the same program, another game is called What's Going Down in the Cemetery? A label for a particular part of speech, such as "adjective," appears on a tombstone. Words are shown surrounding the stone. The student clicks on a word that matches the part of speech indicated. The student must hurry or the part of speech fades away. The correct response gains points while an incorrect response loses time. A timer is located in the upper left corner of the screen. As stated in the manual, "Remember, the Grim Reaper is coming—you must move quickly." Throughout the same program, a candle burns to indicate player health. The slower a player is at completing all the games, the more the candle burns. The punishment for slow play is to be sent to the center of a labyrinth to answer knowledge questions in order to build up the candle again. It is discouraging that lack of speed, a skill that is reflexive and not academically based, is penalized by the need to demonstrate knowledge.

In recent educational reforms, we have moved children toward more complex and multifaceted tasks, requiring longer time to think at higher levels and apply knowledge. This is in opposition to most literacy software. Not only are children discouraged from taking their time to think carefully, but also, in many cases, the game will end or the player is penalized. Children are discouraged from quality knowledge construction or metacognitive self-checking. This impulsive response mode is not something we want to encourage in most children. It is even more problematic for learners with diverse needs. Students with processing difficulties who are often told to slow down and check their work will not find the same message in these programs. In a world that is moving constantly faster, literacy software perpetuates the need for speed, sometimes at the cost of learning. Think time, cautious thoughtfulness, the ability to weigh all options, careful selection—these values are belittled and in some cases punished in these programs.

Go for It?

The place of accuracy is another area in which implicit values are transmitted. In some cases, children learn that it is more important to be correct than to take a risk and try different solutions. For some students, particularly those with learning problems, this may establish a pattern of learned helplessness.

For example, in Reading Galaxy, there are differing penalties for guessing. In Meteor Match, students are discouraged from making guesses because each incorrect match costs them one credit. Make an incorrect match after the credits have run out and the round is lost completely. Students can reread passages at any time during a game, but this lowers the values of current and future questions about that passage by 20% with each hint. There are also limited chances, so incorrect tries use them up. Students who are unsure may find themselves frozen with the fear of costly mistakes.

This is juxtaposed with the differing types of feedback given when an incorrect response is made. In some cases, if a certain amount of time passes and the student has not made an attempt, a verbal prompt is given to encourage a response. For example, a voice may ask, "Hey, are you out there?" In other programs, a prompt is given to remind the student that there is an option available for assistance. The prompt may say, "Click on a letter to hear its sound." Most programs allow one to three hints before giving the correct answer. This seems to foster a certain amount of problem-solving behavior. Most incorrect attempts are rewarded with a positive response, such as, "Good try, try again." In some cases, there is an unpleasant beep or sound that makes getting a wrong answer undesirable.

Teachers and parents should carefully examine the feedback mechanism in particular programs. In some instances, programs may cause children to act as if paralyzed when they do not know an answer, rather than use what knowledge they have to attempt a response. We want to encourage risk taking in order to foster inventiveness and creativity. There is a poster in some classrooms that states, "You'll always miss 100% of the shots you don't take." This is a powerful message for our children—one that does not seem to be reinforced on the computer screen. Children with different levels of self-esteem may react differently to prompts. Students with difficulties such as attention problems may find that some programs reinforce the impulsivity they are trying to control. A certain amount of thoughtful risk taking is positive in order to learn new things; we should explore to what degree that element is found within a program before deciding on its use.

Can't We All Get Along?

Social skills among characters are also an issue of note. In some cases, rude behavior between characters on opposite sides (such as good versus evil) is accepted and encouraged. When a student is successful at the program, a variety of bad things happen to the villains. In many cases antisocial behavior such as aggressive acts or verbal abuse is part of the "fun" of winning. Discourse includes sarcastic remarks, would-be humorous comeback lines and idioms meant to provoke laughter at the villain's expense.

Children have always been amused by physical humor. One could make the case that it is harmless because it is not real. However, like the violence seen in cartoons and movies, it may desensitize children to the realities of violence. In addition, some children may have trouble distinguishing between what is acceptable in make-believe programs and the real world. Many parents and schools have begun programs that teach and encourage cooperative and caring behavior. Why would computer software containing characters who behave in unacceptable ways be selected and used?

There are some cases in which characters employ positive attributes, primarily the characters on the student's team. For example, the Clue Finders all cooperate with each other and are an interdependent team. The mission is not successful unless all members (via the student) work together. These types of programs teach compassion, acceptance of diversity and individual differences, teamwork, and cooperation. They are a welcome addition to the field.

Winning Is Everything

The ultimate goal of programs demonstrated a variety of motivation and reward structures. Intrinsic rewards, such as helping others versus winning and accumulating points, send differing messages to students.

In many cases, students play for points. These points translate into items that are purchased within the program. With some software, you must earn enough points to maintain viability. Your character needs certain basic items, such as food, energy and so on. If you do not win enough, you virtually go broke and die. In other programs the goal of increased learning is more important. Students chart their previous progress and play against their own performance. The goal is improvement and learning rather than winning in the traditional sense.

There are other more explicit distasteful concepts related to winning in certain programs. For example, in Reading Galaxy, a well-designed program in many ways, students wager part or all of their earned Starbucks before playing certain games. With gambling recognized as an addictive behavior in some adults, the appropriateness of encouraging and promoting this with young people is questionable. Greediness, materialism, consumerism, social status attached to wealth, and other negative values are problematic for our children in many aspects of their lives. Literacy software should not be another place that reinforces the notion that wealth = power = status over knowledge, skills, and kindness.

In summary, tacit values are implied subtly throughout literacy software. The value-laden messages described here are patterns that exist in many programs. The findings in this area caution parents and teachers to look below the surface aspects of software programs. What is contained beyond the content and motivation may not be worth the academic gains.

Proactive Parents and Teachers

The findings of this study are only a beginning in terms of examining software with an eye toward subtle values. Teachers and parents can use the strategies presented here as an evaluation mechanism or as the basis for ongoing discussion with students.

Try Before You Buy

Literacy software is marketed in a variety of ways. Marketing is done to appeal to various constituencies with diverse motivations. Targeted populations include classroom teachers and parents. These groups are generally interested in supplementing and extending their child's curricula. The focus of the advertisements, therefore, is often the impact on test scores or the increase in specific skills, rather than values.

As parents and teachers seek appropriate software, they are most often concerned with the ease of use and motivational qualities. To this end, many manufacturers have borrowed an approach from video games, providing points, skill levels, and certificates as incentives. In some programs, as noted, speed is rewarded over accuracy and long-term retention. However, these aspects are difficult to decipher prior to purchase and trial.

Packaging is also an interesting aspect of computer software. What manufacturers put on a box to attract a child's and/or parent's attention when scanning a store shelf must be deemed worthy of pulling in the consumer. In many cases, the software has bright colors and few details about the characters or settings. The more unusual and incredible may be emphasized to draw attention, whether or not this is an actual focus of the program itself. Many boxes or advertisements include the words "Recommended by teachers" or "Designed by educators" to carry a seeming endorsement, yet little information is available regarding the actual qualities that earned this recommendation.

As discussed earlier, some software has become an extension of an existing toy market. For example, there is a plethora of Disney movie-related software that piggybacks on the marketing associated with Disney products. Mattel has built on the Barbie market, and dolls such as Working Woman Barbie come with a CD-ROM that allows girls to create customized stationery and daily planners for Barbie in her business-related occupation. Of course, the doll also comes complete with a tight-fitting "professional" outfit, including extremely high-heeled red platform shoes. There are software programs associated with other media phenomena such as Teletubbies, Blue's Clues, Bear in the Big Blue House, and Pokémon. In cases such as these, the software package and any potential educational benefits are a small part of million-dollar advertising campaigns.

Parents and teachers should not purchase literacy software without the opportunity to evaluate it for themselves. Although students may enjoy particular programs, there may be inherent undesirable values that are not obvious to the young player. Parents who are concerned with gender issues, stereotyping, or rewarding risk taking over safe accuracy will most likely not find reviews that address these factors. Figure 4 includes a sample evaluation that can help

FIGURE 4   Sample Evaluation Questions for Examining Values Within Literacy
Software

Action/Plot
- How fast does the child have to work? Is speed a critical factor in processing?
- What happens when there is no response? Does the program prompt in a friendly or sarcastic way? Is it counted as "wrong" if a child takes too long to respond?

Form
- What are the settings? Are they realistic in any way? Is there violence?

Actors/Words
- Who are the main characters? Who are the ancillary characters?
- What does each do? How important are they?
- What do they look like? Are they appealing? Are they negative?
- How do they speak? Are their words realistic? Are they sarcastic?
- Are the villains antisocial to other characters in language or behavior?
- Is diversity represented in terms of age, race, gender, abilities, etc.?

Proximity/Movement
- Is the program too busy and confusing?
- Which items are largest and most important? Which are secondary? What does that say to the child?

Culture/Context
- What symbols and names do I notice? What does that represent?
- Is anything other than the dominant culture shown as important and valuable?

Technical Effects
- What technical effects are most noticeable? What do they emphasize?
- Do the production device and elements send any mixed messages in terms of what is important or positive?

uncover some of these areas. Libraries and some retail stores offer opportunities to try software prior to purchase, as do some Internet sites. This is critical for parents and teachers concerned with the subtle messages in these programs.

Software for Girls: Not All Good News

Literacy software has primarily addressed drilling of specific skills such as spelling, vocabulary, and phonics. Within the literacy software available, none was specifically designed for females. Developers purport that their products are gender neutral. This study and others question the accuracy of that claim. The findings of this study would seem to support software programs marketed specifically to female students. However, a growing interest in this market niche has raised some serious issues related to gender and technology.

Programs do exist that are designed for school-age girls. Although these are not generally focused on literacy skills, they all integrate reading, writing, and listening. Developers claim to have attended to the research on preferences of girls regarding play style, characters, and focuses (Miller, Chaika, & Groppe, 1996). In fact, Laura Groppe used this research as the springboard to create a company, Girl Games, designed to develop and market software for girls (Maisel, 1997). Another company, Girl Tech, was begun by researcher and educator Janese Swanson after a successful career at Broderbund that included development of educational software including the Carmen Sandiego series. Both Girl Games and Girl Tech seek to provide girls with software that addresses their preferences in a positive and affirming way, rather than merely changing the activities or characters in existing programs. Although neither company has a purely educational focus, the goal is to get girls interested in and using computers so they will have the skills necessary for the future and will not lag behind their male peers.

Not all girl-focused programs are so positive. As mentioned earlier, Mattel has several programs focused on the popular and controversial Barbie character. Although some are story and literacy related (for example, Barbie as Rapunzel), others include Barbie Fashion Designer (in which girls design clothes that can be printed on special paper-and-glue-backed fabric and "made" for a real doll to wear). Mattel also manufactures software that allows girls to design their own hair wear, tank top patterns, and tattoos and then print these on special paper for real use. Other programs for girls focus on designing stationery, diaries, and address books (such as The Babysitters Club Friendship Adventure). There are also programs that allow girls to design hairstyles and makeup on models' faces, and complete makeovers on their own digital images.

Some programs for girls are based on popular television and movie characters, such as *Sabrina the Teenage Witch* and the movie *Clueless*. Most of these are not educational in the purest sense and are more akin to video games. There are programs that are art oriented, such as Paint 'n Play Pony, which allows girls to design and dress their own pony, raise a virtual pony, write stories about their horses, and read stories about famous horses. IBM/Crayola also markets the Magic Princess and First Ladies paper-doll–making programs, in which girls learn about clothes and noteworthy women, based on historical periods from ancient times to the present. Players can design clothes, read a diary from a girl of the time period, and learn about the history behind the fashions. The clothes and doll can be printed for play. In this respect, there is a modicum of worth in that historical female figures who may have been ignored or given little attention in textbooks are in the spotlight.

In terms of values, there is a series of software that is marketed directly to girls that includes some questionable features. The Purple Moon series, marketed by Mattel, began with Rockett's New School. Rockett, the main character, is an eighth grader who is entering Whistling Pines Junior High. She encounters unfamiliar faces and has several decision-making points, in which the player decides which direction the game takes. Rockett's items include a camera, a sketchbook, a diary, and an electronic "Girl Message Getter." The aspect of the adventure that raises some question regarding values is the ability to uncover secrets in other students' lockers. Rockett has the ability to see personal items belonging to other characters in order to learn more about them. This information can then be used to influence later decisions. The manual even states, "Be on the lookout for teachers' private space. Click on their objects to find out more about the grown-ups at Whistling Pines Jr. High!"

This progresses in the second program, Rockett's Tricky Decision. In this episode, Rockett is worried about which of two parties to attend, depending on which popular students are attending. Again sneaking into private areas is encouraged. Rockett is able to sneak into the teachers' lounge when the door is unlocked. The manual states, "Even though it says, 'No Students Allowed,' you may still get in!... If you click on a teacher's name plate, you may hear some of their thoughts out loud....You might be able to read interoffice memos, student reports—and report cards—plus private mail to the teachers. Notes from parents and who knows what else." Other episodes include Rockett's First Dance, Rockett's Secret Invitation, and Rockett's Camp Adventures .

Certainly the goals and skills put forth as the objectives have positive intent: to foster independent problem solving and decision making in an arena girls say is important to them, that of social interactions. There are other positive aspects. Rockett's friends include a variety of girls from diverse backgrounds in terms of race, although all appear to be middle class. The series has grown to include Rockett's Adventure Maker, in which girls design their own adventure, including setting and dialogue. Related programs include Secret Paths to the Sea and Secret Paths in the Forest, which include a group of multiethnic girls who discuss family problems in a realistic way. Also, there is The Starfire Soccer Challenge, which presents girl athletes in a somewhat positive manner (although there is still an aspect of decision making based on social impact versus morality).

Parents and teachers must seriously question what would cause software developers who seem to have such lofty goals and who produce these other quality programs to encourage girls using the Rockett programs to emulate behavior that is dishonest, immoral, and illegal. The danger in allowing girls to use such programs without questioning and discussing the negative aspects is obvious. Tacit approval may be perceived if nothing is said, or if this aspect is dismissed as merely part of the game. In such a realistic setting, girls may certainly be confused as to the morality and ethics involved, particularly where lines are blurred between fantasy and reality in other programs as previously discussed. It is disheartening that in the name of gender-specific software designed to promote technology use by females, such offensive values are clear and promoted. Parents and teachers must be vigilant as new marketing and development plans targeting girls take form.

Children: Critical Viewers

As with any resource, joint viewing of software programs with children is advantageous. Children remain relatively passive viewers, even when interacting as a player. They generally are not aware of the deeper messages behind the images in front of them. It is the responsibility of teachers and parents to assist them in becoming critical of the world around them, including the virtual world of the computer. Evaluation questions that focus on the underlying values can be used to spark such discussions (see Figure 4, p. 95).

The findings of this study support in-class discussions around some of the issues raised. Even a simple plan in which children self-select programs to use during computer time and then are asked to explain the rationale for their selections can be done with students in primary grades. Older students are well equipped to conduct their own deep-viewing analysis facilitated by a teacher or parent. The insights they will gain as they view with new eyes and notice aspects that were not as obvious to them can be powerful.

Parents and teachers have become more aware of the impact of aspects of media on children. Violence and stereotypes in television programs, cartoons, books, movies, and video games have all received renewed attention in light of societal issues such as bullying and scapegoating. Instructional programs designed to foster character education and qualities such as respect, cooperation, and responsibility abound in many schools. Technology is infused throughout home and school life for many students. It remains an area where potentially undesirable values or messages may sneak unnoticed into children's experience and beliefs. It is imperative that teachers and parents not only become critical viewers themselves, but assist students in gaining the necessary tools and questions to explore all dimensions of the new virtual "neighborhoods" and "friends" they are meeting via computer programs.

Conclusion

In summary, technology presents another area requiring careful analysis on the part of parents and teachers. Typical reviews are generally limited to aspects such as ease of use and curricular alignment. As shown in this study, children are exposed to subtle messages laden with values, much like what is found in television and movies. Although this medium purports to be interactive, it does not allow or promote a critical view of the value issues related to setting, characters, and language. When parents and teachers remain silent regarding these issues, students may come away with more than just increased literacy skills. They may be the unknowing recipients of value messages that perpetuate existing stereotypes and foster implicit views of inequality based on race, class, and gender.

References

Agalionos, A., & Cope, P. (1994). Information technology and knowledge: The non-neutrality of content-specific educational software. *Journal of Educational Policy*, 9(1), 35–45.

Bender, E. (1987, February). *Evaluations of microcomputer courseware/software: A content analysis of published reviews*. Paper presented at the Annual Convention of the Association for Educational Communications and Technology, Atlanta, GA. (ERIC Document Reproduction Service No. ED2855270)

Caftori, N. (1994). Educational effectiveness of computer software. *T.H.E. Journal*, 22(1), 62–65.

Chappell, K.K. (1996). Mathematics computer software characteristics with possible gender-specific impact: A content analysis. *Journal of Educational Computing Research*, 15(1), 25–35.

Christiansen, L. (1997). Unlearning the myths that bind us. In B. Bigelow (Ed.), *Rethinking our classrooms: Teaching for equity and justice*. Milwaukee, WI: Rethinking Schools.

Collis, B., & Ollila, L. (1990). The effect of computer use on Grade 1 children's gender stereotypes about reading, writing and computer use. *Journal of Research and Development in Education*, 24(1), 14–20.

Comer, P.G., & Geissler, C. (1998, March). *A methodology for software evaluation*. Paper presented at SITE 98: Society for Information Technology & Teacher Education International Conference, Washington, DC. (ERIC Document Reproduction Service No. ED421140)

Ellsworth, N.J., & Headley, C.N. (1993). What's new in software? Selecting software for student use. *Reading and Writing Quarterly: Overcoming Learning Difficulties*, 9(2), 207–211.

Heyboer, K., & Mayo, C. (1993). Software to swear by. *Teacher Magazine*, 4(4), 22–23.

Hodes, C. (1995). *Gender representations in mathematics software*. Research report. (ERIC Document Reproduction Service No. ED380277)

Houston, G. (1998). *Setting as a multidimensional influence on the characters in multicultural literature* [Online]. Available: http://www.ceap.wcu.edu/Houston/Multicultural.html

Jonassen, D.H. (2000). *Computers as mindtools for schools: Engaging critical thinking*. Upper Saddle River, NJ: Prentice Hall.

Kincheloe, J.L., & Steinberg, S.R. (1999). Series editor foreword. In L.M. Semali & A.W. Pailliotet (Eds.), *Intermediality: The teachers' handbook of critical media literacy*. New York: Westview.

Macaul, S.L., Giles, J.K., & Rodenberg, R.K. (1999). Intermediality in the classroom: Learners constructing meaning through deep viewing. In L.M. Semali & A.W. Pailliotet (Eds.), *Intermediality: The teachers' handbook of critical media literacy*. New York: Westview.

Macnamara, S. (Director) (1998). *Casper meets Wendy* [video]. Twentieth Century Fox.

Maisel, A. (1997). *Software for girls: A market is discovered* [Online]. Available: http://www.superkids.com

Miller, L., Chaika, M., & Groppe, L. (1996). Girls' preferences in software design: Insights from a focus group. *Interpersonal Computing and Technology: An Electronic Journal for the 21st*

Century. 4(2), 27–36. Available: MerMILLER IPCTV4N2 on Listserv @Listserv.George town.edu.

National Association for the Education of Young Children. (1996). NAEYC position statement: Technology and young children—ages three through eight. *Young Children, 51*(6), 11–16.

Pailliotet, A.W. (1998). Deep viewing: A critical look at visual texts. In J.L. Kincheloe & S. Steinberg (Eds.), *Unauthorized methods: Strategies for critical teaching* (pp. 123–136). New York: Routledge.

Semali, L.M., & Pailliotet, A.W. (Eds.). (1999). *Intermediality: The teachers' handbook of critical media literacy.* New York: Westview.

Singer, L.A. (1997). Native Americans on CD-ROM: Two approaches. *MultiMedia Schools,* 4(1), 42–46.

Taylor, L.S., & Napier, G. (1992, November). *The portrayal of economic deprivation in thirty selected works of children's literature.* Paper presented at the Annual Meeting of the Mid-South Educational Research Association, Knoxville, TN. (ERIC Document Reproduction Service No. ED 353600)

Valenza, J.K. (1997). Girls + technology = turnoff? *Technology Connection, 3*(10), 20–21.

Children's Literature Cited

George, J.C. (1974). *Julie of the wolves.* New York: HarperCollins Juvenile.

Krumgold, J. (1984). *...and now Miguel.* New York: Harper Trophy. (Original work published 1953)

Yep, L. (1975). *Dragonwings.* New York: Scholastic.

Section III

Content Area Connections

When teachers have connected with students and their families, they are better prepared to explore values across the curriculum through literature, multimedia, and literacy events. Using historical fiction picture books for interdisciplinary lessons, teachers and students may explore the moral power of stories through the content areas. Using technology in the classroom, they may consider the values practiced in a classroom community that promote collaborative reading, writing, listening, speaking, and viewing. Finally, using scientific inquiry, children with special needs in literacy development may experience learning communities where caring, sharing, respect, and responsibility produce positive outcomes.

Chapter 6

Historical Fiction Picture Books and Values: An Author's Reflections

Deborah Hopkinson

Before my first picture book was published in 1993, I had little insight into the imaginative ways that educators incorporate literature into values learning and other areas of the elementary curriculum. Then I received a call from a teacher asking me to visit her school to speak about *Sweet Clara and the Freedom Quilt*. I asked whether she had read about the book in the local paper.

"Oh, no," she said. "I found out about *Sweet Clara* at a curriculum workshop on mathematics."

Mathematics? At first I was puzzled. What did the story of a girl who creates an escape map in a quilt have to do with mathematics? But as I soon realized, educators are immensely creative in the ways they incorporate picture books into curriculum units covering a wide range of topics, from mathematics to social studies, from language arts and geography to values and character education.

Values and Historical Fiction

Historical fiction picture books provide a rich resource for classroom discussion of values, especially in the context of looking at values as a component of social studies and history education. In a 1999 article in the *Phi Delta Kappan*, Sam Wineburg wrote, "Coming to know others, whether they live on the other side of the tracks or the other side of the millennium, requires the education of our sensibilities. This is what history, when taught well, gives us practice in doing" (p. 488).

Historical fiction and nonfiction picture books are often children's first introduction to the study of history. Historical fiction creates opportunities for young readers to come to know others, as they read and identify with characters from other times and places. Through this process, children get practice not just looking at the world through different eyes, but looking at different worlds. They can better understand what values are, and how they vary and change throughout cultures and times. At the same time, children can begin to identify, articulate, and understand their own personal, family, and community values.

Tarry Lindquist, in an article published in Scholastic's online *Instructor* magazine, outlines a number of reasons she teaches with historical fiction. Historical fiction, she maintains, piques students' curiosity, puts people back into history, presents the complexity of issues, and promotes multiple perspectives. She notes that the genre introduces young readers to characters who have different points of view, and who deal differently with problems—in other words, people who have different values.

Exploring Values: An Author's Perspective

As my understanding of how educators use historical fiction picture books in the classroom has expanded, the way I approach my writing has changed as well. Although I do not choose topics based solely on their potential for classroom use, I am now much more aware of how historical fiction and nonfiction picture books may be incorporated into the curriculum in a variety of ways, including values exploration. To facilitate the use of my own books in the classroom, I provide links to online lesson plans and classroom activities on my Web site (see http://people.whitman.edu/~hopkinda).

In the following sections I explore some of the activities and ideas educators have shared with me about the ways in which my books can be incorporated into the classroom. Similar activities, of course, can be developed for many other titles. At the end of this chapter I have included a sampling of resources for activities and lesson plans for use with my picture books, as well as an annotated bibliography of other recommended picture books.

Sweet Clara and the Freedom Quilt

> Sometimes I think I'm like Sweet Clara, you know, struggling, so I know how hard it is, but I think most people are struggling. When I sew, my fingers always get poked and get cuts. (letter from a fourth grader)

In *Sweet Clara and the Freedom Quilt*, Clara has been separated from her mother and sent to work in the fields of Home Plantation. After Aunt Rachel teaches her sewing, Clara becomes a seamstress in the Big House, where she first hears people talking about the Underground Railroad. One impediment to escape, Clara discovers, is the lack of a map to show the way. Clara decides to sew a quilt that will have all the information she needs to escape. By the time the quilt is done, she has memorized the route, and she leaves the quilt behind for others to follow to freedom.

I wrote *Sweet Clara and the Freedom Quilt* after hearing a National Public Radio story on the history of African American quilts. Although the story is historical fiction, a recent book titled *Hidden in Plain View: A Secret Story of Quilts and the Underground Railroad* (Tobin & Dobard, 1999) explores the oral traditions that link quilts and the underground railroad.

The focus in *Sweet Clara* is not the journey on the Underground Railroad itself, but on Clara's determination and ingenuity in designing her quilt, as well as the support she receives in doing so from her community. Teachers have told me they have used the book with students to discuss values such as resourcefulness, courage, and sharing.

From my experience discussing the book with children in schools, students do see Clara as courageous. But, with prompting, they can also identify the courage evinced by other members of Clara's community, who secretly share information that enables Clara to create the quilt.

Sweet Clara has inspired a number of lesson plans and creative classroom activities. Educator Patricia Robeson designed a geography-economics lesson plan for Montgomery County Public Schools in Maryland, sponsored by the Council on Economic Education in Maryland and the Maryland Geographic Alliance, that uses the book to introduce fairly complex economic concepts such as scarcity, production, opportunity cost, and resources (see http://www.mcps. k12.md.us/curriculum/socialstd/grade5/Sweet_Clara.html). After reading *Sweet Clara*, students are asked to describe the environment of Home Plantation and how it was changed to meet people's needs. They must also identify the human, capital, and natural resources of the plantation. The teacher introduces the concept of opportunity cost: "Opportunity cost is the single most valuable opportunity given up when a choice is made. What was Clara's opportunity cost when she chose to run away?" The students are then able to discuss such concepts as the value Clara places on freedom and family when she decides to find her mother and flee to Canada. Clara's escape provides an opportunity to discuss what risks we are willing to take for our values.

Other lesson plans use *Sweet Clara and the Freedom Quilt* to introduce children to societal values in connection with slavery, as well as the ideals and convictions that led individuals to participate in the Underground Railroad. In schools I have visited, students often make quilt squares or create a classroom quilt as a community project. I once visited a school in which each student in a Title I classroom had made a quilt square and had also written a short paragraph about what freedom meant to him or her. During my visit, the students read these aloud to me. When I go to a school, I expect that my job is to give something to the students. But these students gave much more to me.

Other educators use the book to initiate a simulated Underground Railroad experience. Students are asked to articulate what they think they would do under similar conditions. Or they may be asked to write from the perspective of the various people involved in the Underground Railroad to explore different and often conflicting values.

Birdie's Lighthouse

> I have a connection to Birdie because when my dad left I had to raise money. I learned that if you work hard enough you can do anything. (letter from a third grader)

Birdie's Lighthouse is the diary of Birdie Holland's 10th year in 1855, during which she and her family move from their small Maine fishing village to Turtle Island, where her father has been named the lighthouse keeper. Birdie is relieved her father will not be going to sea anymore, but life on the bleak island is not easy. Birdie's diary records her feelings as she struggles to adjust to her new world.

In writing this story, I wanted to explore values such as bravery, responsibility, and community. As Birdie begins to help her father take care of the lamps, she begins to feel responsible for the ships that depend on their light. Reading the logbooks of other families who lived in the lighthouse gives her a sense of continuity. Birdie's sense of personal responsibility and courage are what prompt her to brave the storm when her father is ill to make sure the lighthouse stays lit.

Although Birdie and her family are isolated on their lighthouse island, they are nonetheless an integral part of a supportive fishing community. The values of that community are reflected through Birdie's journal entries and the letters she writes to her cousin, who takes in her old cat, and her brother, who goes to work for a fisherman.

One activity that teachers have used to explore values with this book is to ask students to create their own journal of what they would miss if they moved to an isolated place. They can also discuss why Birdie chooses to brave the storm to keep the lights bright.

Many educators find that a multifaceted approach to history—nonfiction, historical fiction, old photographs, letters, CD-ROMs, role-playing, and field trips—is an effective way to provide students with a sense of the past. With this in mind, I was delighted to discover an excellent online lesson plan using historical journals developed by the Vermont Historical Society that I think would work especially well with *Birdie's Lighthouse* (see http://www. state.vt.us/vhs/educate/diaries.htm). Similar activities could be done using other historical journals, too.

The Vermont Historical Society lesson plan includes online excerpts from historical journals of two 19th century Vermont schoolchildren, as well as activities and questions to stimulate classroom discussion. The lesson introduces the concepts of continuity and change, both in the external facets of daily life, as well as in changing expectations and values of families and society. Students are encouraged to think of themselves as historical researchers, making lists of what they know about the diarists' lives, and what further information they might be able to find through other sources. At the same time, as they contrast their own lives with that of the Vermont schoolchildren, they can explore how values have changed with regard to work, education, the roles of women, and expectations of children.

A Band of Angels

> The Jubilee Singers became such a success they were invited to sing for thousands of people all over the United States and Europe. They even sang at the White House for President Grant and in England for Queen Victoria. (from A Band of Angels)

A Band of Angels: A Story Inspired by the Jubilee Singers is based on the life of Ella Sheppard Moore, born February 4, 1851. Ella's father was able to work extra to earn money to buy freedom for himself and Ella, but before he could purchase Ella's mother, she was sold away.

When Ella was in her teens, the Civil War ended, and so did slavery. Left penniless when her father died, Ella earned $6 from odd jobs and hired a wagon to take her to Nashville, Tennessee, where Fisk School, a school for former slaves, had been established. There, Ella joined the school's chorus. But Fisk was in danger of closing unless more money could be found, and the chorus agreed to travel north to give concerts to raise money. Nine young singers set out in October of 1871. At first, audiences did not respond to the classical songs they performed. But when the singers began to share the spirituals they had learned from parents and grandparents, they succeeded.

A Band of Angels lends itself well to discussions of heritage and of the value of education. The book can also be tied into black history units, musical heritage, the history of schools and education, Reconstruction, and African American music.

Whenever I visit schools, I ask students if they would be willing to help their school just as the Jubilee Singers did. Although the younger students all say yes, sometimes fourth and fifth graders are not so sure.

The illustrations in picture books also offer opportunities to explore values with children. *A Band of Angels* takes place in 1871, soon after the U.S. Civil

War. One of the pictures in the book shows the singers huddled in the rain outside a hotel where a man is turning the sign to read, "No Vacancy." When I show slides of this book during school visits, I always ask the children to tell me why they think this is happening. I then show them a picture of Jubilee Hall, the first permanent structure for the education of black students that was built at Fisk through the efforts of the Jubilee Singers. Younger students may not yet be ready for a detailed discussion of the history of civil rights in our country, but through the art in picture books, the issues can be introduced.

Maria's Comet

> I am afraid they will say no,
> afraid they will say
> a girl should only look through the eye of a sewing needle.
> But perhaps they can see I need more,
> And that in my heart, I have already set out. (from *Maria's Comet*)

Maria's Comet is based on the life of Maria Mitchell, who was born August 1, 1818, in Nantucket, Massachusetts, to a large Quaker family. As a child, Maria (Ma-RYE-ah) inherited her father's passion for astronomy. Her life of obscurity ended when she received international recognition after her discovery of a telescopic comet on October 1, 1847. In 1848, she became the first woman member of the American Academy of Arts and Sciences, and later became a professor at Vassar College.

Maria was perfectly suited for her Vassar post, which combined her love of science with a commitment to women's education. In 1873, along with other leaders such as Lucy Stone, Susan B. Anthony, and Elizabeth Cady Stanton, she helped found the Association for the Advancement of Women, serving as president in 1875. She retired in 1888 and died in 1889.

Maria's Comet can be tied to units on science and literature, women's history, astronomy, and young people who followed their dreams. The book reflects the everyday chores of a 19th century girl, and it can provide a springboard for discussion about changing attitudes toward women's education.

Often when I show slides from the book, I pause to show Maria asking her parents if she can study the stars. "What do you think they said?" I ask. Students often guess "no," although Maria's parents said "yes." I use this question to introduce the values placed on women's education in the past, and women's changing roles in society. The book is also an opportunity to explore other values, such as a love of learning.

Conclusion

The study of history is often the study of values in conflict. Using historical fiction and nonfiction picture books in the classroom enables students not only to expand their understanding of history, but also to increase their awareness of what values people held in the past and how they have changed. In the process, educators have opportunities to help students develop a more sophisticated awareness of their own personal, family, and community values.

References

Lindquist, T. (accessed 2001, May 22). Why & how I teach with historical fiction. *Instructor* [Online]. Available: http://teacher.scholastic.com/lessonrepro/lessonplans/instructor/social1.htm

Tobin, J., & Dobard, R.G. (1999). *Hidden in plain view: A secret story of quilts and the Underground Railroad.* New York: Doubleday.

Wineburg, S. (1999). Historical thinking and other unnatural acts. *Phi Delta Kappan, 80*(7), 488–499.

Children's Literature Cited

Hopkinson, D. (1993). *Sweet Clara and the freedom quilt.* New York: Knopf.

Hopkinson, D. (1999a). *Maria's comet.* New York: Atheneum.

Hopkinson, D. (1999b). *A band of angels: A story inspired by the Jubilee Singers.* New York: Atheneum.

Hopkinson, D. (2000). *Birdie's lighthouse.* New York: Aladdin.

Recommended Web Sites for Historical Fiction

Classroom Activities and Lesson Plans

Access Indiana Teaching and Learning Center
   http://tlc.ai.org/index.html
   A site with many links, lesson plans, and numerous resources for educators.
Educational Resources Information Center
   http://www.accesseric.org
   A good source for activities and lesson plans.
History/Social Studies Web Site for K–12 Teachers
   http://www.execpc.com/~dboals
   Access to a wide range of Internet resources in history and social studies.
Internet School Library Media Center Historical Fiction Page
   http://falcon.jmu.edu/~ramseyil/historical.html
   This site includes bibliographies, listing of authors, awards, lesson plans, and numerous links.
Teachnet
   http://www.teachnet.com
   A resource for educators that includes shared curriculum ideas, activities, and lesson plans.

Sweet Clara and the Freedom Quilt

Classroom Projects on the Underground Railroad
  http://www.ugrr.org/learn/jp-proj.html
  Includes information on codes and passwords and creative writing assignments.
Female Voices in Picture Books
  http://www.scils.rutgers.edu/special/kay/fempic.html
  Kay E. Vamdergrift's bibliography of picture books with strong female voices.
Geography and Economics Lesson
  http://www.mcps.k12.md.us/curriculum/socialstd/grade5/Sweet_Clara.html
  Excellent lesson plan on *Sweet Clara* covering economic concepts.
Sweet Clara Teacher Cyber Guide
  http://www.sdcoe.k12.ca.us/score/sweettg.html
  An excellent supplemental unit for *Sweet Clara* providing activities and Web resources.

Birdie's Lighthouse

Historical Fiction
  http://falcon.jmu.edu/~ramseyil/historical.htm
  Bibliographies and a discussion of historical fiction.
Learning With Lighthouses
  http://groton.k12.ct.us/WWW/cb/lwl.html
  Great ideas on using lighthouses (grades 3–5) for geometry, math, language arts, and
  science.
Lighthouse Links on the Web
  http://www.maine.com/lights/www_vl.htm
  This teacher reference site includes links to lighthouses, lightships, and life-saving stations.
Using Historical Journals in the Classroom
  http://www.state.vt.us/vhs/educate/diaries.htm
  A lesson plan using online historical diaries, developed by the Vermont Historical Society.
The Weather Unit
  http://faldo.atmos.uiuc.edu/WEATHER/weather.html
  A variety of weather-related lesson plans that can be tailored to elementary levels.

A Band of Angels

Fisk University History
  http://fisk.edu/history.html
  Background information on Fisk University.
Lesson Plan for "Wade in the Water"
  http://www.mhschool.com/teach/music/sharethemusic/program/sample_wade.html
  A sample fourth-grade lesson plan focusing on the spiritual "Wade in the Water."
The Songs of Freedom
  http://www.ties.k12.mn.us/ugrr/lessons/week4/855160211.html
  Songs of the Underground Railroad lesson for grades 3–5.

Maria's Comet

The Constellations and their Stars
  http://www.astro.wisc.edu/~dolan/constellations/constellations.html
  An excellent site for information on stars and constellations.

Maria Mitchell

http://www.lkwdpl.org/wihohio/mitc-mar.htm

Biographical information on Maria Mitchell.

Maria Mitchell Association in Nantucket, MA

http://www.mmo.org

Home page of the association established in Maria Mitchell's name, dedicated to furthering science education, encouraging women in science, and service as a science resource for Nantucket Island.

Annotated Bibliography—Historical Figures Who Followed Their Dreams

Atkins, J. (1999) *Mary Anning and the sea dragon*. Ill. M. Dooling. New York: Farrar, Straus & Giroux.

A beautifully illustrated book on Mary Anning focusing on her discovery of the first sea reptile fossil.

Brighton, C. (1999). *The fossil girl: Mary Anning's dinosaur discovery*. Brookfield, CT: Millbrook Press.

A fictionalized biography using comic strip frames depicting the discovery of an ichthyosaurus by Mary Anning in 1810.

Brown, D. (1997). *Alice Ramsey's grand adventure*. Boston: Houghton Mifflin.

The amazing story of Alice Ramsey, who drove across America in 1909 in 59 days.

Hearne, B. (1997). *Seven brave women*. Ill. B. Andersen. New York: Greenwillow.

This beautiful book is a celebration of the lives of ordinary women and a reminder that we do not have to be heroic or have our names in history books to lead rich, fulfilling lives.

Joseph, L. (1998). *Fly, Bessie, fly*. Ill. Y. Buchanan. New York: Simon & Schuster.

A picture book inspired by the life of Bessie Coleman, the first black woman aviator.

Martin, J.B. (1998). *Snowflake Bentley*. Ill. M. Azarian. Boston: Houghton Mifflin.

Both the lyrical text and the Caldecott-winning illustrations support the story of a life devoted to a personal passion, in this case Wilson Bentley's accomplishments in photographing snowflakes.

McGill, A. (1999). *Molly Bannaky*. Ill. C.K. Soentpiet. Boston: Houghton Mifflin.

A historical fiction picture book about Benjamin Banneker's grandmother, who marries Benjamin Bannaky, a man who had been her slave.

Miller, W. (1997). *Richard Wright and the library card*. Ill. G. Christie. New York: Lee & Low.

This handsome picture book retells an episode from the autobiography of the writer Richard Wright, who was unable to get a library card in Memphis in the 1920s.

Mora, P. (1997). *Tomas and the library lady*. Ill. R. Colon. New York: Knopf.

A tribute to the life of Tomas Rivera and the librarian who aided him. Rivera began his life as a migrant worker and eventually became a university chancellor.

Pinkney, A.D. (1994). *Dear Benjamin Banneker*. Ill. B. Pinkney. San Diego: Harcourt Brace.

A picture book exploring the life of another self-taught astronomer, African American Benjamin Banneker.

Schroeder, A. (1996). *Minty: A story of young Harriet Tubman*. Ill. J. Pinkney. New York: Dial.

A fictionalized account of the childhood of Harriet Tubman.

Sis, P. (1996). *Starry messenger*. New York: Farrar, Straus & Giroux.

Galileo's triumphs and tragedies are made accessible to young readers in this amazing Caldecott honor book.

Stanley, D. (1996). *Leonardo Da Vinci*. New York: Morrow.

A beautiful and fascinating biography of Leonardo da Vinci.

Weller, F. (1997). *Madaket Millie*. Ill. M. Sewell. New York: Philomel Books.

The story of a Nantucket girl, Millie Madaket, who trained dogs to patrol beaches and conduct lifesaving rescues.

Winter, J. (1998). *My name is Georgia: A portrait*. San Diego: Harcourt Brace.

A portrait of artist Georgia O'Keefe and the development of her distinct artistic style.

Chapter 7

Technology and Values:
Connecting With Classroom Literacy Learning

Elizabeth A. Baker

O ur society functions on some basic principles of collaboration, mutual respect, and responsibility. Schools commonly encourage these princi-ples in tacit and explicit ways. For example, teachers expect children to respect classmates during class discussions as well as during recess. At the same time, schools are rapidly purchasing technology. In 1995, 98% of schools reported owning a computer (Coley, Cradler, & Engel, 1997). There was spec-ulation that all U.S. schools would be online by 2001. I visited a classroom that had 26 children and 35 computers. I wanted to know if these children were learning basic values to function in our society. What I found was a strong collaborative community of children who actively took responsibility for their learning in a respectful environment. The purpose of this chapter is to describe this classroom, consider the values these children learned by participating in this classroom, and discuss challenges the teacher faced.

Classroom Description

Setting and Participants

I entered this classroom in January and stayed until the end of the school year in early June. I observed and assisted 4 or 5 days each week for 6 to 8 hours each day. My descriptions are based on these observations and the time I spent working with Ms. Jones (pseudonyms are used for the teacher and children) and the students in her room.

My observations occurred in a fourth-grade classroom that was located in the southeastern United Stated in a suburban public school. This classroom had a variety of technologies (see Figure 1) in addition to textbooks, trade books, and magazines. The most frequently used software included word pro-cessing (e.g., ClarisWorks) and graphic programs (e.g., Kid Pix, HyperStudio). Kid Pix provided access to multiple graphics that were easily edited, enlarged, shrunk, flipped, and pasted into documents. Kid Pix gave students slide show and animation formats. HyperStudio also provided a slide show format. The

HyperStudio slides could be randomly accessed whereas Kid Pix slides could not shift from a predetermined order. As with Kid Pix, students pasted clip art, edited clip art, and scanned images into HyperStudio products. Furthermore, HyperStudio provided verbal recording abilities and access to video from laser disc players. Thus, HyperStudio provided the expression of meaning with text, spatial images, and sound.

The students in this classroom were selected by a board of faculty members from a pool of applicants within the school. The board purposely selected a representative sample of the school population with regard to race, gender, and academic ability. The class consisted of 13 boys and 13 girls. The teacher described the class as "average" in ability, citing that no student qualified for special, remedial, or gifted services. There were one African American boy, three African American girls, and one Hispanic girl. The remaining children were European American. Forty-four percent of these children received free lunch. Twenty of these students had been in a third-grade technology classroom.

Ms. Jones was a seasoned teacher with more than 20 years of classroom teaching experience. She had received various awards for her outstanding teaching and was considered to be a very good teacher. When I worked with Ms. Jones, it was the first year that she had taught fourth grade or taught in a technology-based classroom.

FIGURE I   Technologies Used in This Classroom

Technologies	Most Frequently Used Software	Frequently Used Digital Sources of Information
35 computers (Apple IIe, Macintosh SE, Macintosh Quadra)	America Online	CD-ROM encyclopedias (Grolier's, World Book)
10 printers	HyperStudio	filmstrips (commonly included narrated audiotapes)
2 televisions	Kid Pix	
2 CD-ROM drives	word processing	
1 external drive (predominantly used for capturing video)		laser discs
1 VCR		videotapes
1 video camera		World Wide Web
1 laser disc player		
1 modem		
1 telephone		
1 scanner		

Using Technology

Ms. Jones based her instruction on inquiry projects and process writing (see Figure 2). The inquiry projects started with topics from the district curriculum, such as oceans, geometry, poetry, and regions of the United States (see Figure 3, p. 116). To begin an inquiry project, Ms. Jones announced a topic and the students silently read their textbooks to identify questions and points of interest. Then they formed inquiry teams with classmates who had similar interests. These teams found materials about their topics by searching the Web, laser discs, CD-ROM encyclopedias, trade books, magazines, videotapes, learning kits with narrated film strips, and telephone interviews (usually with parents, sometimes with professionals such as zookeepers).

FIGURE 2   Synthesis of Daily Schedule

Time	Activity
8:45–9:30	Students entered room: • Students got books and materials they would need from their classroom lockers and put them on their desks • Students began work on whatever assignment the teacher had on the board; assignments typically included instructions to write a journal entry, work on an independent book report and presentation, work on a team unit of inquiry, correct assignments returned by the teacher
9:30–9:45	Whole-class time: • Class recited the pledge of allegiance and sang a patriotic song • Class reviewed morning tasks, including strategies and materials for accomplishing such tasks • Teacher returned and reviewed graded assignments • Class worked on an English lesson based on what the teacher observed the day before during individual and team work times (e.g., if students needed guidance on how to outline or use commas)
9:45–11:10	Independent projects or team inquiry units: • Independent projects included individual compositions usually representative of a specific genre, and book reports • School library: Students selected a book for an individual book report or gathered materials related to the unit of inquiry • Study Buddies: 45 minutes every 2 or 3 weeks, a second-grade class entered the room with a composition assignment; each second grader was paired with a fourth grader who helped with typing, editing, and revising the composition assignment
11:10–11:20	Whole-class time: • Teacher asked students to evaluate their progress during the morning • Teacher announced, based on students' comments, what they would do after lunch (e.g., continue morning projects or shift to something else) • Teacher gave directions for what the students should do when they returned from lunch

FIGURE 2   Synthesis of Daily Schedule (continued)

Time	Activity
11:20–12:00	Lunch and restroom
12:00–12:20	Odds and ends This time was used for a variety of activities, including • Finish morning work • Individual or team presentations • Math lesson • Handwriting lesson (1 or 2 times a week)
12:20–1:00	P.E. and water break
1:00–1:05	Whole-class time: • Teacher discussed how they would spend the afternoon
1:05–3:20	Odds and ends This time was used for a variety of activities, including • Handwriting (1 or 2 times a week, for about 20 minutes) • Math (about 30 minutes of instruction and activity) • Music (the teacher team taught music with another teacher for about 30 minutes one day a week) • Work on individual or team projects • Individual or team presentations
3:20–3:30	Whole-class time: • Class reviewed homework assignment • Class gathered materials to go home • Teacher shared school announcements

The students completed 11 inquiry projects between January and June. On the average, these projects took 6 to 8 school days with 30 to 120 minutes of work per day. Each day, the teams met to discuss what they had found since the previous day (while at home, the students often read more sources or discussed the topic with their parents). The inquiry projects culminated with a session in which the students taught the class what they had learned about their topics. In order to teach the class, the students had to figure out how to communicate their topics to their classmates. The teams used technology to develop presentations that typically incorporated bulletin boards (made with computer graphics and captions), newspapers (composed and printed on computers), multimedia slide shows, animations, and skits (composed and revised on computers with multiple copies printed for students in skits).

Ms. Jones incorporated the writing process within the inquiry projects. At the beginning of the year, she discussed how the writing process involved brainstorming, drafting, editing, revising, and publishing. She posted this process on a classroom wall in the form of a staircase. Throughout the year,

FIGURE 3   Inquiry Process

Initiate Inquiry
- Based on the district's curriculum, Ms. Jones announced an inquiry unit topic (e.g., oceans, aerospace, geometry, poetry)
- Students silently read district textbooks to find topics they wanted to investigate
- The class met and discussed topics they found interesting and formed inquiry teams based on similar interests

Conduct Inquiry
- Inquiry teams (three or four students on each team) went to the school library to find information about their selected topics (e.g., books, magazines, CD-ROM encyclopedias, and learning kits with videotapes, filmstrips, and photographs)
- Inquiry teams met with the teacher to share what they found in the library and discuss resources in the classroom (e.g., books, magazines, multimedia CD-ROMs, e-mail, Web sites, phone, laser discs)
- Inquiry teams met to discuss their findings and how they would present their findings to their classmates

Culminate Inquiry
- Each student submitted a summary of his or her information to Ms. Jones
- Ms. Jones reviewed the summaries and either approved them for presentation or recommended further inquiry
- Students presented their findings to their classmates by giving each student a blank outline about their topic (for note taking) and orally presenting their topic with supporting materials (e.g., video, filmstrips, animations, multimedia slide shows, and student-made newspapers, magazines, and books)
- Using the blank outlines, the class took notes during presentations and asked questions so they could understand the topic and complete the blank outlines
- Students took a stimulated recall test of the presentations

she reminded students about which step of the process they were following. For example, during a poetry unit, the whole class analyzed poetry and then brainstormed topics for poetry together. Then the students went to their seats and brainstormed their own topics. Ms. Jones circulated the room and discussed the topics with each student. If the students' topics were sufficient, Ms. Jones told them they could begin drafting.

Before the students were allowed to publish their compositions, they were expected to request feedback from two or three other classmates. The class talked about how the process of giving appropriate feedback should include sharing at least three positive comments before making any suggestions. To culminate the writing process, the students printed out their compositions; in other words, they published their work. These publications were then used during their inquiry presentations, posted on bulletin boards, handed out for classmates to take home (e.g., newspapers), or added to the class library for classmates to check out (e.g., reports about regions of the United States).

Values Students Learned

Collaboration and Respect

The students actively collaborated in this classroom. Respect for one another's ideas and capabilities was paramount for this collaboration. For example, in the following excerpt, Jessica had just composed a story about how a girl named Chelsey found a robot and named her Ashley. Before Jessica printed her story, she invited two classmates, Chuck and Lisa, to read her story from her computer screen. The excerpt begins while Chuck was reading Jessica's story out loud. Chuck and Lisa took turns reading and making suggested changes. The material in italics represents text from Jessica's story.

Chuck: *Then* [a girl named] *Chelsey started school. Ashley* [the robot] *started home and cleaned house. A week wented by.*

Jessica: Went by.

Chuck: Went by. You should just cut off that -ed; it should be *a week went by.*

[Jessica edited her text]

Lisa: *Chelsey said, "What do you want to do, Ashley"*... You need to um...[Lisa pointed to the screen]

Chuck: *"What do you want to do"*... Oh, put a question mark right there. [He pointed to the screen and Jessica edited her text]

Lisa: *When they woke up...*

Chuck: *When they woke up though?*

Lisa: *They wached TV.*

Jessica: *When they woke up they* [Chuck edited the text and changed *though* to *they*]

Lisa: There is a *t* there [referring to the *t* missing from *watched*]

Chuck: Oh yeah, I forgot...

Lisa: *...played games and went outside, and they played with their friends*

Chuck: ...that needs to be capitalized... [reference not clear]

Jessica: *Then, after that, they went to the zoos and farms. At one farm they rode the bull. The bull killed Ashley. We was so* [mad] *at the bull but I...*

Lisa: Made at the bull? [although Jessica pronounced *mad*, it was spelled *made*; Jessica then fixed it]

Chuck: It keeps saying *after* [many of the sentences began with *After*].

Lisa:	Why don't you make friends with another robot in the story?
Jessica:	Well
Lisa:	Make it a happy ending.
Jessica:	Well, I don't want it that happy...
Chuck:	That was a very good story...
Jessica:	OK, so can I read yours next?
Chuck:	Yep.

Collaboration, based on mutual respect, occurred throughout this dialogue. Jessica respected Chuck and Lisa's abilities enough not only to ask for their feedback but also to incorporate it.

The students in this class collaborated continually. Ms. Jones noted that as the students became accustomed to working with one another, they respected their peers' input so much they requested to collaborate even during individual activities. For example, she told me that during an individual writing project, the students asked to work together:

> I kept stressing, "This is your poem; you are doing it by yourself." What did we find? [Students] congregating, commenting on each other's poems... And whenever I say, "Study your spelling," [they say,] "Can we study with somebody else?" I think because we do such a big part of the day with the group work [inquiry projects], they are used to interacting. I do not think that they would do that if we had not been spending an hour and a half or two every day doing these group projects.

Making Choices and Taking Responsibility

Making choices and taking responsibility for learning occurred throughout the inquiry projects and process writing. The students chose their topics (e.g., ocean tides, tidal waves, and the topography of the ocean floor), sources of information (e.g., science textbook, trade books and magazines, CD-ROMs, laser discs, videotapes, filmstrips), and presentation formats (e.g., animation, bulletin boards). Making choices and taking responsibility for learning also occurred during *individual* projects. Specifically, the students chose which genre they wanted to explore. They chose what format they would use to report to the class about the book (e.g., multimedia slide show, written script and performance of character impersonation, written and oral "sales pitch" for the book). As a consequence, the students appeared to have ownership of the information they gathered and made decisions about how they would present their projects to their classmates.

To illustrate how the students made choices and took responsibility for their learning, I will share the story of an inquiry team of four students who investigated ocean tides, tidal waves, and the topography of the ocean floor. The ocean unit occurred over 3 days and required 6 designated inquiry team meetings. (Refer to Figure 3, p. 116, which depicts the process of this inquiry unit.)

On the first day of the inquiry, the students silently read their science textbooks and chose what topics they wanted to investigate. During the next day, they went to the school library and found additional information from trade books, videotapes, magazines, CD-ROM encyclopedias, and learning kits with narrated filmstrips. They returned to the classroom and found more information from the Web, laser discs, and multimedia encyclopedias. The following excerpt begins when the team got together to share their findings and decide who would focus on which topics for further research. The ellipses indicate instances in which the students were interrupted and did not complete their statements.

Randy: OK, we have got to have some parts [topics].

Richard: OK, me and Randy are going to do waves.

Randy: We are going to do waves and tides...

Wally: I am going to do earthquakes [under the ocean].

Randy: I know, you [Wally] are earthquakes. Simon, what would you do then since your dad was a sea diver or whatever?

Simon: I am going to talk about what the bottom looks like.

Randy: What the ocean bottom looks like, OK... OK, let's [write] this stuff down.

Wally: OK.

The team members then listed each other's names and their selected subtopics on their clipboard pads. Next, the team decided how they would present their information to the class.

Randy: OK, what do you think would be the best [way to present] for our topic?

Simon: OK, what would be good for my thing [the ocean floor] is like I could do, we could do a bulletin board.

Wally: I want to [do an] animation of two [continental] plates hitting...and they are all shaking and everything.

Randy: OK, we could do two [presentation formats], OK?

Richard: Tides would make a good animation...

Randy: Well, that would be a pretty good animation.... [Simon,] could you do [an animation of] a deep-sea diver?

Simon:	I could do a poster.
Wally:	On a bulletin board.
Richard:	Yeah...
Randy:	Naw, let's just do animation.

The students continued to discuss how they might express their research findings. For instance, Wally suggested that he could animate how continental plates shift to illustrate what causes an earthquake that in turn creates a tidal wave. Richard decided that he too could make an animation of high and low tides. Randy concurred that an animation of the tides would effectively communicate how tides are affected by the sun and moon. However, Wally remained unconvinced that an animation would help him teach the class about topography of the ocean floor (even if he added a deep-sea diver who explored the ocean floor). As this example illustrates, the students talked about their ideas around particular research topics and decided which media (e.g., animation, bulletin board) best illustrated the meanings they hoped to convey. In the end, Wally did an animation of earthquakes under the ocean floor, Richard did an animation of the lunar phases and ocean tides, Randy did an animation of a tidal wave and an illustration of the parts of a wave, and Simon did an illustration of the topography of the ocean floor.

On the morning of the third day of the ocean inquiry, Ms. Jones called the class together. She told the students that their next task was to find information that was critical to their topics and valuable for sharing with their classmates. Ms. Jones conducted a minilesson about the uses of indexes and the outlining of information while reading. Ms. Jones then told the students to take notes while they read, with the goal of developing an outline for their presentation. Before dismissing the students for silent reading, she asked who had checked out a video from the library and encouraged students to consider videos as sources of information.

After working on this unit for 3 days and meeting with team members during 5 designated times, the students met to discuss their presentation. As shown in the following excerpt, Randy spontaneously initiated a discussion about the strategies they use to prepare for oral presentations.

Randy:	Hey, Richard, do you write down your info [so you can memorize it for the oral presentation]?
Richard:	Well, I did but...
Randy:	Do you write it down on the computer normally?
Richard:	Well, all I do is just type it on the computer; that is all I do.

Randy:	You do? I don't. OK.
Richard:	Why?
Randy:	Because, see, if you type it on the computer, that's like your memory banks, the computer. If you keep on reading it, your memory banks is [sic] in your head, so that tells you all your information.... Try to get all the information you can. Just read books. See, reading books helps a lot more than writing down your information and studying it, because if you read books you understand your topic a lot more than you do if you are just writing, copying your information out of a book like most people do and keep on studying it.

Randy has apparently discovered a new way to prepare for oral presentations—just read books. While Randy only mentions books, he actually got information from Web pages, multimedia encyclopedia articles, laser discs, videotapes, magazines, filmstrips, and conversations with classmates, the teacher, and his parents. Randy explained to his team members what it meant for him to make sense of the topic they were researching. In effect, he communicated to his team members that it was not enough to memorize the information or to write the information down. Instead, for him to understand the material, it was more important for him to read various sources on the research topic and discuss his findings with others. A few minutes later, the team presented their findings to the class.

Challenges Encountered

Although I am unable to provide an exhaustive list of the challenges that Ms. Jones faced, I can list several that were consistent. Specifically, the students commonly had difficulty (a) recognizing that some multimedia products were flashy and contained little content, (b) creating multimedia products that had informative content, and (c) understanding why sources could have conflicting or inaccurate information. Similarly, Ms. Jones had to (a) verify the information the students incorporated in their presentations and multimedia products and (b) provide privacy for students who did not like the fact that everyone could see their computer screens while they composed.

Flashy Multimedia Products

The students commonly liked multimedia products that showed action, had sound effects, or did something unique (i.e., had distinctive transition features). Ms. Jones helped the students understand that although these features were interesting, without content they offered little educational value. For example, the students enjoyed watching animations of the development (and crashes) of airplanes, jets, and space rockets. These animations, however, did not include explanations for why certain designs were successful or unsuccessful. Ms. Jones showed students how to outline information and determine whether CD-ROM encyclopedias, Web pages, and other multimedia products were simply "flashy" or contained pertinent content information. Although teachers in traditional classrooms typically do not have to deal with this challenge, it can be argued that these children may benefit from the ability to differentiate between flashy and informative materials.

Creating Informative Multimedia Products

Similar to the previous challenge, the students liked to create multimedia products that were flashy. Ms. Jones had to help the students evaluate their own multimedia with the same criteria they used to evaluate commercial multimedia. For example, an inquiry group wanted to teach the class about the dangers of drugs and alcohol. Their initial multimedia slide show simply showed a black lung and a crashed car. Ms. Jones had to ask the students to outline the content they wanted to convey and think of ways to convey that content. Although a black lung and crashed car may be incorporated into a multimedia product, they needed to make clear connections between their content and their multimedia. Students writing traditional paper-and-pencil papers also need to elaborate on their ideas so their audience understands the connections between paragraphs and their topic. The students in this technology-rich classroom, however, had to learn how to orchestrate their content among various sign systems (i.e., animations, video, text, narrations, sound effects, etc.) (see Baker, 2001).

Conflicting and Inaccurate Information

The students were not limited to classroom textbooks. They had access to Web pages, magazines, trade books, videotapes, and other sources. Sometimes the students found conflicting information in different sources as well as information that was simply inaccurate. For example, one student found three different heights for the tallest Himalayan mountain. Ms. Jones helped the students understand that information changes as we make new discoveries or use better technology. When the students found conflicting information, Ms. Jones encouraged them to compare the publication dates as well as confirm the information in two or three sources. Traditionally, teachers do not need to worry about conflicting or inaccurate information because the students use published textbooks. While Ms. Jones had to face this challenge in her classroom, these students learned that not all information is accurate and there are ways to examine accuracy.

Verify Student Information

While the students needed to evaluate the accuracy of the information they read, Ms. Jones had to verify that the information they presented to one another was correct. Unlike traditional classrooms, Ms. Jones could not simply check the classroom textbook to verify the information because the students could extend the information provided in the textbook by using information from Web pages and many other sources. To address this challenge, Ms. Jones taught her students how to cite references and be ready to show her where they found the information they were reporting to the class. Herein, these students had the opportunity to learn how and why authors cite source materials.

Need for Privacy

When I asked the students if they could see classmates' computer screens, they fluently listed whose screens they could read from their seats. In addition, the students in this classroom commonly walked around in order to collaborate, gather materials, and work with various technology peripherals. While walking around they could read anyone's computer screen. In other words, the documents that the students composed on their computers were public within this classroom (Baker, 2001). Although this "publicness" may facilitate collaboration, some students may be intimidated. Ms. Jones dealt with this challenge by establishing rules that required students to tell an author two or three things they liked about a composition before they made any suggestions. These rules appeared to be sufficient for this classroom. However, other teachers may need to take additional precautions. For example, some students may prefer to compose at a computer that is in a study carrel or separate from classmates' seats.

Discussion

My observations occurred in an unusual classroom—it had more computers than students. Nonetheless, schools are rapidly purchasing technology, and many classrooms may resemble this technology-rich classroom in the near future. I was encouraged to see the level of collaboration, respect, and responsibility for learning that occurred in this environment. While Ms. Jones encountered some challenges along the way, they too appear to be valuable learning opportunities. For example, the students in this class learned that just because an animation or multimedia slide show looks slick, it may have minimal substance. Conversely, they learned that when they use technology to communicate information, they can create animations with many features, but unless they add substance, the presentations have minimal value. Because the technologies gave the students access to many sources of information (e.g., Web pages, CD-ROM encyclopedias, laser discs, phone interviews, e-mail), the students had to learn to deal with conflicting and inaccurate information. Although Ms. Jones had to help students with this challenge, these students emerged from this class with the ability to confirm and disconfirm the accuracy of information. Due to the vast number of sources, the students also learned how to reference their information. Both verifying information and referencing information are important skills.

This classroom may not resemble other technology-rich settings in terms of online communications. Ms. Jones did not actively pursue opportunities for students to collaborate with learners in other settings via e-mail or other online communications. Observations in such settings would provide additional insights into ways that technology can foster important community values.

AUTHOR NOTE

The author would like to thank the teacher and students who graciously invited her into their daily explorations with technology. She would also like to thank the following people who helped her evaluate her observations and offered alternate considerations: Charles K. Kinzer, Deborah W. Rowe, Robert Sherwood, Susan Bunch, and Joy Whitenack.

For additional information about how Ms. Jones used the inquiry approach and the process writing approach, see the following Web site: http://www.readingonline.org/articles/baker/

For additional information about various implications of integrating technology and literacy instruction see the following articles:

Baker, E.A. (2000). Integrating literacy and tools-based technologies: Examining the successes and challenges. *Computers in Schools, 16*(3), 73–89.

Baker, E.A., & Kinzer, C.K. (1998). Effects of technology on process writing: Are they all good? In T. Shanahan & F.V. Rodriguez-Brown (Eds.), *Forty-seventh National Reading Conference Yearbook* (pp. 428–440). Chicago: National Reading Conference.

Baker, E.A., Rozendal, M., & Whitenack, J. (2000). Audience awareness in a technology rich elementary classroom. *Journal of Literacy Research, 32*(3), 395–419.

References

Baker, E.A. (2001). The nature of literacy in a technology rich classroom. *Reading Research and Instruction, 40*(2), 153–179.

Coley, R.J., Cradler, J., & Engel, P. (1997). *Computers and classrooms: The status of technology in U.S. schools.* Princeton, NJ: Policy Information Center, Educational Testing Service.

Chapter 8

Inquiry and Literacy Learning in Science: Connecting in a Classroom Community

Patricia Ruggiano Schmidt

All of the children seem involved and interested in studying the desert. I've never seen them work so well together and offer as much information in class discussions. Even Karlton, one of my children with special needs, is making significant contributions. (Mrs. Stone, second-grade teacher)

Mrs. Stone's thoughts were similar to those of other teachers on her second-grade team at Meachem Elementary, an urban school, as they observed the implementation of inquiry learning in science. This chapter demonstrates how inquiry learning naturally connects with reading, writing, listening, speaking, and viewing, and how it acts as a means for bringing children with special literacy learning needs into a classroom community in which children care, share, and respect themselves and others.

Inquiry Learning and Literacy Learning

Inquiry learning/teaching is based on a constructivist approach (see Confrey, 1990; Fosnot, 1996; Piaget, 1970) that perceives children as "little scientists" who experiment, solve problems, and discover how the world functions. Children are encouraged to become more active classroom participants as they connect with their own environment and the studies at hand and formulate high-level questions (Chaille & Britain, 1991). Therefore, the teacher must act as the facilitator who sets broad objectives, plans experiences to help students establish basic knowledge, gathers materials and resources, models questioning behaviors, and guides discovery processes (Birnie & Ryan, 1984; Hawkins, 1965; Raphael & Pearson, 1985). Based on previous personal and school experiences, students connect the known to new experiences and begin to question, make predictions, and discover (Rumelhart & Ortony, 1977). As the teacher anticipates specific answers to questions for a unit of study, the students usually respond not only with answers but also with information beyond what the curriculum requires, and they generate even more questions for further study (Birnie & Ryan, 1984; Hawkins, 1965; Schmidt, 1999).

125

Furthermore, the activities students experience while learning create interest in what is being learned (Dewey, 1969). And if that interest is sustained, successful learning can take place, which leads to the confidence necessary to collaborate with other children and the teacher (Davydov, 1995).

Akin to inquiry learning is the sociocultural perspective (Vygotsky, 1978), a constructivist approach for literacy development. It also requires that teachers consider each child's prior knowledge, home culture, and other social experiences and connect them with units of study. In the process, not only does a unique classroom culture emerge, but one that values individual ideas and social interactions (Moll, 1990). The key to both inquiry learning and the sociocultural perspective is collaborative communication, a social endeavor initiated and practiced by all members of the community (Bloome & Green, 1982). Thus children who experience inquiry and the sociocultural perspective for literacy development learn to share their own knowledge and appreciate that of others.

Background

In 1996, as part of a New York State Systemic Initiative program, three second-grade tenured teachers and I received a grant for the collaborative study of children's scientific inquiry. I am an elementary education professor at a small, private liberal arts college. The setting for our study was Meachem Elementary, a K–6 school in an urban district. It was built in the 1930s and was recently remodeled with special attention to the maintenance of original woodwork, masonry, and style. It housed approximately 660 children, with free lunches provided to 36% of its population. The student population was 58% European American, 36% African American, and 6% Native American, Asian, or Arabic. Almost 95% of the faculty and staff were European American.

Early on, our team noted the positive student responses to inquiry learning and decided to systematically observe six children with special needs in literacy learning. Over 9 weeks, we collected and analyzed videotaped lessons, written classroom observations, children's interviews, children's products, and teachers' journals. A school administrator, three preservice teachers, a college mathematics professor, a college chemistry professor, and an educational researcher were involved as participant observers to help us record and analyze the data. It was a collaborative effort that contributed to our understanding of inquiry learning and literacy learning as social phenomena.

The Second-Grade Program

The second-grade classrooms included learning centers with similar materials and an abundance of fiction and nonfiction literature for children to explore daily. All the classrooms had adopted a district-wide literature-based program, and all included individualized writing workshops with time each day for direct whole-group instruction related to grammar, punctuation, and spelling. Additionally, math manipulatives were in use for whole-group and small-group instruction, and all content areas included videos, field trips, and teacher-created and commercially prepared worksheets.

The Inquiry Unit

The 2-month unit of study titled "Insects in My Back Yard" included three key components: (1) kinds of insects found in the children's environment, (2) life cycles of the butterfly and mealworm, and (3) impact of insects on our lives. The concept map depicted in Figure 1 shows the teaching objectives for the unit.

The teachers gathered videos and literature, scheduled special guests and field trips, and surveyed science kit materials. They integrated math into lessons where appropriate, and ensured that math materials were available. Science classes began with minilectures and basic directions for inquiry activities. The children then studied individually, in pairs, and in small groups. At the end of classes, the teachers brought children together for whole-group summaries, the sharing of discoveries, and questions for the next class.

FIGURE I   Concept Map

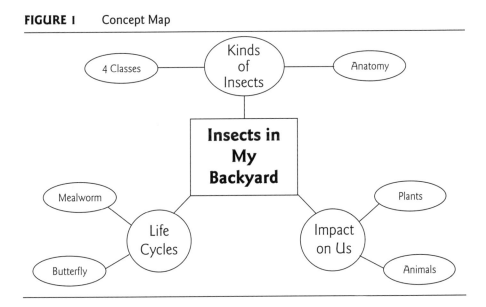

FIGURE 2   K-W-L-Q Chart

What I Know	What I Want to Know
What I Learned	**More Questions to Answer**

Teachers decided to follow the K-W-L-Q process (Ogle, 1986; Schmidt, 1999) to help the team and the children frame questions in a consistent format throughout the unit. The children used the chart shown in Figure 2 for their questions and research.

The teachers believed this chart would act as an organizer for inquiry. For *K* (What I *Know*), the students recorded prior knowledge of an insect. For *W* (What I *Want* to Know), they generated questions about the insect. Next, the students perused the literature, talked to people, visited places, and viewed videos to find answers to the questions. For *L* (What I *Learned*), they wrote information they had discovered. Finally, the box for *Q* (More *Questions* to Answer) was the place to brainstorm more questions, so that students would see that learning is a continuous, cyclical quest.

Children's Responses to Inquiry Learning and Literacy Learning

The team selected two students from each classroom who were officially labeled or were in the process of being labeled learning disabled in oral and written language. There were three African American children and three European American children, four boys and two girls. All the children responded in positive ways to inquiry learning and literacy learning during science lessons.

First, the children maintained a greater focus during lessons. They followed directions, developed their own questions for individual and whole-class study, used the literature available to discover information for assignments and wrote/dictated/drew the information gained.

Second, the children's interactions with their classmates became more positive. They worked successfully with self-selected or teacher-selected buddies. In some cases, for the first time other classmates actually chose to work with these children. Both partners searched for and shared information about the task at hand, listened to their partners, and discussed findings.

Third, orally and in writing, the children demonstrated clear understandings of the three major concepts in the "Insects in My Back Yard" unit:

- They described and explained the form and function of body parts and replicated the anatomies of insects studied.
- They described and explained the life cycles of the mealworm and butterfly.
- They discussed the impact of insects on our lives and explained their duties and purpose in the world.
- They read their final insect reports in class and answered questions posed by their classmates.

In summary, the children's observable behaviors during inquiry learning not only promoted literacy learning but also reinforced values such as caring, sharing, and respect for the individual—elements necessary for building a classroom learning community. The next section of this chapter is devoted to a description of each child (pseudonyms are used) and his or her individual responses to inquiry learning and literacy learning.

Duke

Duke, an African American male, was slightly below the average weight and height for second grade. He had spent the early period of his life with his mother. He now lived with his grandmother, who provided a healthy environment; his mother maintained weekly contact. He began kindergarten severely delayed in social and academic skills and often became distracted from the task at hand. At the beginning of the second-grade school year, he accomplished little reading or writing. He moved from one center to another and rarely maintained focus on any book, puzzle, math manipulative, or word game. Considered emotionally disabled, he was capable of reading beginning second-grade materials, but had difficulty sitting long enough to read aloud in a group setting and share in discussions.

Focus. During inquiry learning in science, Duke demonstrated a focus on literature that he had not exhibited previously. He was fascinated with insects and the freedom to talk about what he was learning. At three rotating work stations, he pored over the books on insects and made comments to his classmates, such as, "Hey guys look at this!" "I bet you guys didn't know this about ants!" and "I found something cool about bees...wanna see?" If students did not respond, he would read alone, sounding out words and narrating pictures. Often, nearby children would join him and listen intently.

During whole-group discussions, Duke regularly contributed. This was new behavior because he usually had difficulty listening or keeping his hands to himself. He also followed teacher read-alouds and shouted correct answers to questions. When incorrect, he would lean forward and listen to other students' answers or those read from a book.

Duke was totally absorbed when he created an insect with modeling dough. He molded the three body parts, formed antennae with black pipe cleaners, neatly placed raisins for eyes, and shaped brown pipe cleaners for the legs. He created wings with tissue paper and proceeded to show class members his invention. He described his insect to the class, correctly naming the head, thorax, and abdomen as well as the legs and antennae. He also stated newfound information: "Not all insects have wings."

Finally, Duke showed his engagement during a Jeopardy!-type game as the class created a flip book. The children were directed to write questions they wanted to ask the class, and to illustrate and write the answers inside the book. Duke verbalized his questions and the teacher wrote them. Some of his questions included, "What is the heaviest beetle?" "What makes an insect an insect?" "Why isn't a spider a insect?" He also raised his hand and correctly answered questions composed by classmates.

Interactions. Duke showed for the first time more positive interactions with individuals and the group during the insect unit. When the teacher selected Jess as Duke's partner, she hoped they would at least try to get along, because they had a history of problems together. Their assignment was to search for information about insects in the available literature at the reading center. To her surprise, Duke handed the clipboard to Jess and a serious conversation began:

Duke: Killer bees sting you. They sting you and die.

Jess: Dragonflies hang around pools. Spiders got eight legs, so they aren't insects.

Duke:	Insects have six legs. Spiders got eight. They's arachnids. It's in that book. I read it.
Jess:	What do insects eat?
Duke:	They eat bugs. Bugs eat bugs.
Jess:	I think they eat leaves too.
Duke:	And they eat bugs.
Jess:	[leafing through pages in a book] I know there is a book about praying mantis and scorpion ants.
Duke:	They have pinchers.
Jess:	Tarantulas give poison.
Duke:	They spiders and they is arachnids! Write that one down!

Another positive example of Duke's interest in sharing his learning occurred when he was able to get his whole table involved in observing and writing in their mealworm journals. Duke, while studying his specimen under a magnifying glass, described it: "Look, it's brown and like a squiggly. I see the eyes! Do you see the eyes and the teeny tiny legs? Wooooo! Man oh man! Crazy! Look at that! See that, Kesha! Hey! Don't yours have that?!! Jonny, amazing! How many parts is there? Write that down!" The table began discussing and recording the similarities and differences about color, shape, speed, number of segments, eyes, and so on.

Information Gained and Shared. Duke would easily spend 30 minutes with a classmate reading books and searching for information about a particular insect. When a classmate asked, "What makes an insect different from other creatures?" Duke quickly responded, "It has an exoskeleton. It's a protector on the outside. It has its skeleton outside." This information had never been discussed in class, but Duke had learned this during book exploration.

A guest speaker who was an expert on insects presented insects as helpful to humans and as pests for humans to control. Duke asked numerous questions and offered many answers to questions. When the guest asked, "Are insects helpful or harmful?" Duke emphatically replied, "Both! Bees are good because they make honey, but bad because they sting you. Bees are social insects, too."

Duke researched beetles and dictated the following: "They can grow to 6 inches in length; they are pets for African children; they have an extra hard exoskeleton; they live in rainforests, deserts, caves, beaches, forests, and fields; they are called armored insects; they go through metamorphosis." The teacher was amazed at the information Duke had gained and his ability to explain his understandings.

James

James, a European American child, had a slight build but was of average height and weight, with blond hair and blue eyes. James had struggled during reading and writing since kindergarten. For most of second grade, he completed work only if the teacher was next to him. He usually acted tired and disinterested in schoolwork, putting his head down on the desk or staring off into space. However, James appeared to have friends in class, and on the playground he raced around energetically. His mother stayed at home to care for him and a younger sibling. James's father was away at college but returned home for weekends. He called nightly to talk with the family and discuss schoolwork with James.

Focus. James began listening and sharing information in small- and whole-group discussions during the insect unit. He was intent on finding information and listening to talk about worker and queen bees at the literature station. When studying Venn diagrams to show similarities and differences between spiders and insects, James, while rocking back and forth on the floor, explained, "They both have spiracles. Put it in the middle of the Venn diagram. Spiders are arachnids. They got eight legs."

James had his hand raised most of the time during class discussions. For the first time, he focused on his written work, independently composed four questions for the class book, and read his questions to the class. When students answered the questions, he modeled the teacher by encouraging them, "Tell me more."

Interactions. James often became the center of group discussions during this unit. Previously, he had not been interested in conversing with classmates unless the talk related to free time and nonacademic activities. Due to his prior knowledge of insects, he enjoyed having opportunities to share.

With two other boys in the class, James chose the praying mantis for a research project. They studied books in the classroom and library and enthusiastically discussed their findings. James often asked to return to the library with his group to find new information. The librarian was amazed at the intensity and focus of this triad as they worked quietly together, finding books and sharing them at the library table.

Students would often ask James questions about insects and would get thorough explanations. When one student asked, "What makes an insect an insect?" James quickly replied, "Three body parts, six legs, spiracles, and an exoskeleton. The exoskeleton is the outer hard covering of the insect that protects it. It says crunch when you step on it." When another student asked, "What do worker ants do?" he replied, "They work for the queen ant." He then listed several specific jobs for the worker.

Occasionally during small-group discussions, a disagreement would arise. If James overheard, he would run to the table of insect books to find proof. He would promptly return with a book, point to the answer, and settle the dispute.

Information Gained and Shared. James became a resource for the rest of the class. As part of a Jeopardy! game, the children began discussing why the praying mantis would or would not make a good pet. James, with hand raised high, explained, "It eats everything. It can eat its brothers and sisters. It snaps their heads off just like a person's head. They actually don't eat people because people are too big."

Over the next 2 months of the unit, James gained information beyond the expected unit objectives. He especially enjoyed working on Venn diagrams that compared and contrasted insect similarities and differences. He would cut out a sentence about a particular insect, read it carefully, and glue it to the proper area of the diagram. When he discovered that a species of praying mantis could be purple, he decided to write a report about it. With the aid of the teacher, he learned to type the report on the computer. Finally, he drew and orally explained to the class the sequence of stages for the butterfly: "eggs, larva, pupa, adult, caterpillar, butterfly." He also took great pleasure in writing, explaining, and pronouncing the term *metamorphosis.*

During journal writing, while examining mealworms, James could be seen rocking back and forth in his chair for 10 minutes before actually recording his lesson observations. He would finally stop and begin writing and filling the page with information. Inquiry learning activities gave James the time to organize his thoughts and record observations and information.

Karlton

Karlton, an African American male, was of average height and weight for the second grade. He was always neatly dressed and groomed. He was the oldest of three male siblings, with a baby brother born in the spring of the school year. Karlton's parents showed great interest in his education and understood that he was academically delayed. He started the school year with limited letter recognition and, due to what appeared to be mental fatigue, he could only hold a pencil long enough to write five to eight words. He showed a complete lack of confidence in both reading and writing because he had difficulty forming letters and pronouncing the simplest words. He would stop all work and put his head down whenever he met frustration. He was considered severely disabled in language development.

Focus. Karlton rarely focused at length on any subject, but this all changed with inquiry learning. Near the beginning of the insect unit, the class saw a 10-minute video about insects in the backyard. Karlton watched with great interest while sucking his finger. He commented, "Eeeoo, that's nasty! There's a praying mantis." After the video, when Karlton was paired randomly with one of the top female students in the class, he smiled and eagerly joined her. When the teacher arrived to check what they had learned, Karlton enthusiastically took the lead, explaining, "Some ants have green heads. Some butterfly wings are the color that matches the trees so you can't see them. They has wings with eyes to scare birds. Ya know, praying mantis got little spikes."

After a guest entomologist brought in her extensive collection for the children to study, the class spent the next day exploring 30 books. Children were divided into groups of five to study six books for 20 minutes. From their perusal, they were asked to choose an insect they wanted to study. Karlton chose to study the praying mantis and became particularly excited when he found information and pictures. He explained to his neighbor, "Muhamut, look what I found! A praying mantis! This other insect on the page is a snack for the praying mantis. The praying mantis is the same color as the plant it's sitting on, and it can blend in!" Karlton went to lunch chattering about the insects in the books.

Karlton was also at ease with mealworms, gently touching them and carefully observing them with a magnifying glass. He dictated his findings to the teacher, counting worm segments, describing colors and parts, explaining worm movement, and drawing a detailed picture.

Interactions. Before the unit, Karlton never had problems with classmates, but he rarely became involved in conversation. During the unit, Karlton worked in pairs and small groups and made it known that he really liked this arrangement. After several lessons, he exclaimed, "This is fun! I like it with people."

Karlton was the first to discover the mealworm pupa stage. When he turned over the worm, he noticed small wings folded together on the bottom of the worm. He became very excited and brought his worm around to show the students at the various tables. "Look! My mealworm shed. Its legs became wings." That day, when he dictated his journal entry, he repeated his new information.

The group activities in the insect unit that focused on discovery seemed to serve as a means for promoting conversations among students. Karlton was able to express himself naturally. He had information to share and people to listen.

Information Gained and Shared. Karlton appeared to learn more information than ever before during the insect unit. For example, in the class flip book, he easily composed questions and illustrated the answers. He dictated the following questions: "What do butterflies do when it snows? What do butterflies drink? What does the praying mantis do when it's in trouble? What does a praying mantis eat?" His illustrations were detailed and his answers were correct.

With modeling dough, pipe cleaners, and raisins, Karlton and another student, Natoya, quickly constructed an imaginary insect and placed it on a large index card. They labeled each part, demonstrating knowledge of insect anatomy.

Karlton also completed an accordion book following his mealworm study. He dictated the description of each stage and illustrated the four stages of the life of a mealworm. This was a new experience for him in school. In other subjects and units of study, Karlton had been unable to retain information, question, or explain.

Natoya

Natoya was a 7-year-old African American female at the typical height and weight for second grade. Her colorfully braided and beaded hair and immaculate, stylish outfits always matched. She often dramatically displayed vivacious mannerisms and an excellent command of oral language. Additionally, she sang and danced in perfect tune and rhythm. Natoya's supportive family encouraged her talents and gregarious attitude; she appeared to be a happy child from a loving home. Because Natoya's reading and writing were weak for the second grade, she was assessed for a learning disability. The evaluation was inconclusive because her brothers displayed similar developmental lags in the language area. Therefore, Natoya was not labeled, and her teacher, Mrs. Stone, was told to monitor her carefully over the year.

Focus. During the unit, Natoya actively sought information about ladybugs and loved being able to share her knowledge with others. During book explorations, she remained focused as she searched the pages. Her talk of insects often continued on the way to the lunch room.

Natoya joined two other girls to study ladybugs. She recorded her own work as she perused books, shared information, and sought information from her buddies.

When the mealworms arrived, the class listened to directions for setting up the habitat. Natoya followed directions perfectly, handled her mealworm carefully, and helped the children around her with confidence. She also sustained an interest in the mealworm sensory trials even though it was repetitive.

Interactions. Natoya was a social child and interacted with classmates easily, but before the unit her talk was usually related to parties, clothing, songs, friends, and relatives. This changed during the insect unit as she shared, discovered, and questioned. Her prior knowledge of ladybugs drove her initial interest, but soon she was sharing books in pairs and was able to speak with authority on many kinds of insects. During the mealworm molting, she announced, "I know what's making them turn white; they are shedding." Other children had thought they were having babies or were sick. Natoya asked, "Why are they shedding? Do they turn white because they're getting older?" This caused a flurry of questions and comments from students around her.

Information Gained and Shared. Natoya had recorded a great deal of information about her ladybug, but she needed help organizing it and reading what she had written. First, with help from the teacher, she made decisions about what she wanted to include and wrote a sloppy copy. When she finished her final copy with an illustration, she proudly read all the information:

> Ladybugs can be different colors. They are all over the world. They eat aphids. They are beetles and they can fly. They eat flowers and they lay eggs. They made [mate]. That's when the husband and wife get married and they made [mate] and then they both die. The babies are born in a leaf. They like pollen. They suck the flower. They can sting and poison and they can hurt. I can sing a ladybug song. I was a ladybug at a party. I had these wings with toilet paper. I had red with black spots. My mother made this for me.

Natoya enjoyed studying insects, and flourished through her reading, writing, and conversation during inquiry activities.

Kyle

Kyle, a European American male of average height and weight, was labeled learning disabled in reading and language. Each day he received help in the resource room with his classmate Lonnie. Kyle often wore sweatpants and appeared to be in constant motion. His closely cropped blond hair revealed several noticeable cowlicks. A quick smile, articulate oral language, and an agile athletic ability hid his disorganization and lack of focus. During class discussions, he would forget to raise his hand and shout answers. His mother, an educator, was interested in his academic success. Kyle portrayed himself as a science expert and, with sparkling eyes, spoke of discoveries made in the outdoors with "Pops," his grandfather. He was quick tempered, extremely competitive, and both bragged about his own accomplishments and diminished those of his neighbors. He kicked, pushed, and interrupted others, although he usually followed this behavior by saying "excuse me." Consequently, he had developed no friendships among classmates.

Focus. After watching a video about backyard insects, Kyle actively participated in a 30-minute class discussion, listening to questions and answering numerous questions asked by others. During that time, he was the most noticeably involved child in the class.

Initially, Kyle avoided book exploration during the unit. While his partner looked up information about bees, Kyle studied, under a magnifying glass, a dead wasp that he found on the classroom interior window sill. They both shared the information discovered. Soon after, during silent reading time, Kyle asked if he could read a book about bees, wasps, and hornets. He wanted to determine the kind of wasp he was examining and knew he needed a book.

Writing was a task Kyle usually avoided, but he proudly wrote his observations about the life cycle of the mealworms and butterflies. During a class discussion about the words *larva, pupa,* and *metamorphosis,* he eagerly moved to a seat near the blackboard. Equipped with his journal and a pencil, he began copying definitions from the blackboard.

When Kyle used modeling dough to create a queen bee, the model was accurate in detail. He surrounded her with eggs, and labeled the card that she rested on. He remained focused and needed no repeated directions or guidance throughout the activity.

When the mealworms arrived, Kyle became the expert handler. He offered assistance to others in the class by determining whether a worm was alive or dead. He went to the class culture and acquired new mealworms for other classmates.

Interactions. In the past, Kyle preferred to work alone and usually did not stay on task. During this unit, he often showed initial dislike for working with a buddy, but he would eventually settle in and produce good work. When he and his partner, Patrie, were required to write statements about their prior knowledge of insects, they took turns and recorded 20 statements within 5 minutes.

While examining mealworms, Kyle would work alone for a short while and then be off to help classmates as they attempted to discover information about their worms. One day, when Kyle's worm was two-thirds beetle, one-third mealworm pupa, students hovered around his desk to watch this new creature. He then whirled around the room, looked at other worms, and returned to his desk. He talked to himself and his worm as he tried to figure out what was happening before his eyes: "What is going on!? It's changing to something else! Oh my God! What is it?" He invited others over to help him figure it out; they were mystified and shared their own questions and comments. He allowed others to talk without interrupting.

Toward the end of the unit, the assignment was for students to work in pairs and record how insects could be helpful and harmful. Kyle begged the teacher to let him work alone, but a calm, soft-spoken student named Annette asked the teacher if she could work with him. Kyle, with a surprised look on his face, nodded assent. The two quietly recorded excellent lists of helpful and harmful insect attributes.

Information Gained and Shared. Kyle had a lot of prior knowledge about insects before he began the unit, and he was able to formulate numerous questions for his own research and that of others. He asked, "Why do wasps have pollen on their faces?" He discovered, "It sticks to the faces so that they can have it for later."

When asked about his own learning, he expounded on his latest findings:

> Do ya know, killer bees come from Africa and do not live here in this city. Killer bees like hot places like Texas. Only the lady bees work on the honey, not the boys. I know why queen bees are not camouflaged. It is because they are territorial and do not leave the nest. The queen bee doesn't help get the honey because she is too busy laying eggs and doing the main things around the hive. Bees do not collect pollen during the rain, because the pressure of the rain will push them to the ground.

When describing the mealworm transition from larva to pupa, he explained, "Watch how he gets out. He pulls his way out moving his legs. I found him. He's an adult beetle now. He's prying his way out. Let nature do it. Never help him out yourself!"

Lonnie

Lonnie, a European American female of average height and weight for the second grade, began the school year with no friends. She appeared quiet and withdrawn and often put her head down on the desk or table, staring at nothing and devoid of expression. She would rarely talk with anyone or smile and, if provoked, she would withdraw in silence. She was labeled learning disabled in math, reading, and language in the fall and received special help one hour each day in a small group with the resource teacher. Her hair was usually tangled, and her clothes were mismatched and inadequate for the cold weather. Similarly, Lonnie's mother, a single parent, appeared tired, pale, and distracted. She had little to say during parent-teacher conferences and explained that, because the family had moved often, Lonnie had already attended two other schools.

Focus. Lonnie became much more focused and verbal during the insect unit. When asked to list what she and her partner, Nanette, knew about insects, they thought of 16 facts in 5 minutes. Lonnie did not write, but she gave her share of ideas.

After exploring a book on caterpillars with the teacher and her group, Lonnie willingly shared information with the whole class, an unusual behavior for her. When she had contributed several bits of information, the teacher looked to the next student. Instantly, Lonnie clearly stated, "But I'm not finished sharing ALL the information." She continued, "Caterpillars are harmless, but their enemies think they are wasps, so they leave them alone. Caterpillars have fake eyes to scare birds."

From the beginning of the unit, Lonnie expressed her dislike of insects, "Yuk, they're disgusting. I hate this." Despite her aversion, she remained focused on inquiry activities and produced very good work. Much to the teacher's surprise, one morning Lonnie drew an insect picture, cut and pasted extra bug pictures from the class math project, drew a picture of the environment that included the pasted bugs, and wrote a poem on the back about the bugs.

Interactions. During the inquiry science lessons, Lonnie began choosing workmates and was also chosen by others. She shared in the large group and demonstrated some animation.

One day, she brought in a book about insects, and while the teacher held it, she pointed to pictures of interest. She explained about 10 pages and added that she would leave the book in class for others to share. Without teacher prompting, the children enthusiastically thanked her.

Information Gained and Shared. Lonnie chose to investigate butterflies with Katie. First, they wrote what they knew about a butterfly: "I know butterfly's are pirrett." Then they composed questions to be answered in their research: "Do butterfly's eat? Do they Bit? Do they have baby's?" Finally, they looked up information and recorded their ideas:

1. the Butterfly have black and oeige [orange] waige [wing]

2. they fold together ther wing's when they sleep

3. they fly the rnd [around] the Day

4. thy fly 2000 Aiewrs [hours]

5. it is diffet [different] to a dutterfly to mohe [moth]

6. Sometime the butterfly's red yellw bah [black]

Lonnie and Katie found the answers to their three questions and recorded more information for their reports. Lonnie read the butterfly research report in class with ease, another new experience for her. When observed completing the final draft, she was never distracted while writing and drawing the illustration.

Lonnie's modeling dough insect was also an amazing creation. She had been in the resource room when the classroom teacher asked the students to make an insect with three different colors. Upon returning to the classroom, she created a perfect bee. Without any directions, she accurately labeled the body parts. Other students commented, "Lonnie, it looks just like a bee."

Lonnie often added information to class journal entries by drawing pictures that illustrated the entries. She also answered the class-generated question—"Why do mealworms shed their skins?"—in an interesting manner. She wrote, "The worms shed because they don't feel good in their old shell." In fact, Lonnie seemed to emerge from her own cocoon during the insect unit.

Inquiry Learning, Literacy Learning, and Classroom Community

Inquiry learning and literacy learning, as social phenomena, were naturally connected in the three second-grade classrooms. The classrooms provided a setting for literacy learning because students were constantly reading, writing, listening, speaking, and viewing to explore and discover. All children were encouraged to question, share their work, and learn from other classmates. This gave children with special needs in literacy learning the confidence to contribute and respond in alternative ways. As a result, they met with academic and social success in this classroom culture of inquiry.

The teachers claimed that this was the first unit of study in which the six students actually demonstrated understandings of all major concepts, making it difficult to distinguish them as students with special needs. Therefore, a key outcome of inquiry learning and literacy learning appeared to be the emergence of authentic classroom learning communities.

Much of what was accomplished in these three classrooms can be attributed to the teachers who designed the inquiry unit. They learned as they studied the process. They became carefully attentive observers who were more responsive to the needs of children. They created an atmosphere of inquiry and questioning with activities and discussions that drew on prior knowledge and facilitated connections between the known and the new. Consistent with constructivist approaches (Confrey, 1990; Fosnot, 1996; Piaget, 1970; Vygotsky, 1978), the children not only were acting like little scientists as they constructed their own understandings, but also were sharing information and learning from others.

Choice played a role as the children took control of their own learning by selecting classmates with whom to work, topics to study, and alternative ways to demonstrate learning. They drew from their own prior knowledge of insects and connected easily with the experiences they had both in and out of the classroom through field trips, videos, guests, actual insects, and literature. From these experiences, children read fiction and nonfiction books, observed real insects, recorded information, proposed research questions, answered questions, delivered their own oral presentations, and read their own reports. Soon, what could be described as a "healthy hum" became the norm in the classrooms as children talked about their observations and discoveries. They remained on task for longer periods of time and developed positive relationships with classmates during inquiry lessons. Their active involvement through questions, investigations, use of appropriate tools and techniques, critical thinking, and communication of logical explanations seemed to indicate that their own levels of expectations, as well as their teacher's, rose in a community of learners.

Like the students in Slavin's research on cooperative learning (1990), the six children had opportunities to share their talents and information with classmates, thus encouraging the development of cooperation and community. In accordance with Lickona's beliefs about character education (1991), the six children appeared to develop self-respect and respect for others, thus empowering them to participate positively in the learning environment. Therefore, the three teachers of Meachem Elementary leave us with a strong suggestion: Inquiry learning and literacy learning can help teachers connect classroom community with child and child with classroom community to build an authentic learning environment in which everyone's knowledge and experiences are valued.

AUTHOR NOTE

This study of classroom community is part of a larger study related to inquiry learning and literacy learning soon to be published in *The Reading Teacher*.

Three second-grade teachers—Susan Gillen, Teresa Colabufo, and Rhaenel Stone—were major contributors to this article. They would like to thank and recognize additional members of the research team who collected and analyzed data. The preservice teachers were Julie Falk, Shana Fogarty, and Todd Hicks. The school district math supervisor was William Collins. The Le Moyne College professors were Edwin Baumgartner, Mathematics Department; Cathy Leogrande, Education Department; and Michael Masingale, Chemistry Department.

References

Birnie, H.H., & Ryan, A. (1984). Inquiry/discovery revisited. *Science and Children, 27*(7), 31–34.

Bloome, D., & Green, J. (1982). The social contexts of reading: A multidisciplinary perspective. In B.A. Hutson (Ed.), *Advances in reading/language research, Volume 1* (pp. 309–338). Greenwich, CT: JAI Press.

Chaille, C., & Britain, L. (1991). *The young child as scientist: A constructivist approach to early childhood science education.* New York: HarperCollins.

Confrey, J. (1990). What constructivism implies for teaching. In R.B. Davis, C.A. Maher, & N. Noddings (Eds.), *Constructivist views on the teaching and learning of mathematics* (pp. 107–122). Reston, VA: NCTM.

Davydov, V.V. (1995). The influence of L.S. Vygotsky on education, theory, research and practice (S.T. Kerr, Trans.). *Educational Researcher, 24*(3), 12–21.

Dewey, J. (1969). *The school and society.* Chicago: University of Chicago Press. (Original work published 1899)

Fosnot, C.T. (1996). *Constructivism: Theory, perspectives, and practice.* New York: Teachers College Press.

Hawkins, D. (1965). Messing about in science. *Science and Children, 2,* 5–9.

Lickona, T. (1991). *Educating for character: How our schools teach respect and responsibility.* New York: Bantam.

Moll, L.C. (1990). *Vygotsky and education: Instructional implications and applications of sociohistorical psychology.* Cambridge, UK: Cambridge University Press.

Ogle, D.M. (1986). K-W-L: A teaching model that develops active reading of expository text. *The Reading Teacher, 39,* 564–570.

Piaget, J. (1970). *The science of education and the psychology of the child.* New York: Orion Press.

Raphael, T.E., & Pearson, P.D. (1985). Increasing student awareness of sources of information for answering questions. *American Educational Research Journal, 22,* 217–237.

Rumelhart, D., & Ortony, A. (1977). The representation of knowledge in memory. In R.C. Anderson, R. Spiro, & W. Montague (Eds.), *Schooling and the acquisition of knowledge* (99–135). Mahwah, NJ: Erlbaum.

Schmidt, P.R. (1999). KWLQ: Inquiry and literacy learning in science. *The Reading Teacher, 52,* 789–792.

Slavin, R.E. (1990). *Cooperative learning: Theory, research and practice.* Englewood Cliffs, NJ: Prentice Hall.

Vygotsky, L.S. (1978). *Mind in society: The development of higher psychological processes* (M. Cole, V. John-Steiner, S. Scribner, & E. Souberman, Eds. and Trans.). Cambridge, MA: Harvard University Press. (Original work published 1934)

Schoolwide Connections

S choolwide programs for character education have naturally made use of literature, multimedia, and literacy events. Reading, writing, listening, speaking, and viewing have been basic to program creation and design. Those presented in the next chapter include a variety of ideas and plans that emerged from community, family, faculty, administration, staff, and, of course, student participation. They represent community values promoted by families and schools to educate their students. Schools and communities connected for common purposes and explored values using combinations of materials and strategies that could be described as unique schoolwide programs for character education.

Chapter 9

Schoolwide Approaches for Teaching Values Through Literature and Multimedia: Connecting Across Classrooms

Matthew L. Davidson

So, you want to develop a schoolwide approach for teaching values through literature and media? Well, imagine for a moment the conversation that might ensue should this topic arise in the faculty lounge:

> Harry the History Teacher quips, "Sounds fine to me. Whose values will we teach?" Then Erin the English Teacher adds, "I agree with the concept, but what do you mean by *literature*? Are we talking Shakespeare or Judy Blume?" Finally, Pat the Protective Principal cautions, "Don't forget, this year we're under the new standards and that means additional requirements to last year's overloaded schedule. When and where do you propose we add this to our day?"

Maybe this sounds like a conversation your school has had. Maybe it sounds like precisely the kind of conversation your school wants to avoid. Effective schoolwide approaches for teaching values through literature and media invariably generate discussions similar to this fictional one. Avoiding, squelching, or circumventing such inquiries is not the solution; rather, creating a successful schoolwide approach requires precisely that you engage in just such exploratory conversations.

The second premise of *The Seven Habits of Highly Effective People*, by Stephen Covey (1989), encourages individuals to "begin with the end in mind" so that their lives follow a preconceived plan rather than the whims of chance—sound advice for schools as well as individuals. Schools beginning without the end in mind generally find the initiative over before it begins, or they arrive at an unintended (or undesired) destination. It is important at the outset to form a historical perspective on the strengths and weaknesses of previous efforts, as well as a shared vision of the current goals. To begin consideration of these issues, we turn to understanding character education and its various uses of literature, past and present.

Resurgent Interest in Character Education

Character education is an old idea with resurgent interest in the United States, and although many agree that values should be taught, there is still widespread discussion regarding what should be taught, as well as how it should be taught. However, although ethnic, religious, and ideological diversity undoubtedly—and thankfully—define the United States, there is overwhelming support for character education and the proactive instruction of universal core ethical values. The Character Education Partnership (1996a) documents support for character education by President Bill Clinton, both houses of Congress, state governments, and the National Education Association. The National School Boards Association (1996) states, "Educating for character has been a central mission of America's public schools since the earliest days of our Republic" (p. iii). That same report documents that "nearly half (45%) of the 399 districts responding said they were already offering character education, and 38% of the 217 districts that do not offer it are thinking of providing it within one to two years" (p. 5). Phi Delta Kappa has begun a major high school character education initiative involving more than 40 high schools (Frymier, 1996). To date, more than 20 states have received grants totaling approximately $20 million; up to 10 more states received funding in 1999, and numerous additional states have applied for funding (Character Education Partnership, 1999).

Character education is certainly not without its critics. In the article "How Not to Teach Values: A Critical Look at Character Education," Kohn (1997) raises several important points for consideration, including the dangers of narrowly defining moral character (exclusively behavioral) and narrow approaches for developing it (indoctrination). Nevertheless, Kohn acknowledges supporting broadly defined comprehensive character education approaches such as those advocated by Lickona (1991), the Character Education Partnership (1995), and the Child Development Project (cf. Cage, 1997; Kohn, 1997). So, then, if what goes by the name "character education" does not mean the same thing each time it is used, how are we to meaningfully distinguish one version from another?

Comprehensive Character Education

What is it that separates comprehensive broad-based character education from its more narrow forms? First, broad-based character education begins by trying to form an understanding of the whole moral person. Berkowitz (1995) argues that "like Humpty Dumpty, the moral person has been shattered into bits" (p. 3). That is to say, practitioners and theoreticians frequently focus on promoting knowledge *or* promoting reasoning *or* promoting behavior, when in reality these elements are of equal importance. Lickona (1991) defines moral character comprehensively as having cognitive, affective, and behavioral dimensions. This theoretical outline suggests attention to the complete moral person—head, heart, and hand. Therefore, the goal of teaching values through literature is not simply to increase students' knowledge of values; the goal is also to transform how students feel (moral affect) and what students do as a result of this new body of knowledge (moral action). Comprehensive character education attempts to develop the complete moral person by avoiding the indoctrination and behavioral manipulation that Kohn rightfully rails against. In addition, comprehensive character education attempts to intentionally provide opportunities for students to expand their knowledge, their motivation, and their habits—intellectually and morally—throughout all phases of their school experience.

History of Literature in Character Education

Teaching values through literature has been a hallmark of moral education since the time of Aesop's Fables, when internalizing the moral of the story was presumed as easy as simply hearing the story again and again. The use of literature as a form of direct moral instruction was also a visible part of the earliest formal character education efforts. In the 1920s, character education proponents used the McGuffey Reader as a literature-based character education text (Leming, 1997). In those early efforts to teach values using literature, the approach was direct, the method was didactic, and the purpose was to transmit moral knowledge. Residual influences from early character education efforts are visible in the current philosophies of certain character education theorists today (e.g., Bennett, 1993, 1995; Kilpatrick, Wolfe, & Wolfe, 1994) who suggest that the very act of sharing moral stories increases moral literacy. However, moral education researchers such as Leming (1997) note that despite the claims of advocates for this type of approach, there is a relatively sparse body of research actually examining the effects of literature on moral development. Further, research by Narvaez, Gleason, Mitchell, and Bentley (1999) suggests that "reading moral stories to children does not guarantee that they will understand the moral message or theme as intended by the author" (p. 482).

Increasingly, teaching methodologies have focused on broader uses of literature in moral development and education. For example, the research of Narvaez et al. (1999) investigates the mediating influence of developmental differences on moral theme comprehension. In addition, research by Leming (1997) examines the use of literature as a character education strategy for developing moral knowledge, moral commitment, and moral action—a significant expansion of developmental constructs that previously focused on just moral knowledge. Character education approaches such as those used by the Child Development Project (CDP) now utilize literature in a multidimensional approach for improving children's general cognitive-social problem-solving skills, and for developing positive resolution strategies for use in problem situations (Solomon, Watson, Delucchi, Schaps, & Battistich, 1988). Thus, the developmental net cast by broader theoretical approaches uses literature for a variety of developmental purposes aside from a more narrow interest in simply promoting moral literacy.

Which Values? Whose Values?

Despite its timeless presence, it seems that potential controversy looms around the topic of teaching values using literature. Most controversy over values and values education is rooted in false assumptions and misunderstandings. Which type of values should be taught: religious, democratic, civic, personal, moral, or universal? Depending on the context, any and all of these values might seemingly be important. For example, the Baltimore County Public Schools built its character education effort around values from the U.S. Constitution, including honesty, human worth, dignity, justice, equality, and due process (Lickona, 1991), whereas a religiously affiliated school might choose to build around spiritual values such as mercy, justice, and love. The Character Education Partnership (CEP), a nonpartisan U.S. national coalition promoting character education, argues for the teaching of universal core ethical values as the basis of good character (1995). According to the CEP, core ethical values should meet the tests of "reversibility" (would you want to be treated this way?) and "universalizability" (would you want all persons to act this way in a similar situation?). Defining values in this manner provides a solid foundation for building community consensus on how we would like to be treated, and how we would like others to act. Defining values using these two criteria assists schools in the quest to find the shared values that unite us, rather than aimlessly worrying about the controversial values that divide us.

How, exactly, might a school or classroom decide on which core values to focus on? At Lansing Middle School in the state of New York, Phyllis Smith-Hansen, a sixth-grade teacher, assembled a representative focus group of parents, teachers, and students to help her choose the most appropriate core values for her sixth-grade character education intervention. This process demonstrates one concrete strategy for involving stakeholders in a collaborative, noncontroversial process for determining the critical questions of which values and whose values should be emphasized. The focus group followed four steps:

1. They brainstormed common problems for this age.
2. They identified the positive core values developmentally matched to the problems identified.
3. They sorted the core values into categories around common themes.
4. They rated the categories for relative importance.

In the end, the group concluded that they should focus on respect, responsibility, tolerance, and honesty. Not only did they have their core values, but they were also able to define the core values in a developmentally appropriate match from their focus group data. For example, Figure 1 displays the cluster of data around the core value "responsibility." For sixth graders in this school, the operational definition of the core value "responsibility" focused on particular nuances: responsibility for personal work ethic, responsibility for having a positive attitude, and responsibility for continuing to persevere despite initial failure.

For the past 5 years, I have worked under the direction of Thomas Lickona as a research associate at the Center for the 4th and 5th Rs (Respect and Responsibility). My work involves helping schools plan, implement, and evaluate a comprehensive character education program that is custom built around the center's general blueprint. The center promotes a 12-point comprehensive approach to character education (nine classroom strategies and three schoolwide strategies) that uses all aspects of school life as deliberate opportunities for character development (see Figure 2). These are broadly defined categories that each school will address in unique and different ways. Regardless of the varied ways schools accomplish the general tasks, all schools seeking to establish a comprehensive approach eventually incorporate each component. That is, schools cannot simply do cooperative learning and call it comprehensive character education.

FIGURE 1   Lansing Middle School: "Brainstorming Data"

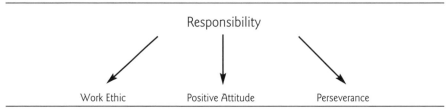

FIGURE 2   A Comprehensive Approach to Character Education

The Center for the 4th and 5th Rs promotes a 12-point comprehensive approach to character education, one that uses all aspects of the school life as deliberate opportunities for character development. The inner part of the wheel below shows nine character-building strategies for the classroom; the outer rim shows three schoolwide strategies.

THE COMPREHENSIVE APPROACH TO CHARACTER EDUCATION

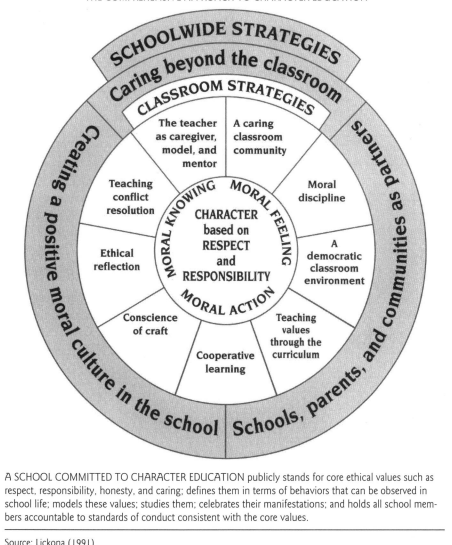

A SCHOOL COMMITTED TO CHARACTER EDUCATION publicly stands for core ethical values such as respect, responsibility, honesty, and caring; defines them in terms of behaviors that can be observed in school life; models these values; studies them; celebrates their manifestations; and holds all school members accountable to standards of conduct consistent with the core values.

Source: Lickona (1991)

This chapter is built around the center's theoretical model. There are certainly other approaches to teaching values through literature, but this broad outline provides a sound theoretical blueprint that encourages individual creativity. Although literature plays a crucial role in the nine classroom strategies, this chapter will elaborate exclusively on the three schoolwide strategies featured in the comprehensive approach to character education. Listed under each schoolwide strategy are several concrete examples of how literature can be used to develop that particular strategy.

Schoolwide Strategies

Strategy 1: Creating a Positive Moral Culture in the School

The first of three schoolwide strategies in the comprehensive approach, "Creating a Positive Moral Culture in the School," represents the underlying support for all subsequent moral structures in the school. It could be argued that all other 11 strategies in the comprehensive approach are in essence directed toward developing a positive moral culture, one that supports the development of a child's intellect and character. Literature provides numerous opportunities for developing intellect and character while simultaneously creating a positive moral culture in the school. The following examples represent schoolwide practices that use literature to promote moral culture in the school.

Heartwood: An Ethics Curriculum for Children. Created by a team of teachers and Eleanore Childs, a Pittsburgh criminal defense attorney, the Heartwood Ethics Curriculum is a multicultural, literature-based ethics curriculum built on seven core values essential to all cultures and communities: courage, loyalty, justice, respect, hope, honesty, and love. It intends to reverse the trends of juvenile behavior by providing youths with knowledge of core universal values and examples of positive social character through the memorable medium of literature.

Heartwood has assembled a plethora of literature supporting each of the seven core attributes. Like character education, Heartwood is not an add-on program; rather, the literature and related activities are integrated throughout the existing curriculum. Incorporating cooperative learning styles and conflict resolution skills into the process unites the message and the medium so that students practice the skills of character while they learn the content of character through literature. Heartwood extends beyond the classroom through various carry-home activities designed to involve families in the learning process (see Figure 3). Students gain knowledge and familiarity with models of good character through literature and experience real opportunities to practice similar actions in their own lives, in and out of the classroom.

FIGURE 3   Heartwood "Whole-School Involvement" Suggestions

1. Heartwood Display Area
Designate one area in your school to display Heartwood activities weekly or monthly. A display case or table can be arranged to highlight the attribute being discussed. Your school's Web site could also feature a Heartwood area. Visit www.kamalii.k12.hi.us to see Kamalii Elementary School's Heartwood projects on display.

2. World Cultures Fair
Stories from different countries tell us about cultures, but the stories also contain lessons about life. We can learn things of value by listening to or reading stories from many cultures. Collect tales from different ethnic backgrounds and celebrate the nationalities represented with a World Cultures Fair. Each classroom could choose one country to research and then share findings in drawings, songs, games, and storytelling. The whole school population could share ethnic dishes at lunchtime. Parents could volunteer to prepare the foods.

3. Cookbook
Make a school cookbook with recipes representing the cultural backgrounds of the students and their parents. Include attribute recipes. For example, a recipe for Honesty might include 1 heaping cup of truth, 1 tablespoon of integrity, a dash of friendship, and a generous portion of courage; simmer until needed, and serve to everyone.

4. Assembly
A class (or several classes) could prepare and present to the whole school a play that celebrates the positive aspects of the attribute being studied. The play might be based on a Heartwood story or a historical event.

5. Heartwood Quilt
On cloth squares, students can draw with markers symbols that represent the concepts of the Heartwood character attributes. Sew them together to hang in the hall. Parents or grandparents could help convert the hanging into a real quilt. The quilt could also be made of felt squares.

6. Heartwood Village
Have students replicate houses represented in the Heartwood stores (Hogan, palace, African village hut, farmhouse, Greek tavern, teepee, windmill, etc.). Label and display the buildings together. Invite a younger class to visit your village. Discuss the meaning of community and how your school can be a community.

7. Media
Invite a local newspaper, television station, or radio station to do a feature on how Heartwood attributes are infused throughout the school.

Source: The Heartwood Institute (2001)

Recent research on the Heartwood curriculum by Leming (2000) provides empirical support documenting that it was successful in developing a shared moral language between students and teachers, instilling respect for people, creating a more caring and stronger academic classroom and school environment, increasing respect for diversity, and decreasing racial prejudice in program students (grades 1–3). This research suggests the Heartwood Curriculum provides the structure and resources to help schools develop a positive moral community in the school.

Homegrown Character Education Programs. The Heartwood Curriculum offers schools a prepackaged program with predetermined core attributes and supporting literature. However, other schools are creating a positive moral culture through homegrown character education programs using literature-based character education resources built on their school's core values, their available resources, and their desired outcomes. For example, at Brookside Elementary in Binghamton, New York, Principal Lynn Lisy-Macon involved her entire staff in the planning and execution of their character education program. First, teachers, staff, and parents came to an agreement on their core values; these included responsibility, respect, tolerance, and friendship. Teachers and staff were then given the freedom to bring the concepts to life according to their own interests and talents, and in accordance with the interests and talents of their students. The school librarian, Marge Day, assembled recommended readings by grade level around each of the school's core values (see Figure 4). Once it began to search its own reserves, Brookside found that it had plenty of literary resources and expertise that simply needed to be focused toward the school's effort. The literary list provides the school with a resource that is age appropriate, fosters knowledge and discussion around the school's value themes, and allows teachers creativity and autonomy.

Teaching values through literature, indeed character education itself, appeals to many districts because of the low upstart and maintenance costs. Most efforts require only the cost of planning, staff development, and an overhaul of existing resources. Schools do not need to recreate the wheel; they simply need to dust off forgotten resources and refocus existing resources. At the middle and high school levels, most schools already have a literature and history curriculum packed with moral exemplars, great works of literature, and other rich moral education reserves. Tapping into these resources requires a unifying focus and a collaborative atmosphere in which colleagues can share their experience and expertise toward a common focus and mission.

FIGURE 4   Sample Entries From the Literature List at Brookside Elementary School Supporting the Core Value of Tolerance

Title	Grade	Classification
All the Colors of the Earth by Sheila Hamanaka	K to 2	Tolerance of Human Difference
Come Home With Me by Aylette Jenness	3 to 6	Tolerance for Other Cultures
Are You My Friend? by Alma F. Ada	K to 3	Acceptance of Difference
How Many Days to America? by Eve Bunting	2 to 4	Tolerance of Others' Beliefs
Be Good to Eddie Lee by Virginia Fleming	2 to 3	Tolerance of Special Needs
Autumn Street by Lois Lowry	4 to 6	Acceptance of Racial Difference
Shy Charles by Rosemary Wells	K to 2	Self-Acceptance

Dear Super-Citizen. Enders Road Elementary in Fayetteville, New York, has developed a strategy for creating a positive moral culture in the school while assisting students to develop the skills of ethical reflection. Students correspond with Super-Citizen, a fictitious character who helps students resolve moral dilemmas. Students' questions are posted under the giant blue mural of Super-Citizen. As the school studies a particular value, students begin to wonder about the exceptions, the complexities, and the dualities—because neither literature nor life present simple either-or dilemmas. For example, a student might write,

> Dear Super-Citizen, my friend stole some bubblegum from the store last night. Even though I didn't steal any, I feel bad. Is it more important to be honest and report what happened, or be a good friend and not say anything?

Principal Storrier and his staff take turns answering students' letters and grappling with the critical nuances of their core values and the dilemmas that arise from competing values. Student letters are shared with the whole school community so that all can benefit from the discussion (where required, student privacy is protected). This strategy provides students with a forum for considering the complexities of ethical behavior and provides an opportunity for students to develop their writing skills as they compose the letters.

The Enders Road approach offers a model for active reflection by students and staff on value themes in literature. Research by Narvaez et al. (1999) suggests that providing students with adult reflections on the moral theme is a critical aspect of effectively using literature to develop character. They state, "Research in narrative comprehension has demonstrated that children do not understand narratives in the same way adults do: Children remember less of the story overall and have difficulty making inferences to connect goal-action-outcome chains of events" (p. 478). In other words, discussion and explication of the themes and dilemmas, through age-appropriate means such as the Super-Citizen activity, provides a critical piece for comprehending the complexity of the moral themes presented in literature and in life. Through systematic reflection and in-depth discussion, the power of literature can be fully realized. Moral culture is developed within the school as all community members share in the collective sense-making around difficult value themes. Students are not simply memorizing the moral of the story; they are also gaining moral reasoning skills and moral affect that comes from authentic engagement of the issues.

A Book That Changed My Life. One of the classroom strategies in the comprehensive approach—the teacher as caregiver, model, and mentor—holds additional possibilities when considering ways to create a positive moral culture

FIGURE 5   Five Strategies for Promoting Literature and Multimedia

1. Teacher/Student Book Club
Establish a book club in which teachers and students gather once a month to discuss a literary work related to the school's value theme. Teachers with content expertise on the work might collaborate with one or two students to provide introductory remarks on the background of the work and then act as facilitators for whole-group discussion of the work.

2. Literary Guest Speakers
Invite regional or national writers, poets, and other literary experts to speak about their work, their reading habits, and literary influences in their own life.

3. Summer Reading
Assemble a representative group of teachers and students for each grade and choose one critical literary work related to the school's value theme. Students and teachers will read the book over the summer and then discuss the work at the beginning of the new school year.

4. Dramatic Reading
Provide opportunity for the school community to hear or participate in a dramatic reading of a literary work. For example, create an assembly for African American awareness month in which students and faculty collaboratively prepare dramatic presentations of important literary works such as Martin Luther King's "I Have a Dream" speech.

5. Parents' Reading and Discussion Night
Coordinate a parent reading and discussion format so that two or three times a year parents come together to discuss a literary work or a parenting resource related to the school's value theme.

in the school. The same complaint is repeated over and over in teachers' lounges: "Students today don't have heroes and heroines like we used to." However, teachers often avoid or miss out on the opportunity to be a hero or heroine for their own students. If we want students to love literature and feed on its wisdom, we should act as caring mentors who model those actions in our own lives.

The library at Le Moyne College in Syracuse, New York, shared one technique for modeling the importance of literature in the lives of teachers, faculty, and staff. In the front lobby of the library a glass case displayed books of particular impact in the lives of professors and an accompanying description of how it changed or affected their lives. The technique could be used with younger students as well. Particularly at the middle, secondary, and postsecondary levels, it is important for students to know how a particular piece of literature influenced the lives of their adult models.

This technique also models teachers as lifetime learners who read literature in order to understand life, consider its complexities, and contribute to ongoing character development. Robert Coles (1997) is perhaps the most prominent modern educator to share the influence of literature on his moral and intellectual life. If teachers begin to share the affect of literature in their lives, students and teachers may begin to share more common heroes and heroines.

Jenkins (1997) argues that for teachers to adequately present the complexities of literature, they must have a critical literary base of their own from which to draw; that is, they must be engaged in a learning process themselves. Teaching values through literature, like character education itself, is not something we do *to* students; it is something we do *with* students. Simply put, literature provides a bridge of common experience across ages and cultures. Figure 5 provides five suggestions for collaborative relationships with students (especially grades 6–8) in the investigation of literature and multimedia.

The School That Reads Together. Wellwood Middle School in Fayetteville, New York, has developed a Sustained Silent Reading (SSR) prototype designed to involve the entire school in reading and discussing literature together. Once a week (or once a month, depending on available time) classes are shortened to allow 40 minutes during which students and staff can read and discuss literature related to the theme of the month. For example, one month their effort focused on the core value of respect. They created the acronym RESPECT— Respect Every Single Person Especially Classmates and Teachers. Principals, custodians, bus drivers, coaches, parents, teachers, and staff were encouraged to read and discuss literature with students. In general, this activity establishes literature as a central component of the entire school and communicates to students that adults are interested and committed. It is just one additional idea from a whole host of ways to begin creating a positive community around the shared experiences of values and literature. This approach is also substantiated in the research done by Narvaez et al. (1999), suggesting that students need to understand the moral themes from different, and more sophisticated, sources.

The Loving Well Project. One of the most potentially divisive aspects of character education is the question of sex education. According to "Character-Based Sex Education in Public Schools," a position paper by the Character Education Partnership (1996b), "sex education should teach students to see that sexuality is an area of their lives that calls for the presence of virtues." One program, The Art of Loving Well, has managed to bring divided parties to the peace table through a multicultural literature-based curriculum designed to educate adolescents on the sexual and social values inherent in the relationships of life and love. Developed at Boston University and field tested over 4 years by nearly 100 teachers and 10,000 students in inner-city, suburban, and rural communities of Maine, Massachusetts, and South Carolina, the Loving Well curriculum (Ellenwood, McLaren, Goldman, & Ryan, 1993) seeks to examine the virtues of successful human relationships, be they romantic, family, business, or other. Reflecting on characters, behaviors, and situations in literature reveals many truths to the observant adolescent. It provides glimpses of the best human virtues, such as loyalty, patience, love, and courage, as well as the worst human tendencies, such as manipulation, abuse, stereotyping, and exploitation. Figure 6 displays the first of three sections of the Loving Well program.

In *The Moral Intelligence of Children*, Robert Coles (1997) argues that adolescents are not naive, lawless rebels who never contemplate right and wrong. On the contrary, Coles suggests, adolescents are astute critics of adults and the inconsistencies between what adults preach to others and what they practice in their own lives. He states, "I do believe that it is important for all of us not to regard adolescents, most of them, as lawless, as beyond the kind of moral anxiety that most of us have learned to have—[that] they have been brought up to have" (p. 147). The Loving Well project focuses on the human need in adolescents to examine how and why we treat each other as we do. Figure 7 offers a sample of some reflective activities provided in the Loving Well curriculum for interacting with a story about love. In general the curriculum provides students with authentic opportunities to develop a positive vision for a lifetime of healthy relationships.

FIGURE 6 "Section One: Early Loves and Losses" From *The Art of Loving Well*

Title	Author
Little Briar-rose	The Brothers Grimm
A&P	John Updike
President Cleveland, Where Are You?	Robert Cormier
If Only	Anonymous
Ancestor	Jimmy Santiago Baca
The Old Grandfather and His Little Grandson	Leo Tolstoy
A Distant Bell	Elizabeth Enright
Welcome	Ouida Sebestyen
Fifteen	Bob Greene
Boy Meets Girl	Peter Stone & Carl Reiner

Student Poetry
"Being Male"
"Do You Think"
"Uncertainty"

Source: Ellenwood, McLaren, Goldman, & Ryan (1993)

FIGURE 7   Sample Activities for the Story "Appointment with Love" From *The Art of Loving Well*

For Discussion

Have you ever had a long term pen pal? How is getting to know someone through letters different from getting to know them in person?

It has been said that character is destiny. In other words, the way our lives unfold is determined by those qualities that make each of us unique. Short as this story is, it reveals a great deal about its characters. What adjectives would you choose to describe Lieutenant Blandford? To describe Hollis Maynell? What is at the core of their passionate attraction to one another? Are there signs that this relationship will be a happy and lasting one?

Creative Writing: Crystal Ball

What happens after this romantic meeting in Grand Central Station? How does this love story play out? Set the scene in a time and place at least 20 years later. Who are your characters? Are Lt. Blandford and Hollis Maynell still together? Have other people come into their lives? Although you are focusing on a future moment, let your story reveal what has gone on in intervening years. Remember that specific details will bring your story to life. Be prepared to read your narration to the class and explain what led you to predict the destiny you describe.

Unit Activity: Your Appointment With Love

Your ideas are likely to change as you grow older, but the stories in this section should help you think about the kind of person you'd like to meet some day under the clock at Grand Central Station. Think about yourself, your values, the person you hope to become, the life you hope to lead. What is it that excites you? What kind of person do you find most attractive? Try to write the descriptions both of yourself and of the person you hope to meet. It might be helpful if your class brainstorms the qualities that might be included in these descriptions. For example, is a sense of humor more important to you than athletic ability? What about honesty and loyalty? Do your prefer large parties or quiet evenings at home?

Source: Ellenwood, McLaren, Goldman, & Ryan (1993)

Strategy 2: Schools, Parents, and Communities as Partners

Thomasina Portiss, a frequent speaker on character education and an expert in securing parent and community involvement in character education, tells the following story about a troubled turtle:

> An unassuming turtle was meandering down the road when she came upon a gathering of snails scattered about the road. Distracted and confused, she went off the road and got stuck on a fence, where she remained waiting for the next passerby to set her free. When help arrived, the turtle was asked how she managed to get hung up on the fence. She responded: "I don't know, it happened so fast."

Like the turtle in the story, the moral character of children is something that develops so slowly, yet so fast. Children acquire moral knowledge from every person, place, and situation they experience. Intended or not, children receive strong value positions even when we do not intend to send them.

The second of the three schoolwide strategies, "Schools, Parents, and Communities as Partners," focuses on the all-important task of uniting schools, parents, and communities as partners in the moral education of children. Children spend an average of 6 hours per day in school, which leaves the overwhelming majority of time for character development in the hands of the child's "other teachers": parents, family, coaches, church members, other community members, and the media. If, as Heraclitus once said, "character is destiny," then there must be consistent, coherent attention given to the issues of character in all elements of a child's life—home, school, work, and play.

Table Talk and Literacy. A Harvard University study of low-income families (Zernike, 1996) found that "good dinner conversation was the single best predictor of how well a child learns to read—even better than reading from an early age" (p. 1). According to the report, "of the more than two thousand 'rare' words the researchers recorded in two years, over 1,000 were heard at the dinner table—compared with only 143 from books." Does this research suggest the demise of an anthology arguing the need to teach values through literature? Certainly not. Rather, this research suggests the need to connect with parents, who were, are, and always will be the child's primary educator. It should also indicate to schools the importance of forming a solid partnership with parents and communities.

Consider the following question: If table talk is a primary factor in determining child literacy, what impact would moral discussions at home have on a child's *moral* literacy? Literature offers schools a vehicle for encouraging moral discussions and reflections in the home in a nonintrusive, unpretentious manner. For example, schools can encourage students to record their own family's history. Each family story describes real-life heroes and heroines involved in real-life hardships. Or, schools can encourage families to read and discuss a play or short story as an attempt to begin, or rejuvenate, family discussions vital to the moral literacy of youths.

The Taming of The Tube. If Shakespeare were alive today, he would undoubtedly find countless topics to satire. He might, for example, alter his classic *The Taming of the Shrew* and construct *The Taming of the Tube*, a satire about families communicating around, over, and through the television. Having already acknowledged the profound impact that something as minor as family dinner talk can have on child literacy, it is equally important to recognize that increasingly busy schedules at home and work make it a real challenge for parents and children to engage in meaningful dialogue on a consistent basis. And, although the total time available for families has decreased, television viewing has continued to increase. Regardless of which media statistics you choose to consult, or what you perceive to be the actual outcomes of these trends, the bottom line is that television viewing is a reality schools must face in a thoughtful manner. On the one hand, schools should seek innovative ways to cut into a portion of the time devoted to television; on the other hand, schools should begin to develop critical viewing skills in students so as to utilize the teachable moral moments presented by the media. At the very least, schools must encourage parents and children to increase awareness of their television viewing habits and the educational impact of those habits.

At Enders Road Elementary in Fayetteville, New York, the school has made a concerted effort to create the time and atmosphere at home for reading and discussion to occur. The Enders Road TV-Turnoff is an annual event designed to create time for reading and discussion, as well as a lasting awareness of television's influence on our families. At the beginning of the program, families chart their television habits prior to the turnoff. Classroom discussions explore alternative activities for students and families to include in place of television. An evening of alternative entertainment at the school includes music, skits, and a reading of Shel Silverstein's poem "Jimmy Jet and His TV Set." Families prepare for the weeklong TV-Turnoff by turning off the television once a week in the weeks leading up to the entire week without the television. Students conclude the experience by recording and sharing how they spent their time in the absence of television. The point here is not simply to advocate an end to television viewing. Rather, the event seeks to promote reflection on current television habits and to present some positive alternatives to television.

Television can be a source of excellent research for students. The No Put Downs Project in Syracuse, New York, asks students to watch television for a period of time with notebook and pencil in hand. Students record insults, degrading comments or actions, and other disrespectful and unkind behaviors they observe. The exercise usually yields notebooks packed with examples of the moral messages sent by television. This recognition is the first step to developing the ethical sensitivity to begin questioning the message, not simply modeling it.

When it comes to the issue of television, the old adage "If you can't beat 'em, join 'em," may contain some useful wisdom for educators. Schools throughout the United States are attempting to join forces with local media to support their character education efforts. At many schools, local television stations feature reports on the school's character education efforts. These reports frequently attempt to define the value under discussion, to share a concrete example of someone who exemplifies this value, or to highlight specific situations in which this value is particularly important. Other attempts to work with the television media offer pathways to a middle ground in the attempt to control the impact of television on students.

Newspaper Involvement. In St. Louis, Missouri, schools, parents, and communities have joined together on a newspaper feature called "Character Matters," a series designed to help parents use the *St. Louis Post-Dispatch* as a resource for instilling character and respect for values in young people. This feature shares the word of the month, lesson plans, feature stories, parent guides, and other useful resources supporting character education in the school and community. Aside from the obvious support this feature offers the schools' efforts, it also helps prevent uninformed community naysayers from derailing them. The column dissipates fear that the schools' effort to teach values contains some hidden agenda by opening the program for the community to observe, discuss, and take part in.

The *Tennessean*, a newspaper published in Nashville, began an effort to turn the tide of juvenile crime by publishing a biweekly eight-page tabloid to teach positive character attributes and life skills. An ardent supporter of first amendment rights, the *Tennessean* worked with a committee of parents, teachers, and community members to establish core values essential to the entire community. This feature has managed to turn distant words and foreign concepts into real-life lessons of local heroes and heroines. The articles describe specific examples of how virtue is lived in their own community, thus avoiding the danger of making virtue a state of being reserved for heroes and heroines of fairy tales and other worlds.

Sports, Literature, and Character. Second only to the time spent watching television is the time students spend playing organized team sports. Athletics plays a critical role in teaching values. Unfortunately, in many communities sports are promoting destructive values like poor sportsmanship, cheating, and a win-at-all-cost attitude that undermines the positive potential of sports. Athletics and other youth activities present valuable opportunities in the development of character. Character education cannot be viewed as a subject learned in school; it is a lesson that begins in school and continues throughout a lifetime. Vast reservoirs of untapped potential exist for schools and communities that make an effort to connect athletics and character development.

The PLUS Institute (Personal Learning Using Sports) developed in New Hampshire by Jeff Beedy was created to teach positive values and interpersonal skills through sports. The literature-based Sports PLUS curriculum (Beedy, 1997) integrates reading, writing, and thinking skills through the medium of sports. Through literature, children examine the core values of teamwork, respect, responsibility, fair play, and perseverance; these qualities are reinforced through practical application on the field. The program is reinforced by professional athletes who speak on the importance of literature and character in sports and life. This important program capitalizes on an opportunity to bridge the school and home in character development. It emphasizes the importance of literature, sportsmanship, and good character and provides valuable integrations of moral knowledge, moral affect, and moral action. The PLUS Institute and the Sports PLUS curriculum provides enormous opportunities for committees to connect with schools in an effort to promote, model, and reward good character from the classroom to the athletic field.

Strategy 3: Caring Beyond the Classroom

As character educators, we must convince students that virtue is learned for living. Schools must break down compartmentalized notions of moral behavior; school behavior, home behavior, work behavior, church behavior, and play behavior should be the same. It has been said before that character is what you do when nobody is looking. Students who internalize this understanding of character will begin to live what they have learned, in and out of class.

The third strategy, "Caring Beyond the Classroom," fosters the extension of moral character beyond the classroom. It contains two important elements. First, our moral character should accompany us wherever we are—inside or outside of school. Second, our moral education is not finished when we leave a particular lesson, teacher, or school. Students must see the characteristics of heroes and heroines of other worlds and other times also flourishing in their own world and in the present time. Virtue should never be portrayed as the stuff of pathetic sinners and immortal saints. In reality, on any given day we are all pathetic sinners who fall prey to bad habits despite what we know and desire to do, and on any given day we are saints, if we consider saints as ordinary people doing extraordinary things.

The Giraffe Project. In 1992, the husband-and-wife team of John Graham and Ann Medlock began the nonprofit Giraffe Project, which attempts to recognize and promote "giraffes"—people who stick out their necks for others. The K–12 character education program known as Standing Tall encourages an approach to teaching values through literature perfectly aligned with the broad-based comprehensive approach to character education. Standing Tall brings literature to life as students learn to "hear the story, tell the story, and be the story."

The "Giraffe Story-bank" records countless tales of real heroes and heroines so that students can hear the stories of those who stuck out their neck for someone else. For example, stories center around people like Abdullah Turner and Nero Graham, who led their neighbors in driving out drug dealers, or people like the Earth Angels, a group of at-risk children who take to their neighborhood's crime-filled streets to do clean-ups and recycling. First, students learn about these model characters. Next, students tell the story of similar heroes and heroines in their own lives (sources include television, movies, books, local communities, churches, and home). Finally, they must become the story as they decide various ways to make a positive effect in their lives and in the lives of those around them.

In an era in which the word *news* is almost synonymous with the term *bad news*, it is difficult for young people to develop an optimistic outlook on life and a sense of their opportunities to positively influence the world. There are real heroes and heroines in every community. Virtue, heroism, and genuine kindness often exist in the worst of times and situations. The Giraffe Project takes the concept of values and literature and connects it to the reality of values and life. Sharing good news about good people is one simple yet effective way to extend caring beyond the classroom and into the world while simultaneously promoting values such as caring, respect, and community in an authentic way.

Hometown Heroine. West Point Elementary in West Point, Georgia, is doing its part to extend caring beyond the classroom by celebrating models of virtue from the school and community, along with examples from literature and history. Each week a particular virtue is discussed and concrete examples are shared. These examples are particularly powerful and noteworthy because they are often examples from within the school and community. The following story about Margie McCullough, a cook in the West Point Elementary cafeteria, is included in the lessons on the virtue of punctuality.

> Mrs. McCullough is a cook in our lunchroom. She has worked in our school for 9 years. She enjoys preparing meals for over 500 students and staff every day. She also helps prepare breakfast each morning. She helps fix over 200 breakfast trays every day. To do so, she has to be at work by 6:00 every morning! It is very important for her to be on time for work. Because she is prompt every day we enjoy a delicious breakfast and lunch at West Point Elementary.

This story extols the virtue of a real-life heroine at West Point Elementary, Margie McCullough, and provides a model for students on how the virtue of punctuality is lived. This activity also contributes to the positive moral culture by promoting respect for the members of a community. Again, this is not an extraordinary action, except when it is performed with diligence and consistency so that students begin to see and believe that they can be virtuous people.

West Point Elementary adds an additional element of moral reflection and extension beyond the classroom as students, parents, teachers, and staff are encouraged to write a prose article or poem about a personified character trait.

For example, one exercise asks students to write a letter to Billy Lateman, a person who is always late, and give him advice on how to be punctual. This exercise encourages students to consider solutions for overcoming a bad habit. It could be extended into an exercise asking students to describe what happens to Billy Lateman: Can people trust Billy Lateman? (This promotes proactive consideration of the consequences of our actions.) How do his friends feel when he is always late for ball games and movies? What do Billy's teachers think when he is always late for class? How do his parents feel when he does not come home on time? (These questions promote empathy or consideration of others' feelings.) Are there any good reasons for being late? (This promotes true ethical reflection and role-playing.)

This exercise is important for two reasons. First, it encourages students to think deeply about virtues, virtuous behavior, the consequences of their actions, and the ways their actions will affect other people. This exercise is a form of role-playing that provides students with the opportunities to consider the consequences of acting, or not acting, with good character. Second, the exercise also encourages students to write their own literature for teaching values, an important revelation for students who are learning that literature and character are indeed alive in all our lives. We all have much to learn and much to teach from our personal experiences and from the experiences of those around us.

Heroes in Our World. In 1996, an article appeared in the *Syracuse Post-Standard* of Syracuse, New York, describing the heroics of an 11-year-old girl named Brittany Bartlett, who found herself in a real-life moral dilemma. Brittany was celebrating her birthday with her grandparents at a local shopping center when she found a purse with $800 in it. A member of Girl Scout Troop 344, Brittany called the owner of the purse, who was nearly sick from the shock of losing her purse, including an $800 deposit for her office. Brittany returned the purse and received a $50 reward; however, she showed her true character again by sharing the reward with her sister.

This article demonstrates a real-life moral dilemma with an 11-year-old heroine. It would have a strong message for other students Brittany's age. Undoubtedly there are similar stories to be found and told in all communities and schools, stories that promote caring beyond the classroom and moral exemplars that other children can model in their own lives.

Conclusion

Brittany's story is one of the small victories along the lifelong trail to moral character; teaching values through literature is about finding those victories, sharing them with others, and replicating them in some small way in our own lives. A schoolwide approach to teaching values through literature will attempt to accomplish three strategies: (1) create a positive culture in the school, (2) unite schools, parents, and communities as partners, and (3) extend caring beyond the classroom. A Spanish proverb states, "Three persons helping one another will do as much as six persons singly." I have shared some of the treasures discovered in the effort to teach values through literature, and I look forward to the undiscovered treasures that lie buried in your school, in your community, and in you. Find them, share them, recreate them anew!

References

Beedy, J. (1997). *Sports PLUS: Positive learning using sports, developing youth sports programs that teach positive values.* Hamilton, MA: Project Adventure.

Bennett, W.J. (Ed.). (1993). *The book of virtues: A treasury of great moral stories.* New York: Simon & Schuster.

Bennett, W.J. (Ed.). (1995). *The moral compass: Stories for a life's journey.* New York: Simon & Schuster.

Berkowitz, M.W. (1995). *The education of the complete moral person.* Hilton Place, Aberdeen, Scotland: Gordon Cook Foundation.

Cage, M.C. (1997, March 21). A controversial professor crusades for character education. *The Chronicle of Higher Education,* p. A16.

Character Education Partnership. (1995). *Eleven principles of effective character education.* Alexandria, VA: Author.

Character Education Partnership. (1996a). *Character education in U.S. schools: The new consensus, A report on the developments during 1993–1995.* Alexandria, VA: Author.

Character Education Partnership. (1996b). *Character-based sex education in schools: A position statement.* Alexandria, VA: Author.

Character Education Partnership. (1999). *Character education—A growing national movement* (Vol. 7, No. 2). Alexandria, VA: Author.

Coles, R. (1997). *The moral intelligence of children: How to raise a moral child.* New York: Random House.

Covey, S. (1989). *The seven habits of highly effective people: Powerful lessons in personal change.* New York: Simon & Schuster.

Ellenwood, S., McLaren, N., Goldman, R., & Ryan, K. (1993). *The art of loving well: A character education curriculum for today's teenagers.* Boston: Boston University.

Frymier, J. (1996). Values and the schools: Sixty years ago and now. *Phi Delta Kappa Research Bulletin, 17,* 1–4.

Heartwood Institute. (2001). *The Heartwood Ethics Curriculum for Children* (revised). Pittsburgh, PA: Author.

Jenkins, C.B. (1997). Aristotle comes to the literature circle. *Journal of Education, 179*(3), 59–80.

Kilpatrick, W., Wolfe, G., & Wolfe, S.M. (1994). *Books that build character: A guide to teaching your child moral values through stories.* New York: Simon & Schuster.

Kohn, A. (1997). How not to teach values: A critical look at character education. *Phi Delta Kappan, 78,* 429–439.

Leming, J.S. (1997). Research and practice in character education: A historical perspective. In A. Molnar (Ed.), *The construction of children's character: Ninety-sixth yearbook of the National Society for the Study of Education* (pp. 31–44). Chicago: The University of Chicago Press.

Leming, J.S. (2000). Tell me a story: An evaluation of a literature-based character education program. *Journal of Moral Education*, 29(4), 413–427.

Lickona, T. (1991). *Educating for character: How our schools can teach respect and responsibility.* New York: Bantam.

Narvaez, D., Gleason, T., Mitchell, C., & Bentley, J. (1999). Moral theme comprehension in children. *Journal of Educational Psychology*, 91(3), 477–487.

National School Boards Association. (1996). *Character education in the classroom: How America's school boards are promoting values and virtues.* Alexandria, VA: Author.

Solomon, D., Watson, M.S., Delucchi, K.L., Schaps, E., & Battistich, V. (1998). Enhancing children's prosocial behaviour in the classroom. *American Educational Research Journal*, 25(4), 527–554.

Terrell, K. (1996, October 23). Angel in Eastwood. *Syracuse Post-Standard*, p. A1.

Zernike, K. (1996, May). Declining art of table talk a key to child's literacy. *Boston Globe*, pp. 1, 30.

Character Education Resources

The Center for Learning, PO Box 910, Villa Maria, PA 16155; Tel: 800-767-9090; Fax: 888-767-8080; E-mail: cfl@stratos.net; Web: http://www.centerforlearning.org

Educational publisher of values-based curriculum materials for classroom teachers who champion excellence in education, parents and leaders who support ethics and character, and communities who believe that cultivating knowledge and values is essential to human growth.

Center for the 4th and 5th Rs, PO Box 2000, SUNY, Cortland, Education Department, Cortland, NY 13045; Tel: 607-753-2455; Fax: 607-753-5980; E-mail: Crn5rs@cortland.edu; Web: http://www.cortland.edu/www/c4n5rs

The Center disseminates complimentary articles on character education, sponsors an annual summer institute in character education, publishes a newsletter, offers a browsing library of character education materials and is building a network of "Fourth and Fifth Rs Schools" committed to teaching respect, responsibility, and other core ethical values as the basis of good character.

Character Education Partnership, 1600 K Street, NW, Suite 501, Washington, DC 20006; Tel: 800-988-8081; Fax: 202-296-7779; Web: http://www.character.org

The CEP provides national advocacy and leadership for the character education movement. It is a U.S. nonprofit, nonpartisan coalition of more than 1,000 organizations and individuals who share a common purpose: to foster the teaching and modeling of positive character traits within U.S. schools. CEP works to provide publications, research, and program initiatives that support quality character education implementation.

Chip Hilton Sports Series, Randall and Cynthia Bee Farley, Broadman & Holman Publishers, Nashville, TN; Web: http://www.chiphilton.com

The Chip Hilton Series has inspired and influenced young people for more than five decades. Today's youth can gain lasting values following the adventures of Chip Hilton, the sports-loving hero who will capture their hearts and direct them toward developing strong determination and character.

Developmental Studies Center, 2000 Embarcadero, Suite 305, Oakland, CA 94606-5300; Tel: 800-666-7270; Fax: 510-464-3670; E-mail: denise_wood@devstu.org; Web: http://www. devstu.org

>DSC's mission is to deepen children's commitment to being kind, helpful, responsible, and respectful of others. DSC offers resources to help educators develop a caring, collaborative learning environment where students feel a strong sense of belonging and a strong desire to learn.

Elkind & Sweet Communications/Livewire Video, 3450 Sacramento Street, San Francisco, CA 94118; Tel: 800-359-KIDS; Fax: 415-665-8006; Web: http://www.livewiremedia.com

>Produces In Search of Character video series of 10 videos designed to help adolescents develop into caring, responsible people who make choices based on what is right, rather than what is easy. Each video focuses on a different virtue and includes a discussion guide with group activities, writing assignments, and questions for discussion before and after viewing.

The Giraffe Project, PO Box 759, Langley, WA 98260; Tel: 800-853-7550; Fax: 360-221-7817; E-mail: office@giraffe.org; Web: http://www.giraffe.org

>Since 1983, the Giraffe Project has focused U.S. attention on what can be done to inspire more citizens to act from the heart and to work for the common good. It finds and publicizes contemporary, real-life heroes, people who have stuck out their neck for the common good. Products include *The Giraffe Project Handbook: A Guide To Effective Community Service and Social Action* and a K–12 curriculum package, *Standing Tall.*

Heartwood Institute, 425 N. Craig Street, Suite 302, Pittsburgh, PA 15213; Tel: 800-432-7810; Fax: 412-688-8552; E-mail: hrtwood@heartwoodethics.org; Web: http://www.heartwoodethics.org

>The mission of the Heartwood Institute is to foster moral literacy and ethical judgment in children by educating them in universal virtues common to the world's cultures and tradition and to encourage and enable schools to play a major role in helping children become mature and caring adults.

The Loving Well Project, Boston University School of Education, 605 Commonwealth Avenue, Boston, MA 02215; Tel: 617-353-4088; Fax: 617-353-2909; Web: http://www.bu.edu/education/lovingwell

>The Loving Well Project helps adolescents learn responsible sexual and social values through good literature, which reveals the complexity of life and love relationships. Healthy friendships, romances, and families require sensitivity and insight into ourselves and others. The curriculum includes activities that enable students to learn vicariously from their readings and from conversations with teachers, parents, and friends.

Sports PLUS Institute, PO Box 219, New Hampton, NH 03256; Tel: 603-744-5401, ext. 161; Fax: 603-744-9660; E-mail: plusinfo@sportsplus.org; Web: http://www.sportsplus.org

>Sports PLUS (Positive Learning Using Sports) is a nonprofit organization dedicated to promoting the use of sports as a positive educational medium. The organization believes that within sports lie valuable lessons and potentially powerful learning opportunities. Their goal is to show others how to tap into these lessons and create programs that develop good athletes and good people.

WiseSkills Resources, PO Box 491, Santa Cruz, CA 95061; Tel: 888-947-3754; Fax: 831-426-8930; E-mail: info@wiseskills.com; Web: http://www.wiseskills.com

>The WiseSkills curriculum highlights the words and lives of inspiring positive role models such as Booker T. Washington, Mother Teresa, Mohandas Gandhi, and many other multicultural figures.

Global Connections

Many educators believe that our students' future depends on their ability to make global connections. Children need to understand and appreciate differences among the peoples of the world. By exploring values through literature, multimedia, and literacy events, our students may come to an understanding of universal values that will help them become socially responsible beings who care and share. Literature provides the means for studying people groups around the world. Students can learn about human differences as well as human similarities and explore why values may be similar and different. These new understandings can help students strengthen connections with people from all places.

Chapter 10

Multicultural Books and Values: Connecting With People and Places

Jane Kurtz

In a sense, children's literature has always been about values education. For years, children's books were assumed to instruct first and entertain later—or not at all. As Donna E. Norton (1991) points out in her widely used textbook *Through the Eyes of a Child*, the earliest books used with children "adhered to the sentiment that young readers should read only what would improve their manners or instruct their minds" (p. 46).

In the introduction to *Dear Genius: The Letters of Ursula Nordstrom*, Leonard Marcus (1998) writes that Nordstrom—who served as director of Harper's Department of Books for Boys and Girls from 1940 to 1973 and published such classics as *Charlotte's Web, Harriet the Spy, Goodnight Moon*, and *Where the Wild Things Are*—believed young readers were "ill served by the sentimental illusions and false pieties of their elders." Marcus notes that by the late 1930s, when Nordstrom became an editorial assistant, "the genteel tradition had lost some of its stifling hold on American children's literature" (p. xvii). However, even a person of Nordstrom's stature—an editor of "maverick temperament, high-voltage intellect and grand ambition" who managed to "reexamine, and often to reject, the shopworn taboos and conventions of the genre" (p. xviii)—still had to deal with many a critic or reader who argued that one or another of Harper's books was instilling the wrong values in young readers.

As tastes in children's books began to lean away from the didactic, mainstream children's literature lost most of its obvious and heavy-handed messages. Modern editors and critics tend to spurn stories about some wise elder (whether human, owl, or fish) with infinite wisdom to hand down. But rejecting didacticism does not necessarily mean rejecting any role of children's literature beyond that of entertainment.

The readers of children's books are, for the most part, young people whose minds are working to understand and navigate the worlds they were born into; thus, children's books do generally offer myriad opportunities to learn. A story gripping enough to invite readers to invest their own emotions in the characters' feelings and actions also has the power to spur those readers to think about their own actions and choices. Some of the learning that happens is certain to suggest answers to the age-old question, "Are there certain ways of behaving toward myself, toward other people, toward the community and earth around me that are right, and others that are wrong?" As the characters in stories for young readers struggle for creative and resourceful solutions to their problems, their solutions and epiphanies often shine a small light that suggests certain paths are good, certain paths can be trusted, certain paths lead to depth, imagination, vision, and compassion. It is a rare children's book, for instance, that ends on a bleak note. Even in the recent wave of "gritty" books, most books for young readers carry—at the very least—the message that ultimately no situation is hopeless.

I believe there is a widely accepted moral quality to much of children's literature. But exactly which values should be embodied or how explicit should the messages be? Such questions are much debated these days. The United States is a pluralistic society with a high focus on individual rights and individual family responsibilities, and some people are uneasy with any talk of societal values or norms. At the same time, many U.S. citizens who have spent time in other countries notice, often with a note of longing, that less pluralistic societies tend to do a better job of communicating (as one man living in Japan puts it) that "we do have moral values and they matter." For teachers and schools wanting to emphasize character education, books set in other countries can be a particularly fertile source of wisdom about living a life that once might have been described as one of "high moral character."

My parents moved to Ethiopia when I was only 2 years old, and my family has spent more than 30 years in East Africa. I was raised as what is sometimes called a "third culture kid," immersed in a culture I knew was not completely my own, while at the same time finding myself a visitor in the country of my parents' culture. During my childhood in Ethiopia, I observed the communication of moral values not only through instruction from parents and grandparents but also through ceremonies, time-honored customs, and, yes, stories. It is not surprising to me that the growing number of children's books set in other countries and cultures are useful for educators wanting to communicate the importance of such arguably universal values as cooperation, fairness, kindness, patience, appreciation of diversity, hospitality, and perseverance.

Folktales and Traditional Literature

In the 1960s, self-examination in the children's book world led to cries for stories set outside the United States. Partly in response, the next two decades brought an explosion of picture books based on folktales. Folktales tend to be loaded with moral instruction. Even various Cinderella-type stories, such as T. Obinkaram Echewa's *The Magic Tree: A Folktale from Nigeria* (in which Mbi is provided with a magic *udara* tree through no real efforts of his own), suggest that if a person has patience and endurance, anything may be possible. Such stories also serve as cautionary tales for those who would take advantage of the weak: Beware, for such a person may be strong tomorrow.

Several years ago, I became friends with Kofi Obeng, a student at the University of North Dakota who had grown up in Ghana. When I asked Kofi what his childhood was like, he described in rich and loving detail the atmosphere of the village in the evening when the stories are about to begin. I used some of this description and two of Kofi's stories in *All the Wisdom in the World* (forthcoming from Greenwillow). Kofi and I had long discussions to clarify the "point" that each story was supposed to make, because Kofi was adamant that stories in his village taught children how to behave—to adopt values the elders of the village found important. It is no wonder folk literature used through centuries of oral storytelling in traditional societies can be a way to look at some of the attitudes and traits that many cultures value.

Cooperation

People who have spent their whole lives in the United States can hardly comprehend the sense of cooperation and community that exists in many other countries—how Africans, for example, live by the proverb "It takes a village to raise a child." Sam Gameda, one of my childhood friends from Ethiopia, recently wrote to me about his struggles to find his place between the society he grew up in and his chosen adult home in Canada. Referring to an essay he had just read about Japan, he commented on the issues that rang true with his own life and noted that a fair amount of his personal struggle has had "to do with 'the conflict between personal autonomy and the great extended household known as' (in my case) Ethiopia." That great, extended household is not always easy to live with. It "allows Ethiopians," he says, "even here in North America to lay claim to you—to feel entitled to supersede your personal aims and aspirations." But it also, as he points out, provided him with "nurturing and a sense of belonging" that has not been easy to recapture in North America.

So societies that are more communal than contemporary North American society are bound to be a rich source of stories about people working together. *It Takes a Village* by Jane Cowen-Fletcher, for example, illustrates the realities of the West African proverb, with a story showing the lives of two children in a marketplace in Benin. *Beatrice's Goat* by Page McBrier illustrates the responsibilities that even a young girl has in helping care for the needs of her family.

The stories in *Senor Cat's Romance, and Other Favorite Stories from Latin America* by Lucia M. Gonzalez provide other examples of sharing and cooperation. Still more examples can be found in Michael Rosen's *How Giraffe Got Such a Long Neck…And Why Rhino Is So Grumpy* and Barbara Knutson's *How the Guinea Fowl Got Her Spots: A Swahili Tale of Friendship*.

Activity. Create cooperation webs to show how people work together. I sometimes talk to students about the people who are part of my book team—an author, an illustrator, an editor, an art director, a printer, a publisher, a bookstore owner, a sales representative, a librarian, a teacher. During a school visit, a student raised her hand and said, "I read your book, so am I on your team?" Definitely! My web, which has a book at the center of it, would be incomplete without readers. Who is listed in the web of each student's school day?

Fairness

We may tell our students and children that life is not fair, but in folktales it usually is. At the end of most traditional stories, everyone has exactly what he or she deserves. My first published folktale, *Fire on the Mountain*, is a good example of a story that has variations on every continent. Students can compare the clever ways the brother and sister manage to get justice in *Fire on the Mountain* with the search for justice in other stories. Examples can be found in *In the Month of Kislev: A Story for Hanukkah* by Nina Jaffe, *Misoso: Once Upon a Time Tales from Africa* by Verna Aardema, *Ooka the Wise: Tales of Old Japan* by I.G. Edmonds, *Fair is Fair: World Folktales of Justice* by Sharon Creeden, *Favorite Folktales from Around the World* by Jane Yolen, *A Kingdom Lost for a Drop of Honey and Other Burmese Folktales* by Maung Htin Aung, and *Once the Hodja* by Alice Geer Kelsey.

Activity. Have students locate the regional origins for two picture books, *The Hunterman and the Crocodile: A West African Folktale*, written and illustrated by Baba Wagué Diakité, and *The Rabbit's Judgement*, retold by Suzanne Crowder Han. Discuss how two such similar stories might have developed in geographical areas so far from each other. Create pictures that illustrate some of the similarities and differences between the two books.

Kindness

Many characters in folktales are notable for their kindness. A young girl in Patricia Polacco's *Luba and the Wren*, for instance, takes pity on a delicate wren and saves its life. In thanks for her kindness, the wren grants Luba wishes. She wants nothing more than for her parents to be happy—which at the end of the book they finally are, in their own little *dacha* after experiencing life as rulers of all Russia and even Emperor and Empress of all the world.

Other folktale heroes are mischief makers. Sometimes stories built around scoundrels and tricksters are told just for entertainment, but often a humorous folktale can fit with values education. Verna Aardema, a reteller of many African folktales, tells a classic trading tale in *This for That: A Tonga Tale*. Rabbit, who is lazy and tells lies, gets her just reward in the end—a hearty kick. The other animals agree that "A lie may travel far, but the truth will overtake it."

When I proposed a retelling of an Ethiopian trading story, which became the picture book *Trouble*, my editor commented that she liked the way the Ethiopian version—unlike most similar stories—did not end in punishment for the mischief maker. Tekeleh's father sends him out with a *gebeta* board (the game commonly known as *mancala*) to keep him out of trouble. As the day progresses, Tekeleh makes one trade after another, blissfully unaware of the scrapes he and his goats weave in and out of. It is a story that is meant to amuse and entertain readers, right up until the end when, as one student put it, "The dad doesn't even know that the kid has been getting into trouble all day."

Another boy, however, said, "He gets in trouble but he's good." When I asked him to elaborate, the student pointed out that, in a gesture of kindness, Tekeleh offers his corn and papaya to children who need them. He gives without hope for gain. In a classic scene of hospitality, the mother of the children invites him into the house for something to eat—and helps to bring the circle back around so that Tekeleh ends up back home with a *gebeta* board. Thus even the story of a mischief maker can be used to illustrate kindness.

Activity. Have students write a paragraph about their own propensities for trouble, starting with the opening sentence of *Trouble* ("Trouble always found Tekeleh") but inserting their own names. Then make a chart for comparing trickster stories across cultures. What differences and similarities do students see, and how many trickster stories illustrate the problems with behaving badly? One possibility is Gerald McDermott's *Raven: A Trickster Tale from the Pacific Northwest*, a Caldecott Honor book in 1994, and another is his *Zomo the Rabbit: A Trickster Tale from West Africa*. You can also use Anansi and Coyote stories, Iktomi stories, and stories of Brer Rabbit.

Patience

When I was a child growing up in Ethiopia, I listened to a story that was sometimes told about a woman who was afraid her new husband did not love her and sometimes told about a mother who had "lost the love of her son." In either case, the woman visits a village elder who tells her that her pain can be cured, but only if she will bring him something from a lion—hair from the lion in some versions, the lion's whiskers in others. When she succeeds, the elder tells her to apply the patience with which she approached the lion to her other relationships. This story became the basis for my picture book version of the story *Pulling the Lion's Tail*. Another version of the story, Tololwa M. Mollel's *Subira Subira*, set in Tanzania, features a family grieving for a mother who has died; in this story the daughter of the family, Tatu, works to find a way to care patiently for her angry little brother.

Activity. In writing residencies with students, I point out that a writer's job is to make the reader experience something. And there is one way—or one set of ways—that everyone, from a newborn baby to a grandmother or grandfather, living in North America or Africa or any one of the other continents, uses to experience the world: the five senses. So writers have to use the five senses to pull in their readers. Have students look for ways that I use the five senses in *Pulling the Lion's Tail* and also use comparisons to make a sensory moment vivid. Then have them incorporate the same techniques as they try their hand at writing a story of the patience needed to approach a wild animal.

Respect

In a country that celebrates precocious youth, it can also be hard to imagine the intensity of respect for elders in most traditional societies. In the Caldecott Honor book *Mufaro's Beautiful Daughters: An African Tale*, written and illustrated by John Steptoe, Manyara shows disrespect to an older woman, while Nyasha takes the woman's advice and ultimately receives her reward for being generous, kind, and respectful. A similar motif is found in a Creole folktale retold in *The Talking Eggs: A Folktale from the American South* by Robert D. San Souci and in *Chinye: A West African Folk Tale* by Obi Onyefulu.

Respect for the earth and its creatures is another value held by many traditional cultures. That respect shines through many folktales, including *The Girl Who Loved Wild Horses*, written and illustrated by Paul Goble, winner of the 1979 Caldecott Medal. T. Obinkaram Echewa has created a contemporary African folktale in *The Ancestor Tree*, in which children honor an old storyteller by planting a tree for him.

Respect for all other human beings, even those very different from ourselves, seems to be one of the hardest lessons cultures have to learn. Examples fill our world of how easy it is to make "the other" into "the enemy," including my own first novel, *The Storyteller's Beads*, which shows the mistrust and loathing Sahay, from the Kemant ethnic group in northern Ethiopia, initially feels toward Rahel, an Ethiopian Jew.

In using books to communicate respect for other people's way of life, it can be helpful to go beyond folktales and look at the lives of contemporary children in many settings. *Kele's Secret*, by Tololwa M. Mollel, set in the author's native Tanzania, shows a young boy who is determined to find the secret of his grandmother's smartest hen. He needs both wits and courage to do it. *Ogbo: Sharing Life in an African Village*, by Ifeoma Onyefulu, uses photographs and text to show the cooperative systems of village life in Nigeria. *Animal Dreaming: An Aboriginal Dreamtime Story*, written and illustrated by Paul Morin, follows Mirri as he learns about his people's history. *Erandi's Braids*, by Antonio Hernandez Madrigal, shows a girl in Mexico who, although young, will do what she can to ease her family's worries.

At the Crossroads, written and illustrated by Rachel Isadora, provides a look at apartheid in South Africa through the eyes of the children who wait to welcome their fathers home from the mines. *Jingle Dancer*, by Cynthia Leitich Smith, is the story of a Muscogee-Ojibwe girl learning to dance so she can honor the women who inspire her. *My Painted House, My Friendly Chicken, and Me*, by Maya Angelou, shows village life in South Africa. And *Sitti's Secrets*, by Naomi Shihab Nye, illuminates the journeys and longings of a girl who travels between North America and her grandmother's house in the Middle East.

Approaching the lives of the very poor with respect and curiosity can be especially difficult. My own picture book *Only a Pigeon* shows the daily life of one of Addis Ababa's "street kids"—a boy who shines shoes to help support his family and, although he has no toys and not one change of clothing, still finds a way to be playful and have something to care for. Stephanie Stuve-Bodeen drew from her memories of a week spent with a Tanzanian family in their home (when Stephanie was in the Peace Corps) to write *Elizabeti's Doll*, the story of a girl who makes a rock into her doll. It can be nicely paired with Tololwa M. Mollel's *My Rows and Piles of Coins*, also set in Tanzania, in which Saruni urgently saves and counts every coin toward his dream of buying a bicycle. *Galimoto*, by Karen Lynn Williams, with its striking images of children making toys out of wire scraps, offers another look at how children will find ways to play no matter what they own (or do not own). Two longer powerful books are *Out of the Dump: Writing and Photographs by Children from Guatemala*, edited by Kristine L. Franklin and Nancy McGirr, and *Baseball in the Barrios*, by Henry Horenstein.

Activity. Use the picture book *Bikes for Rent*, by Issac Olaleye, to examine the connections between students' own lives and the life of a child in the village of Erin in western Nigeria. Make a mural showing the students' favorite toys alongside Lateef's bicycle; the chores or jobs the students do alongside the way Lateef earns money to rent a bicycle; the games students like to play alongside the bike games the village boys play. Many additional details of daily life can be compared using the text and illustrations. Also compare and contrast ways African children find to be playful in *Bikes for Rent, Elizabeti's Doll, Galimoto*, and *Only a Pigeon*.

Appreciation of Diversity

In 1613, a man of Inca descent, Felipe Guaman Poma de Ayala, wrote a long letter to King Philip III of Spain. In one of Guaman Poma's drawings—drawn somewhat like a cartoon with little speech balloons—an Incan man asks (in Quechua) "You eat this gold?" A conquistador replies (in Spanish), "We eat this gold." To the Incas, this seemed a reasonable explanation for why the Spanish invaders seemed so determined to get their hands on all that gold.

Such misinterpretations and misunderstandings inevitably arise when one culture comes in contact with another. *Nim and the War Effort*, by Milly Lee, shows how family values can clash with societal values, as Chinese American Nim uses her intellect and courage to beat a classmate in a World War II newspaper drive, only to find that her grandfather is not happy with his granddaughter's new personality. The truth is that values education in the relatively homogeneous atmosphere of a village is easier than in a complicated society in which people do not always agree about what is most important. In a multicultural society in which people cling to heartfelt values out of their own traditions and often fail to understand each other's drives and longings, values education is complicated.

A good way to start encouraging students to appreciate diversity is to point out that all human beings have much in common. Sheila Hamanaka's *All the Colors of the Earth* shows through oil paintings and poems ways that children are essentially the same. *Whoever You Are*, by Mem Fox, begins, "Little one, whoever you are,/wherever you are,/there are little ones/just like you/all over the world." Fox then goes on to talk about differences, but she emphasizes how hearts and smiles and laughs and hurts are the same, all over the world.

Norah Dooley has written several books similar to her *Everybody Bakes Bread*, in which a girl on an errand encounters many different kinds of breads. *A Ride on Mother's Back: A Day of Baby Carrying Around the World* by Emery Burnhard shows details of daily life in 12 different cultures as seen through the eyes of small children being toted by older siblings or adults. *Market!* by Ted Lewin gives a vivid, bustling picture of markets on six continents.

Activity. Read Selby B. Beeler's *Throw Your Tooth on the Roof: Tooth Traditions from Around the World.* Then create your own class book about tooth traditions in the students' families. Or try your hand at playing the many variations of the games found in *Jacks Around the World* and *Dominoes Around the World*, both by Mary D. Lankford.

Hospitality

Differences may be superficial, but they can still be disconcerting or frightening. How can human beings deal with such emotions? A story from Ethiopia's long-ago past tells that when the Prophet Muhammad began his religious teaching, the people of Arabia launched severe persecution against his followers. Muhammad sent them to Ethiopia, "a land of righteousness where no one is wronged." Thus, around A.D. 615, several groups, including Muhammad's daughter, Rockeya, crossed the Red Sea to take refuge in the ancient Aksumite kingdom in Ethiopia. When Arabia demanded the return of the refugees, King Armah, the Christian ruler of Aksum, is said to have replied, "If you were to offer me a mountain of gold, I would not give up these people who have taken refuge with me."

As this story and others from Ethiopia's past illustrate, Ethiopia is a country where the roots of three major world religions—Islam, Judaism, and Christianity—go deep. A fundamental value of all three religions is that of hospitality: You shall not harm, but welcome, the stranger. Patricia Roddy's *Api and the Boy Stranger*, a folktale from the Ivory Coast, illustrates the importance of this concept in many traditional societies. Although people often talk about "tolerance," sometimes I think we might be better off thinking in terms of that ancient value "hospitality."

I also longed for that sense of hospitality when my family came back to the United States for a first visit when I was 7. I remember the well-meaning adults who would say, "This little girl is growing up in Eth-i-OH-pia. Do you have any questions to ask her?" I remember the children's stares and the questions that almost inevitably included, "Did you see Tarzan?"

Customs that truly are different provide an opportunity for open discussions. During my school visits, for example, many children ask me about the shaving of Almaz's head in my book *Pulling the Lion's Tail*. Their questions provide us with an opportunity to talk about mourning customs in all societies, including our own. A glib "we're all the same" approach is the antithesis of true hospitality, because it ignores the ways in which we are truly unique. Students should be taught that societies do indeed differ in customs and values, and that such things can be approached with respectful curiosity and an interest in learning more.

So how do we teach children to greet the people of faraway places with a sense of hospitality? An important key is what we model in our own attitude and approaches: courtesy, kindness, generosity, tolerance, and a respectful curiosity. After all, though meetings among cultures can be ripe with misunderstanding, they can also be a source of pleasure and a thorough education.

Activity. Books such as Margaret W. Musgrove's *Ashanti to Zulu*, Ifeoma Onyefulu's *A Is for Africa*, and Cynthia Chin-Lee's *A Is for Asia* can help students understand that there are many people groups, languages, and customs even within the same country—and certainly within the same continent. (Ethiopia alone has 80 different languages.) Use *The Night Has Ears*, a collection of proverbs gathered by Ashley Bryan, to look at wise sayings that come from across the African continent, a land mass of about 2,000 distinct people groups. See if you can locate the area where each proverb comes from. Let students try their hand at writing fables that could illustrate each proverb. Discuss which ones are unfamiliar and why. Bryan talks about hearing his own grandmother quote many proverbs. Do proverbs pop up in your students' homes? Make a class collection of proverbs, ones students have heard or ones they create themselves.

Resiliency and Resourcefulness

In the 1980s, pioneer investigators began to note that while certain risk factors in children's lives are highly correlated with the development of behavioral disturbances, at the same time there are children who "are at risk and yet develop normally." The researchers began to ask such questions as, "What are the features of children who, in the presence of known potentials for disaster, have managed nevertheless to sustain healthy development?" (Chess, 1989, p. 180). Since then, books, Web sites, and many articles have shown the importance of helping children recognize their ability to be resilient and resourceful. Probably no other theme is so often illustrated in fiction. One analysis of 1,086 stories told or written by Ethiopian children revealed that a whopping 27%, far higher than any other theme, had to do with the notion that "cleverness pays" (Lord, 1970, p. 227).

Resourcefulness and courage often go hand in hand—in stories and in real life. You can no doubt think of many tales similar to Phyllis Gershator's retelling of *Tukama Tootles the Flute: A Tale from the Antilles*, in which a boy ends up in the clutches of a giant and has to persuade the giant's wife, bit by bit, to let him go. *The Drums of Noto Hanto*, by J. Alison James, draws from a real incident, celebrated each year in Japan, in which cleverness and courage allowed a village to avoid a battle they would surely lose. Similarly, Ken

Mochizuki shines a light on a remarkable moment of moral courage in World War II in *Passage to Freedom: The Sugihara Story*. Sugihara, a Japanese diplomat to Lithuania, decides that he must do something about the Jewish refugees from Poland who need visas. He ends up writing up to 300 visas a day until he is reassigned.

Resiliency is also at the core of an enormous number of stories—and why not? Life abounds with examples of the need for perseverance. Henry Ford went bankrupt twice in the early years of his efforts at making and selling automobiles. In the first year, Coca-Cola sold only 400 Cokes. Thomas Alva Edison spent $40,000 to test hundreds and hundreds of different filaments for an electric light. Abraham Lincoln was defeated twice for the Senate and once as vice president before he was elected president.

One of the primary ways to illustrate perseverance and determination is to use quest tales. While reading a collection of folktales from Latin America, I was impressed to find a retelling of an Inca folktale that features a girl as the protagonist. But the version I read, like so many retellings published in the 1970s, felt "generic" to me. I began to read everything I could lay hands on about the ancient Inca kingdom, and out of my research came my own retelling of the story *Miro in the Kingdom of the Sun*. As in the original version I read, the main character sets out to find water from a magic lake in order to save the prince's life and rescue her brothers from prison—and, at the end of her quest, chooses freedom and family over luxury. It is easy to find many, many other quest stories, even other ones in which girls do the questing, such as *The Painted Fan* by Marilyn Singer.

Quest stories provide excellent models of people who are resilient and resourceful in the face of overwhelming odds. The lives of real people can also be fruitful examples. Picture book biographies and bits of autobiographies abound. Just a few to try are Jeanette Winter's *Diego*, about Mexican muralist Diego Rivera; Sherley Anne Williams's *Working Cotton*, in which the author tells of her family's migrant life in California; Allen Say's *El Chino*, the story of Billy Wong, who chased his dream to become a Chinese American matador; and Diane Stanley's *Cleopatra*, the truth behind the stories of a young woman legendary for her beauty who, in reality, was probably not stunningly beautiful but was intelligent, interesting, ambitious, and brave.

Activity. Craig Kee Strete has written a literary folktale titled *The Lost Boy and the Monster*, which can serve as a model (along with many fairy tales) for students to write their own quest stories about their personal challenges. Help them map out the story ahead of time by pointing out that most fictional heroes try to solve their own problems and fail (traditionally three times) before managing to succeed.

Beware "The Africa Unit"

With all the good things to be found in the use of multicultural books, there are also a few pitfalls to avoid. Far too often, for instance, Africa is presented as a smallish, homogeneous country. It may be helpful for students to know that flat maps, by necessity, distort the shape and size of the continents, because the maps flatten all the curves of the earth's surface. Most common maps, based on the Mercator Projection, make Greenland and Africa look about the same size. Actually, Greenland is 2.1 million square kilometers, and Africa is 30 million square kilometers. In fact, the whole of the United States, plus India, plus Argentina, plus Europe, plus New Zealand, plus China would fit inside the continent of Africa. When studying Africa, it is important to present the enormous variety within the continent. In addition to the books already mentioned, *Sand and Fog: Adventures in Southern Africa*, by Jim Brandenburg, is a fascinating book with text and photographs that show how much variety exists in just one African region.

Beware "The Multicultural Unit"

Presenting "the multicultural unit" also poses problems in that it tends to promote the cordoning off of other cultures and sometimes provoke a response of, "Other people are so weird." Multicultural books can be woven in more naturally. For instance, European folktales and fairy tales can be paired with a story such as my own *Miro in the Kingdom of the Sun*. A connection with another continent can be added through *The Girl Who Loved Caterpillars*, by Jean Merrill, a story based on a fragment from an old Japanese manuscript that illustrates that same independence and love of freedom found in *Miro in the Kingdom of the Sun*.

Another of my stories, *Pulling the Lion's Tail*, has been successfully paired with the Newbery Award–winning *Sarah, Plain and Tall*, by Patricia MacLachlan, a theme pairing rather than a geographic pairing. One librarian, expecting to do some explaining about Almaz's father's trip to another village to bring back a wife, found that a surprising number of her students in California had a stepmother they had not met before she married the father.

Art makes a wonderful way to create good connections. In the past 10 years, as computers have taken over the task of color separation, the artwork in picture books has become increasingly colorful and complex. Teachers and librarians who know that many of their students may never set foot in an art museum are making the most of the opportunity to expose young readers to the fine art that illustrates stories. And students can make inspiring connections with books through their own art. I have seen many great art projects used in connection with my books—pigeon mobiles set fluttering from the ceilings of classrooms; Inca symbols drawn onto foam, rubbed with ink, and printed on paper, mimicking a bit of the process illustrator David Frampton uses with his woodcuts; torn paper mountains, chalk dust mountains, painted mountains, with suns rising and setting behind them; homemade *mancala* boards painted with symbols of personal meaning; lions with hair of yarn and paper and fluffy cotton balls. I have also teamed up with teachers or librarians to have students try their hand at illustrating one of my stories before the professional illustrator's work is available—sometimes even doing research, just as professional illustrators do. Some of the best questions about Ethiopia have come from students who have dug for visual resources to accompany one of my tales.

Final Thoughts

In 2000, Harcourt published my book *Faraway Home*, which is about a girl who thinks of the United States as home and struggles to understand her father's homesickness for another home far away. The book was inspired by a real incident that happened to a childhood friend from Ethiopia. When he showed his children a photograph of himself as a schoolboy, his son asked, "But Daddy, why did you take off your shoes to go to school?" In my story, Desta, a young girl, is afraid to let her father leave home to spend some time in Ethiopia with his mother, who is sick. At first, she can see only differences between her childhood and his. Only gradually does she open herself enough to see his world.

As all countries and continents increasingly become a "fruit basket upset," the United States will gather more and more stories from all over the globe, including stories such as *Faraway Home* or Allen Say's *Grandfather's Journey* or Haemi Balgassi's *Peacebound Trains*. Such stories explore the ebbs and flows of people among cultures, sometimes looking at what happens when values clash and change. My hope is that, in this ebb and flow, we will find evermore effective ways to teach children and adults alike to truly understand such grand and luminous words as *hospitality*, *generosity*, *compassion*, *tolerance*, *sharing*, *respect*, and *peace*.

References

Chess, S. (1989). Defying the voice of doom. In T.F. Dugan & R. Coles (Eds.), *The child in our times: Studies in the development of resiliency* (pp. 179–199). New York: Brunner/Mazel.

Lord, E. (1970). *The Queen of Sheba's heirs: Cultural patterns of Ethiopia*. Atlanta, GA: Acropolis Books.

Marcus, L. (1998). *Dear genius: The letters of Ursula Nordstrom*. New York: HarperCollins.

Norton, D.E. (1991). *Through the eyes of a child: An introduction to children's literature* (3rd ed.). New York: Macmillan.

Annotated Bibliography of Multicultural Books

Aardema, V. (1979). *The riddle of the drum: A tale from Tizapan, Mexico*. New York: Four Winds.
The king refuses to let his daughter marry unless one of her suitors can guess what kind of skin was used in the construction of a drum made by a wizard. Through cooperation, a young man is able to solve the riddle.

Aardema, V. (1994). *Misoso: Once upon a time tales from Africa*. Ill. R. Ruffins. New York: Knopf.
The author of this collection retells 12 tales from different parts of Africa.

Aardema, V. (1997). *This for that: A Tonga tale*. Ill. V. Chess. New York: Dial.
In this retelling of a Tongan folktale, lazy Rabbit does not want to work for food and water but coaxes different animals to trade with her instead. In the end, Rabbit gets a kick in the pants for lying and stealing.

Angelou, M. (1994). *My painted house, my friendly chicken, and me*. New York: Clarkson Potter/Crown.
The narrator, a Ndebele girl from southern Africa, shows important pieces of her life, including the wall paintings done by the women of her village. The pages include photographs of the bright designs from the paintings.

Aung, M.H. (1968). *A kingdom lost for a drop of honey and other Burmese folktales*. New York: Parents' Magazine Press.
A collection of traditional tales from Burma.

Balgassi, H. (1996). *Peacebound trains*. Ill. C.K. Soentpiet. New York: Clarion.
While Sumi waits for her mother to come back from serving in the U.S. Army, her grandmother tells Sumi about her own painful escape (via train) from Seoul during the Korean War. The story and paintings both are full of poetry and vivid detail.

Beeler, S.B. (1998). *Throw your tooth on the roof: Tooth traditions from around the world*. Ill. G. Karas. Boston: Houghton Mifflin.
Although children in the United States often put teeth under their pillows for the tooth fairy to collect, children in other countries have different traditions. The customs of half a dozen countries are briefly described, accompanied by whimsical illustrations.

Brandenburg, J. (1994). *Sand and fog: Adventures in Southern Africa*. New York: Walker.
A well-known wildlife photographer uses his pictures to show the Namib Desert landscape, including animals, people, sand dunes, and cities. The text describes cultural practices of people, shows how animals adapt to the dry land, and illustrates the wide variety found in even one region of Africa.

Bryan, A. (1999). *The night has ears: An African proverb*. New York: Simon & Schuster.
Bryan has collected 26 proverbs from different African people groups, some thoughtful and wise, some funny, each illustrated with an intricate design.

Burnhard, E. (1996). *A ride on mother's back: A day of baby carrying around the world*. San Diego, CA: Harcourt.
Babies in 12 different places around the world, carried in slings and wraps and backpacks and arms, view daily activities from their safe perches.

Chin-Lee, C. (1997). *A is for Asia*. Ill. Y. Heo. New York: Orchard.
In this book, every letter of the alphabet introduces some custom or word or object of Asian life, along with a brief explanation to help set the context. The 26 words are written in English and also in one of Asia's many languages, and a note is provided about languages.

Cowen-Fletcher, J. (1994). *It takes a village*. New York: Scholastic.
A young girl in West Africa searches anxiously for her younger brother in the marketplace, unaware that the villagers have been looking out for him.

Creeden, S. (1994). *Fair is fair: World folktales of justice*. Little Rock, AR: August House.
This collection of tales focuses on the notion of fairness all over the world and shows its characters finding ingenious ways to get the justice they seek.

Diakité, B.W. (1997). *The hunterman and the crocodile: A West African folktale*. New York: Scholastic.
In this West African folktale, Bamba, the crocodile, wants to bite Donso, the hunterman. When Donso cries out for help, cow, horse, chicken, and mango tree all turn their backs on him, but a compromise finally shows that all of earth's creatures are interrelated.

Dooley, N. (1996). *Everybody bakes bread*. Ill. P. Thornton. Minneapolis, MN: Carolrhoda.
Exasperated by her children's rainy day bickering, Carrie's mother sends her out into her neighborhood on an impossible task. Carrie samples seven different kinds of bread in her multiethnic neighbors' houses and gathers enough friends for a game of kickball when the rain stops.

Echewa, T.O. (1994). *The ancestor tree*. Ill. C. Hale. New York: Lodestar.
In this Nigerian folktale, an old storyteller dies. Although he has no offspring to plant an ancestor tree for him, the children of the village convince the adults to change traditional customs so that the community will now plant trees for anyone who has lived an honorable life.

Echewa, T.O. (1999). *The magic tree: A folktale from Nigeria*. Ill. E.B. Lewis. New York: Morrow.
Mbi, an orphan boy in a Nigerian village, is mistreated by everyone. One day, a magic tree grows and showers him with fruit. Exercising his wits, he finds a way to use the tree's power to demand better treatment.

Edmonds, I.G. (1997). *Ooka the wise: Tales of old Japan*. Ill. S. Yamazaki. Hamden, CT: Linnet Books.
Originally published in 1961, these 17 folktales show Ooka, a wise Japanese judge, finding various crafty methods to show people the foolishness of their ways.

Fox, M. (1997). *Whoever you are*. Ill. L. Staub. San Diego, CA: Harcourt.
In a simple, rhythmic text, author Mem Fox addresses the children of the world, reminding them that wherever they live and whoever they are, they laugh and cry and hurt and love, just as all human beings do all over the earth.

Franklin, K.L., & McGirr, N. (Eds.). (1996). *Out of the dump: Writing and photographs by children from Guatemala*. New York: Lothrop, Lee & Shepard.
This book chronicles a project in which a photographer gave cameras to children living in a dump in Guatemala City and encouraged them to take pictures and write about their lives. Large black-and-white photographs show families, friends, pets, and sometimes harsh realities.

Gershator, P. (1994). *Tukama tootles the flute: A tale from Antilles*. Ill. S. Saint James. New York: Orchard.
Tukama loves music to the point that he ignores his chores. As his grandmother has warned him, a two-headed giant appears and carries him off. The clever and brave boy is able to use his music to escape.

Goble, P. (1992). *The girl who loved wild horses*. New York: Bradbury.

This Caldecott Award–winning book retells a legend of a girl who understands and loves wild horses with such passion that she chooses to live among them and, eventually, to become a mare.

Gonzalez, L.M. (1997). *Señor cat's romance, and other favorite stories from Latin America*. Ill. L. Delacre. New York: Scholastic.

Each of these six beloved Latin American folktales is told with humor and rhythmic phrases. After each story, a glossary and an explanatory note help set the story in context.

Hamanaka, S. (1994). *All the colors of the earth*. New York: Morrow.

In a poetic text, the author celebrates the children of the earth in all their various colors. She uses natural phenomena to describe the children's skin tones, their hair, and the love of the people who care for them.

Han, S.C. (1994). *The rabbit's judgment*. Ill. Y. Heo. New York: Henry Holt.

In this Korean folktale, a man frees a hungry tiger from a trap, but the tiger then threatens to eat the man. The man calls for justice, and a rabbit finally delivers the verdict that helps him escape his sad fate.

Horenstein, H. (1997). *Baseball in the barrios*. San Diego, CA: Harcourt.

The text and photos in this book show the daily life of Hubaldo Romero Paez, a fifth-grade boy in Venezuela with a huge enthusiasm for baseball. Sprinkled with Spanish words, the text includes details about the many forms of baseball in Venezuela.

Isadora, R. (1991). *At the crossroads*. New York: Greenwillow.

Young children in a South African village wait to greet their fathers, who have been away for months working in the mines. Excitement builds throughout the day, but the men do not end up arriving until the following dawn.

Jaffe, N. (1992). *In the month of Kislev: A story for Hanukkah*. Ill. L. August. New York: Viking.

In this Jewish folktale, a stingy, rich man accuses a poor man's children of stealing the delicious smells of his latkes as the smells drift out his window. A wise and kind rabbi pays for the smells with the jingling sound of coins.

James, J.A. (1999). *The drums of Noto Hanto*. Ill. Tsukushi. New York: DK Ink.

Based on an event from 1576, the people of Noto Hanto know that samurai soldiers from a nearby village are about to swoop down and plunder their village. Using masks and drums, they come up with a clever plan to frighten off the soldiers. The author uses onomatopoeia to capture the sounds of the many drums.

Kelsey, A.G. (1943). *Once the hodja*. New York: Longman.

A collection of humorous stories about Nasr-ed-Din Hodja, a legendary figure of Turkish folktales.

Knutson, B. (1990). *How the guinea fowl got her spots: A Swahili tale of friendship*. Minneapolis, MN: Carolrhoda.

This "pourquoi" tale set in East Africa explains how guinea fowl came by the distinctive coloration that helps the bird camouflage itself in the savanna grasses.

Knutson, B. (1993). *Sungura and leopard: A Swahili trickster tale*. Boston: Little, Brown.

In this folktale from Tanzania, a leopard and a hare accidentally build a house on the same spot. They agree to live together, but it is eventually up to the hare to come up with a plan to save his family from the hungry leopard.

Kurtz, J. (1994). *Fire on the mountain*. Ill. E.B. Lewis. New York: Simon & Schuster.

In this retelling of an Ethiopian folktale, a young dreamer must first survive the cold mountain winds with only a thin cloak to keep him warm and then use his courage (and his sister's wisdom) to convince the rich man to keep his word and give him his reward.

Kurtz, J. (1995). *Pulling the lion's tail*. Ill. F. Cooper. New York: Simon & Schuster.

"Much of what is good comes slowly," according to this Ethiopian folktale. Almaz, a young girl whose mother has died, learns to approach her shy new stepmother with the same patience and courage that she used to approach a lion.

Kurtz, J. (1996). *Miro in the kingdom of the sun*. Ill. D. Frampton. Boston: Houghton Mifflin.

When Miro's two brothers are imprisoned by the all-powerful Inca king, it is up to Miro to use her courage—along with her understanding of the birds' language—to get healing water from the lake at the corner of the earth. The story is full of real details of Inca daily life.

Kurtz, J. (1997a). *Only a pigeon*. Ill. E.B. Lewis. New York: Simon & Schuster.

To Ondu-ahlem, a young "street kid" in the modern city of Addis Ababa, Ethiopia, his pigeons are precious, giving him a way to be playful and have something to take care of.

Kurtz, J. (1997b). *Trouble*. San Diego, CA: Harcourt.

Tekeleh never means to get into trouble, but somehow trouble always finds him. Finally, his father gives him a *gebeta* board (*mancala* game)—but far from keeping Tekeleh out of trouble, the game starts him on an adventuresome day of trades, always one step out of reach of trouble.

Kurtz, J. (1998). *The storyteller's beads*. San Diego, CA: Harcourt.

When Sahay suddenly has to escape from the war and famine that are swallowing her Ethiopian village, she is horrified to discover that one of her companions on the dangerous journey is Rahel, a girl from an Ethiopian Jewish family. Separated by prejudice and fear, the two girls ultimately have to rely on each other to survive.

Kurtz, J. (2000). *Faraway home*. Ill. E.B. Lewis. San Diego, CA: Harcourt.

Desta thinks of the United States as home, but her father is homesick for Ethiopia. When he discovers that he needs to go home to care for his sick mother, Desta is worried about his journey and afraid he will never come back.

Kurtz, J. (forthcoming). *All the wisdom in the world*. New York: Greenwillow.

A young immigrant girl from Ghana comforts her younger brother (and herself) by telling traditional stories from their grandmother's village. Her stories remind them of home and give them the courage to face their new life.

Lankford, M.D. (1996). *Jacks around the world*. Ill. K. Dugan. New York: Morrow.

After setting out a basic history and rules for the game of jacks, Lankford illustrates 14 variations of the game as it is played in different countries. Directions for playing are included along with facts about each country.

Lankford, M.D. (1998). *Dominoes around the world*. Ill. K. Dugan. New York: Morrow.

The game of dominoes has been played from ancient times to the present, all around the world. The author provides facts about such countries as Vietnam, Cuba, Ukraine, and France, as well as instructions for each country's version of dominoes.

Lee, M. (1997). *Nim and the war effort*. Ill. Y. Choi. New York: Farrar, Strauss & Giroux.

Nim, a Chinese American girl, comes up with a clever way to collect more newspapers for her San Francisco school's paper drive during World War II. She reaches her goal, but her actions trouble her traditional Chinese grandfather.

Lewin, T. (1996). *Market!* New York: Lothrop, Lee & Shepard.

With detailed, realistic paintings and poetic descriptions, the author shows markets on six continents. Vendors sell fish, horses, bright clothing, limes, bananas, and a wealth of other goods as the reader takes a look at the world's marketplaces.

MacLachlan, P. (1985). *Sarah, plain and tall.* New York: Harper.

Sarah may not be beautiful, but she brings love and beauty into the lives of two children whose mother died in childbirth. The brother and sister wait eagerly and with some fear to see whether this mail order bride will choose to stay with them on the prairies or return to her New England home.

Madrigal, A.H. (1999). *Erandi's braids.* Ill. T. dePaola. New York: G.P. Putnam's Sons.

Award-winning illustrator Tomie dePaola provides the pictures for this gentle story of a girl who offers to sell her long, black braid so that her family can have money to repair their fishing net.

McBrier, P. (2001). *Beatrice's goat.* Ill. L. Lohstoeter. New York: Atheneum.

A girl who longs to go to school but has to work hard to help her family finally gets her wish after the family receives a goat from Heifer International.

McDermott, G. (1992). *Zomo the rabbit: A trickster tale from West Africa.* San Diego, CA: Harcourt.

Zomo seeks wisdom from the Sky God and is given three huge tasks, which he completes using cleverness and trickery.

McDermott, G. (1994). *Raven: A trickster tale from the Pacific Northwest.* San Diego, CA: Harcourt.

Based on a myth of native peoples from the Pacific Northwest, this is a story of how light came into the world. Raven flies to the Sky Chief's house, steals the sun, and flings it into the sky.

Merrill, J. (1992). *The girl who loved caterpillars: A twelfth-century tale from Japan.* Ill. F. Cooper. New York: Philomel.

Izumi, a girl in 12th-century Japan, is uninterested both in the noblemen who would love to marry her and in other customs of her time. Instead, she is fascinated by living creatures, especially caterpillars. This story is based on writing actually found in an ancient scroll.

Mochizuki, K. (1997). *Passage to freedom: The Sugihara story.* Ill. D. Lee. New York: Lee & Low.

This is the true story, based on Hiroki Sugihara's own words, of his experiences as the son of the Japanese consul to Lithuania in 1940. Together, Sugihara's family decides that the consul should disobey his government and write visas for hundreds of Jews trying to escape the Nazis.

Mollel, T.M. (1990). *The orphan boy: A Maasai story.* Ill. P. Morin. New York: Clarion.

In this Maasai legend, a star becomes a young boy and brings unexpected riches and companionship to a herdsman. When the old man breaks the boy's trust and uncovers his secret, the boy returns to the sky as the planet Venus.

Mollel, T.M. (1997). *Kele's secret.* Ill. C. Stock. New York: Lodestar.

Yoanes, who lives on a coffee farm in Tanzania, has to figure out where his grandmother's most clever hen is hiding her eggs. After he figures out the puzzle, he has to conquer his fears to enter the shed and collect the eggs.

Mollel, T.M. (1999). *My rows and piles of coins*. Ill. E.B. Lewis. New York: Clarion.
Saruni could be tempted by any number of wonderful things in the marketplace, but he is determined to save his rows and piles of coins to buy a bicycle so he can help his family carry things to the market.

Mollel, T.M. (2000). *Subira Subira*. Ill. L. Saport. New York: Clarion.
After their mother's death, Tatu struggles to care for her uncooperative younger brother until MaMzuka, a mysterious spirit woman, agrees to help in exchange for three whiskers from a lion.

Morin, P. (1998). *Animal dreaming: An Aboriginal dreamtime story*. San Diego, CA: Harcourt.
In the Australian outback, Mirri is about to be initiated into adulthood. After studying his people's rock art, he vividly imagines a story from his heritage about the time when the earth was formed and all animals lived in peace and harmony.

Musgrove, M.W. (1976). *Ashanti to Zulu: African traditions*. Ill. L. & D. Dillon. New York: Dial.
Artists Leo and Diane Dillon won a Caldecott Medal for their work in this book, which shows traditions from 26 people groups all over the continent of Africa.

Nye, N.S. (1994). *Sitti's secrets*. Ill. N. Carpenter. New York: Four Winds.
When Mona visits her grandmother in a Palestinian village, she is entranced by the new sights, smells, and other details in this new world—and also by her warm grandmother. When she gets home, she writes an earnest letter to the president, saying that she and her grandmother vote for peace.

Olaleye, I. (2001). *Bikes for rent*. New York: Scholastic.
Lateef works hard for the chance to rent a shiny red bike. After he accidentally crashes it, his hard work not only pays for his mistake but eventually earns him his own almost-new bike.

Onyefulu, I. (1993). *A is for Africa*. New York: Cobblehill.
Using photographs, the author shows her childhood home of Nigeria. Many of the customs and traditions she illustrates are shared by many people groups across the continent.

Onyefulu, I. (1996). *Ogbo: Sharing life in an African village*. San Diego, CA: Harcourt.
In Nigeria, the 6-year-old narrator, Obioma, describes how everyone born in her village becomes part of an age group. The group becomes a kind of extended family, taking responsibility for its members and for making the community a better place.

Onyefulu, O. (1994). *Chinye: A West African folk tale*. Ill. E. Safarewicz. New York: Viking.
In this Cinderella story from West Africa, Chinye must work night and day for her mean stepmother. Her kindness leads her to riches that she shares with others of the village.

Paxton, T. (1991). *Androcles and the lion: And other Aesop's fables*. Ill. R. Rayevsky. New York: Morrow.
This is a retelling of Aesop's fable about a slave who removes a thorn from the paw of a lion and is helped by the lion in turn.

Polacco, P. (1999). *Luba and the wren*. New York: Philomel.
Luba, a young Ukranian girl, helps a frightened wren and is rewarded with a wish. When the girl returns home, though, she finds her parents caught up in greed, wanting more and more from the wren. It is up to Luba to restore their simple, happy home.

Roddy, P. (1994). *Api and the boy stranger: A village creation tale*. Ill. L. Russell. New York: Dial.
In an Ivory Coast village, a thin stranger appears during a feast. Api's family is the only one to show kindness to the boy—and their kindness is repaid by a warning that saves them from destruction by a volcano.

Rosen, M. (1993). *How giraffe got such a long neck…and why rhino is so grumpy*. Ill. J. Clementson. New York: Dial.

In this East African "pourquoi" tale, Giraffe and Rhino are both starving after a long dry period. They ask Man for the help of his magic herbs. As a result, Giraffe grows a long neck and Rhino ends up disgruntled.

San Souci, R.D. (1989). *The talking eggs*. Ill. J. Pinkney. New York: Dial.

This Louisiana Creole folktale tells of Blanche, the youngest child of a poor family, who is kind to a witch and is rewarded with magic eggs. Greedy older sister Rose tries to get the same riches but ends up with snakes, toads, and frogs.

Say, A. (1990). *El chino*. Boston: Houghton Mifflin.

Bong Way Wong, or Billy, grows up in the southwestern United States with an immigrant father who tells his son that he can be anything he wants to be. Alas, Billy is too short to play basketball. But on a visit to Spain, he finds a new love and becomes the first Chinese American bullfighter.

Say, A. (1993). *Grandfather's journey*. Boston: Houghton Mifflin.

Say tells the story of his own maternal grandfather who loves both Japan and San Francisco. He ends up traveling between the two all his life, and whenever he is in one place, he finds that he is homesick for the other.

Singer, M. (1994). *The painted fan*. Ill. W. Ma. New York: Morrow.

In a dramatic story set in ancient China and illustrated by a Chinese artist, cruel Lord Shang wants to marry the peasant girl Bright Willow, but she is in love with one of his grooms. The angry Lord sends the girl on a journey to bring back a pearl from a cave guarded by Red Fang, a demon.

Smith, C.L. (2000). *Jingle dancer*. Ill. C. Van Wright & Y. Hu. New York: HarperCollins.

Jenna, a girl from the Muscogee Nation, is eager to wear a jingle dress at the next powwow, but she has to find the tin jingles to make her dress sing. The very contemporary women of her family pass on their jingles, and Jenna, in turn, is able to carry on their traditions.

Stanley, D. (1994). *Cleopatra*. Ill. P. Vennema. New York: Morrow.

This picture book biography covers the life and world of Cleopatra, contradicting many of the ways the young queen has been misinterpreted. Notes, maps, a pronunciation guide, and a bibliography all help show the period when the Greek Ptolemies ruled Egypt.

Steptoe, J. (1987). *Mufaro's beautiful daughters: An African tale*. New York: Lothrop, Lee & Shepard.

In this Caldecott Honor Book, Manyara and Nyasha, two sisters, are both eligible to marry the Great King. As each sister makes her way through the forest, bad-tempered Manyara is dismissive of those she meets, while Nyasha is kind, winning the love of the king.

Strete, C.K. (1999). *The lost boy and the monster*. Ill. S. Johnson & L. Fancher. New York: G.P. Putnam's Sons.

Lost boy, who lives alone in the forest, is respectful toward the rattlesnake and scorpion he meets, so when the boy is captured by old Foot Eater, a monster who lives in a medicine basket at the top of a tree, the animals help the boy escape.

Stuve-Bodeen, S. (1998). *Elizabeti's doll*. Ill. C. Hale. New York: Lee & Low.

Elizabeti, a girl from a contemporary Tanzanian village, has a new baby brother and a new doll—a lovely rock—that she cares for as tenderly as her mother cares for the new baby. The story unobtrusively works in details of daily village life, such as babies carried in *kanga* cloth.

Williams, K.L. (1990). *Galimoto*. Ill. C. Stock. New York: Lothrop, Lee & Shepard.
   Kondi, a young boy in a contemporary village in Malawi, is determined to find the scraps of wire he needs to make a toy truck, a *galimoto*. Though he encounters many obstacles, he is thrilled to succeed in the end.

Williams, S.A. (1992). *Working cotton*. Ill. C. Byard. San Diego, CA: Harcourt.
   In poetic language, Shelan, the third daughter in a family of African American migrant workers, tells about one long day in the fields picking cotton. The Caldecott Honor Book captures Shelan's way of talking and her matter-of-fact viewpoint of the difficult life.

Winter, J. (1991). *Diego*. New York: Knopf.
   With a text in English and Spanish, the author tells the true story of Diego Rivera, the Mexican muralist whose huge paintings cover many walls. She concentrates on his childhood and the forces that gave him a passion for art and politics.

Yolen, J. (Ed.). (1986). *Favorite folktales from around the world*. New York: Pantheon.
   Grouped by theme, the 160 stories in this collection come from many times and places—40 different cultures. Scholarly notes help those who study folktales put each story into context.

Chapter 11

Magical Tales and Values: Connecting With Heroes and Sheroes

Ann Watts Pailliotet and Michelle Refvik Shaul

In this chapter, we begin with a rationale for teaching values with fairy tales and other magical stories. We follow this with descriptions of activities to help students and teachers explore values. At the end of the chapter we provide annotated bibliographies of Cinderella variations and other magical stories, and a list of further Cinderella readings. The texts selected for the bibliographies reflect and convey the types of democratic values we are proposing in this book: hope, kindness, belief, diversity in thought and action, a fostering of unique talents in oneself, and the celebration and discovery of strengths in others. The texts and activities in this chapter are suitable for a range of readers in grades K to 8. As with all good instruction, we trust that teachers will preview these resources and match them to their students' needs and abilities.

Heroes, Heroines, and Cultural Values

Heroes and heroines embody values that cultures hold most highly (Zipes, 1997). They also reflect aspects of particular cultural conditions (Campbell, 1968). Through their appearance, dress, and symbolic weapons or tools, their traits and actions, their adventures and trials, and their rewards and punishments, heroes and heroines offer instruction about how to think and behave.

In early Greece, Heracles was a popular hero. Brawny, muscular, and short-necked, he carried a club and dressed in a lion skin, symbolizing his brute force and physical power. Heracles was not particularly bright or in control of his emotions; he once shot an arrow at the sun because it was too hot. He also had an uncontrollable blood lust, killing members of his family in a blind rage. However, Heracles also possessed remarkable physical strength, persistence, humility, and obedience toward the gods, which enabled him to complete a series of 12 labors. Heracles was rewarded with immortality by Zeus, his father and patron. This father of the gods was driven by sexual ardor and passion; he was armed with thunderbolts and had a wandering eye for mortal maidens. Heracles and Zeus represented values, qualities, and conditions of emerging Greek society—dominated by men and ruled by competing warlords in scattered kingdoms—where conquest, fierceness in battle, military obedience, and physical strength ensured survival.

Later, Odysseus became a popular hero. He was tall and graceful, reflecting changing Greek aesthetics; his weapon of choice was a long bow—a more sophisticated and crafted weapon than a simple club. Odysseus had physical strength, but he was also a cunning statesman, brave general, quick thinker, talented orator, and resourceful leader—all needed qualities in the increasingly complex social and governmental systems that came with the rise of the demos and city states. Odysseus conceived of the Trojan Horse and outsmarted supernatural foes; he overcame numerous obstacles detailed in *The Odyssey* through guile and thinking, as well as strength and leadership. In contrast to Heracles's fickle and vengeful patron, Zeus, Odysseus found a patron goddess in Athena, who embodied the cultural values and civilized conditions of Athens. She represented industrial arts, domestic crafts, wisdom, rationality, justice, law, order, and meritorious battle. Odysseus also demonstrated fierce loyalty to his kingdom and family. Through disguise, careful plotting, and skill, he triumphed over the suitors who had overrun his home and tested the faithfulness of his wife, Penelope, who embodied desirable female values of the time—resourcefulness, domesticity, and fidelity. Odysseus was rewarded by regaining his rightful place as husband and king, then living a content domestic life while ruling long and lawfully.

Throughout time, heroes and heroines' traits have mirrored the transitional natures of cultural conditions and dominant values (Norton & Norton, 1999). In medieval Europe, fairy tales combined elements of pagan beliefs and Christian morality. In the Victorian era, childhood heroes reflected tensions between the "good child," who flourished in the domestic status quo, and the "bad child," who sought to escape rigid societal norms. In the United States, from the 1970s on, the rise of strong female protagonists in children's literature and the proliferation of heroes from diverse cultures parallel the Civil Rights and feminist movements, as well as the changes in values these movements effected.

Fairy Tales, the Heroic Monomyth, and Magic: Elements That Teach Values

In addition to the traits and exploits of heroines and heroes, other elements in myths and fairy tales convey lessons about values. For instance, Bettelheim (1989) describes how supporting characters, motifs, symbols, conflicts, and magic in fairy tales help children find meaning in life, develop psychologically, and learn about autonomy, pleasure, identity, emotions, self-efficacy, reality, and morality. Of utmost importance to Bettelheim is that fairy tales help children find their "own solutions through what the story seems to imply about [themselves] and...[their] inner conflicts" (p. 25). Bettelheim's emphasis on decision making, personal development, and social learning furthers the kinds of values education we propose in this book.

The Monomyth

Campbell (1990) describes the universal structure of the "monomyth" and motifs within it. He asserts that each stage—with its plots, conflicts, symbols, and settings—models desirable values and actions in the hero, audience, and human condition. These stages are as follows:

1. Divine discontent or the "call to adventure"—in which the protagonist is dissatisfied with existing self or conditions and is called to a greater purpose.

2. The "threshold of adventure"—in which the protagonist departs from current, comfortable surroundings and enters new worlds, often through supernatural means.

3. The Quest, trials, and adventures—including battles with evil, abduction, imprisonment, or "wonder journeys," in which the hero or heroine is tested in foreign lands and conditions, in the process discovering new strengths and values, often with the aid of magical talismans, helpers, or weapons.

4. Apotheosis—the moment of transformation in which he or she triumphs over evil forces and thus discovers his or her heroic traits and values.

5. Reintegration with society—through resurrection, rescue, or return, in which heroes and heroines are rewarded, often sharing their newfound strengths to benefit others.

The monomyth might be seen to parallel processes involved in values formation. Its accompanying motifs and symbols appear across cultures in fairy tales and mass media texts alike (O'Brien, 1995). Cinderella, Alice, Luke Skywalker, and Dorothy all initially express divine discontent with their current situations. Cinderella is then transported to the ball with the aid of her fairy godmother; Alice follows the magical white rabbit down the hole; Luke begins his quest after meeting the mysterious Obi Wan Kenobi; Dorothy is transported over the rainbow to Oz by an unnatural storm. All these protagonists are tested through trials and adventures on their quests. They encounter supernatural creatures and situations, and they are often aided by magical talismans (Dorothy's and Cinderella's slippers; Alice's "drink me" and "eat me" substances; Luke's lightsaber and "the Force"). All reach an apotheosis in which they or others discover their inner strengths. The prince finds Cinderella and places the slipper on her foot; Alice speaks up and rejects the illogical rules at her trial; Luke turns away the mechanized scanner and trusts the Force; Dorothy realizes she has had the power within her to go home all along. At the end of these tales, the heroes and heroines are rewarded by returning home to enjoy and share their adventures, insights, and strengths. All have experienced profound changes in their perceptions, values, and life situations.

Magic

Uses of magic are central to fairy tales and the monomyth. Magic represents opportunity, imagination, unpredictability, love, fate, trust, discovery, kindness, triumph of good over evil, transformation, power, and hope. Often overlooked by society or heroes at their quest's beginning, magic is a key element in their discovery of new insights, values, and powers. Through magical talismans, settings, and helpers, heroes and heroines learn to perceive and use their hidden strengths and unique talents. Magical tales convey many positive values: courage, persistence, resourcefulness, integrity, self-confidence, awareness of opportunity, caring and appreciation of others, pursuit of justice, wit, inner beauty, moral choice, and social responsibility.

In our everyday lives, tales of enchantment encourage us to discover our personal magic—to be good hearted, hopeful, true to ourselves and our ideals, and brave enough to face adversity and not fall prey to the forces that attack our dignity. When we hold to these values we all become heroes. In the tales featured in this chapter's annotated bibliographies, for example, someone with a keen eye, either by magic or kindred spirit, sees real beauty and value within each individual. It is our hope that these tales will enable young readers to discover magic and power in themselves and others.

The Cinderella Story

The tale of Cinderella is nearly universal; there are more than 400 variants from cultures around the world (Yolen, 1977). However, Cinderella's character traits, appearance, behaviors, and rewards vary greatly, reflecting values of the cultures in which they arise (Dundes, 1989). In the popular Disney film version produced in the 1950s, Cinderella reflects many dominant cultural and gender norms of the time. She is a white, slight, blonde, and slim girl who is gentle and kind. She waits passively for her Prince to find her and is rewarded by living in matrimonial bliss "happily ever after." Contrast this tale with that of Nyasha from *Mufaro's Beautiful Daughters* (Steptoe, 1987). Her beauty is dark skinned; she is tall and physically strong. She too is industrious and kind, but she is also generous, community minded, brave, and adventurous. Unlike the Disney Cinderella, Nyasha takes action, sets out on a journey, and makes many ethical decisions. The Cinderella character is also different in some early Chinese variations, in which small feet and grace in motion are central features of beauty. Furthermore, these Cinderellas are crafty, resourceful, able to thwart power, and responsible for honoring their ancestors, reflecting the class struggles and filial duty of Confucian times.

All Cinderellas have the stigma of being different from those around them—of not having adequate clothes, jewels, or physical beauty to compete—but they possess hidden virtues that outshine those with only material possessions or outer attractiveness. Contemporary versions of Cinderella reflect changing values and cultural norms. Protagonists are female or male—all strong characters who learn to perceive their own hidden strengths and talents. Even if they possess requisite material possessions or physical attributes, they often shun stereotypical expectations. In some tales, such as *Fanny's Dream* (Buehner, 1996), common sense is valued over magic intervention. In others, "happily ever after" is often not all that it is cracked up to be. In *The Paper Bag Princess* (Munsch, 1988), Elizabeth tells Prince Ronald that he is "a bum." In *The Frog Prince Continued* (Scieszka, 1994), the hero finds, after his transition from frog to prince, that castle life is dull. He returns to his frog existence, realizing he was happy all along. In *Ella Enchanted* (Levine, 1998), integrity is more attractive to princes than cloying attentions. In *Just Ella* (Haddix, 1999), Ella rejects the empty facade of royalty and leaves to work in a refugee camp.

In the Cinderella variations and other magical tales we offer in the annotated bibliography at the end of this chapter, female protagonists are not weak or passive; nor will they accept the position of pawn. Male protagonists in these tales are more likely to use their heads, hearts, and friends than fists to overcome adversity. All the heroes and heroines in the annotated selections are capable leaders who stand up for what is right, even when their path is difficult.

Rationale for Teaching With Cinderella Variations and Other Magical Tales

There are other compelling reasons for teaching values through magical stories and fairy tales. Given the common elements shared between many mass media and literary texts, connecting fairy tale characters and heroes in mass media and literature may connect literacy environments of home and school. For instance, Dyson (1997) shows how young children are likely to write about heroes and plots they encounter in popular television shows and films. Second, because both adults and children usually enjoy fairy tales, families who read these tales together may increase appreciation of their own literary and cultural heritage. Third, using Cinderella variations and other magical tales may enhance classroom literacy instruction (Worthy & Bloodgood, 1992). Last, these tales were selected for readability to promote intergenerational communication and closeness.

The tales in the annotated bibliography are representative of those most frequently selected by children and recommended by Michelle Shaul, the second author of this chapter, an elementary school media specialist. She writes the following rationale for our bibliography selections:

> In years past, I've encountered select groups of students who sought books about magic; a second group could be coaxed into giving these works a try. With the advent of the Harry Potter series, this trend has changed dramatically. Children are clamoring for books in the magical genre, to keep them sated until the next Harry book appears. The Harry Potter phenomenon is remarkable in its scope. Many children who were formerly nonreaders or reluctant readers are falling in love with words and story. Parents constantly report that their children seek out reading and books, and that the Harry books hold their attention and make them hungry to read more. Boys and girls find magical tales with the male and female protagonists engaging, exciting, and thought provoking.

Literacy Activities for Exploring and Understanding Values in Literature and Mass Media

Many literature response and language activities may be used to teach and learn values. Following are a few ideas.

Cinderella Stories: Comparing Fairy Tales From Around the World

Cinderella is one of the most universal fairy tales. Most plots follow the traditional monomyth format, employ certain archetypes (such as helpers and wise women or men), and contain common motifs (secrecy, city versus country). However, they vary widely in symbolism (e.g., the talismans vary; Cinderella's shoes may be made of diverse materials). Cinderella protagonists are mainly women (with a few exceptions, like the Irish Cinderlad), although their traits vary widely. Because heroes and heroines reflect cultural values, comparative analysis of plot, motifs, and characters in Cinderella stories offers insights into cultural values, particularly social norms for good acts and desirable gender roles.

In whole-group, small-group, or individual read-alouds, ask students to read versions of Cinderella or other fairy tales from diverse cultures throughout the world. Then, using graphic organizers, they can identify and compare characters, conflicts, plot development, rewards, motifs, and themes. Next, through whole- or small-group discussion, students should first identify and then compare and evaluate the values conveyed in these texts.

Comparing Mass Media and Print Texts

Engaging in comparative analyses of heroic values, characters, plots, motifs, decisions/conflicts/rewards, and themes in print and/or mass media texts promotes comprehension, critical viewing, motivation, home-school connections, discussion, and writing skills. Select print versions of Cinderella or other myths and fairy tales, and pair them with films such as *Star Wars*, *The Little Mermaid*, *Aladdin*, *Cinderella*, *Rocky*, or *Beauty and the Beast*.

Activate students' schema and prior knowledge of literary elements by first brainstorming traits that films and fairy tales share. List these on a poster or the blackboard. Read the text and watch the film. Ask students to add to lists individually or in small groups. Then ask students to complete a Venn diagram identifying which aspects are the same and which are different. In particular, ask questions that focus on value messages:

Why do heroes or heroines and evil antagonists look and act the ways they do?

What values do their appearances and actions represent?

What symbols do the films and books share? What symbols are different? What values and messages do these symbols represent?

What conflicts, trials, and tasks do the heroes face? What decisions do they make? Are these the right decisions and actions? What are some alternatives? (This is a great discussion or journal topic.)

Understanding Decision Making

After reading a single story or watching a film, this activity helps students develop comprehension of narrative structures. It also helps them understand how conflict and decision making in stories reflect values. Teachers may model then guide students to map sequences. Use Freytag's triangle (a simple diagram that outlines setting, conflict, and development, or rising action, climax, and resolution), story frames, storyboards, story murals, or reading road maps to diagram plot. (Students may also make board games.)

Discuss the hero's or heroine's conflicts, decisions they make, and what values these plot developments reflect. Identify plot options that embody more positive values. For example, Cinderella might decide to take control of her life instead of being passive. She could take her domestic problems to arbitration or stay past midnight so that the prince will see her and love her as she really is.

In groups or individually, have students rewrite the story so that the heroes make decisions that reflect desirable values. These may be shared through author's chair or compiled into a class book.

Write a Fairy Tale From Another Point of View

The messages and values texts convey are dependent, in part, on the point of view from which they are told. Ask students to retell a well-known tale from another character's point of view. *Cinderella's Rat* (Meddaugh, 1997) or *The True Story of the Three Little Pigs* (Scieszka, 1996) are excellent models.

Directed Reading Think-Aloud or Read-Aloud

Read aloud a text, asking the class prediction, comprehension, and values-related questions. Combine with Freytag's triangle, story frames, storyboards, story murals, or reading road maps to increase comprehension.

Rewriting

In groups or individually, ask students to identify textual elements and values in a tale. Next, have them rewrite the story, changing setting, genre, dialogue, plot, and/or characters to reflect different values.

Letters to Heroes

Heroes appear in our everyday lives. The single parent, the teacher, the friend who diffuses a schoolyard fight, the community mentor who takes time to listen to a child, and the volunteer all display desirable values. Students also are heroes in their daily lives, although few recognize these traits. The student who takes care of a sibling, who performs an act of kindness for a neighbor, or who helps a peer in class is demonstrating heroic traits and desirable values. Ask students to write (and send) a letter to themselves, family members, classmates, friends, or community members about why they are a hero.

Analysis of Visual Elements in Books

As a class, teachers and students should select two or more Cinderella or magical tales and compare covers, colors, styles, points of view, content, and the fit of illustrations with text. Decode messages. What do the images convey about how heroes and heroines should look, act, or feel? Do the students agree? After the analysis of text(s), have students create new book jackets, advertisements, movie posters, videos, or illustrations.

Who Are Our Heroes?

When asked, students will generally identify athletes, mass media personalities, rock stars, and cartoon or popular culture characters as heroes. Through oral discussion or written description, ask students to complete the following steps:

1. Identify what these heroes say and do.
2. Identify their common traits. (Most will be rich, consumer based, and famous because of athletic prowess or media exposure; some may be violent.)
3. Identify strengths and weaknesses of their traits and values by providing real-life scenarios (e.g., Would you want a Power Ranger as a friend in the following situations? Why or why not? Would they visit you in the hospital if you were sick or injured? Would they make time for you if you just wanted to talk? How would they solve a disagreement? Are their behaviors the kinds you would like to emulate?)
4. Identify other heroes from readings and real life who are more balanced or embody positive values. Research them, write them a letter, or e-mail and share your findings.

Sight Poems or Biopoems

Ask students to choose a value such as respect or kindness that reflects the traits of a hero or heroine they have just read about or viewed. Based on this value, students can create sight poems or biopoems. Sight poems may use the letters of a value such as "respect" to begin each line or form a shape, such as a heart. Biopoems use specific elements in an order (e.g., three descriptive phrases followed by four adverbs).

Critical Reading of Values in Advertisements and Commercials

Help students analyze a print- or Web-based advertisement or a televised commercial. What characters, motifs, symbols, products, effects, and persuasive devices are used? What values do these elements represent? What messages are they sending? Who is pictured as a role model? Who is excluded? Who is being targeted as an audience? What are the creators *really* selling? After analysis, ask students to create a new video, slogan, print advertisement, collage, video, drawing, or script using heroes (local or national) who reflect positive values.

Changing Genres

Ask students to rewrite a traditional fairy tale as a screenplay, sitcom, or drama. Stress plot development and dialogue. Alternately, they can create a news report based on who, what, when, where, why, and how. Encourage students to use contemporary motifs, problems, and character descriptions to explore and represent positive values. Students can also create videos of heroes and heroic acts in their own lives.

Group Stories

Using basic story grammar elements (setting, introduction of conflict, development, conclusion), students can create round robin fairy tales that teach positive values. Each student writes a first paragraph and then switches texts with others, adding new paragraphs until the stories are almost complete. The original authors should conclude their stories. The students may read the stories in author's chair or publish them online. Students of all ages love this activity. (For more detailed procedures see Pailliotet, 1998.)

Student-Generated Advertisements or Book Covers for Cinderella Versions

Students summarize and critique values in variations of the story by creating a slogan, advertisement, illustration, and summary.

Journal Activities

After reading a text, students recall and write about similar conflicts in their own lives. Then they write or discuss how their values affect decision making in their lives.

Alternately, students may wish to write about a decision they made recently. They should consider the following questions: How might the heroine or hero from the reading respond? How did you respond? How might you respond now? Which is a better decision? Why?

A Great Sponge Activity

Sponges are short teaching activities. Have a folder of current advertisements or a video of commercials on hand. Make sure they contain a Cinderella-type transformation motif, showing how the characters are transformed by acquiring products such as beer, cars, or medications. Ask students to view the advertisements and answer the following questions: What transforms the character? What is his or her reward? What values does this convey? Do we agree with these values? Why or why not? This activity promotes critical viewing skills.

Movie or Book Reviews

Ask students to write and perform or present a critique of one or more Cinderella stories or other fairy tales. In addition to textual qualities, they should identify and evaluate explicit and implicit values in the story, arguing for or against the relevance of these values in their own lives and contemporary society. Students may choose to work in an oral, print, graphic, Web-based, or video format.

Dear Abby Letters

For this activity, students may choose to identify the main character's problem or decision, and then exchange letters with a peer who writes advice. A second option is for students to write directly to a character, giving advice. Students should identify values and critique them, offering alternatives as necessary.

Puppet Show, Dramatic Readings, or Presentation

Students can write dialogue and present their own contemporary versions of Cinderella or other tales. The audience members must identify values conveyed in the presentation and discuss if they agree with them.

Oral/Cultural History

For this activity, students ask parents, relatives, or community members to tell them versions of Cinderella or other fairy tales. They may also research variants on the Internet or in collections that reflect their cultural backgrounds. Students then hold a storytelling day for peers or younger classmates in which they retell stories and describe how they convey cultural values. This activity may be used as part of a social studies unit, language arts unit, or multicultural celebration day.

Ongoing Studies of the Values Conveyed Through Motifs, Symbols, and Imagery in Mass Media and Print Texts

Motifs, symbols, and imagery, as explained earlier, represent aspects of cultural values. Students may examine a certain motif, symbol, or image across texts, then use it to represent their own values.

Students may create posters with items, interpretations, and examples of the values they find, or an electronic or print class reference book. Common motifs to examine include archetypal characters (heroes/heroines; fairy godmothers/benevolent crone/wise old man; wicked witches/wicked stepmothers; shadows/evil) or plots (the monomyth or hero's quest). Motifs often convey values through juxtapositions or contrasts between good/evil, innocence/corruption or experience, images of light/darkness, city/countryside, nature/technology, water/fire, and moon/sun. Other common motifs include magic, other worlds, heroism, trickery, wishes, disguises, and transformations. Symbols such as colors, shapes, objects, and numbers (particularly 3, 4, and 7) are common to many texts and are used to create motifs.

Rock 'n' Roll Songs

Ask students to look for fairy tale motifs in rock music. What values are conveyed? Students can compare the songs they discover with related poems or short stories that have similar conflicts, imagery, themes, or values. As always, teachers should preview all texts and consider their age appropriateness.

Linking Fairy Tales to Biography

Tales of historic figures reflect many aspects of the monomyth. Our historical heroes, like literary ones, also embody cultural values. For this activity, students research a historic figure and then write, act, dramatically present, or represent their findings through a narrative tale. Most students enjoy this alternative to the usual report.

Collaborative Group Books of Fairy Tales

Compile a book of tales from each student's culture as told by a family member. These may be written and illustrated with a theme or value (e.g., courage, respect) by children and their families.

Seeing Our Heroes and Celebrating Their Values

For this activity, students create bulletin boards, posters, personal journals, computer files, or Web pages with images and written accounts of heroes and heroines they encounter in and out of the classroom. Students should add to displays as they encounter people, in course content, mass media, and their own lives, who embody desirable values. These may be organized under themes such as bravery, persistence, compassion, and intelligence.

Conclusion

Bettelheim (1989) asserts that all children have need for magic and fairy tales because they "answer the eternal questions: What is the world really like? How am I to live my life in it? How can I truly be myself?" (p. 45). We hope that this chapter and the following lists and annotations of magical tales will help children, teachers, and parents explore the answers to these and other questions.

References

Bettelheim, B. (1989). *The uses of enchantment: The meaning and importance of fairy tales*. New York: Vintage Books.

Campbell, J. (1968). *The hero with a thousand faces*. Princeton, NJ: Princeton University Press.

Campbell, J. (1990). *Transformations of myth through time*. New York: Harper & Row.

Dundes, A. (Ed.). (1989). *Cinderella: A casebook*. New York: Wildman Press.

Dyson, A.H. (1997). *Writing superheroes: Contemporary childhood, popular culture, and classroom literacy*. New York: Teachers College Press.

Norton, D.E., & Norton, S.E. (1999). *Through the eyes of a child: An introduction to children's literature* (5th ed.). Upper Saddle River, NJ: Prentice Hall.

O'Brien, P. (1995). If the shoe fits: The many appearances of Cinderella. *Challenge, 13*(4), 12–19.

Pailliotet, A.W. (1998). Reading and writing across the media: Using varied educational technology for literacy learning. In R.M. Branch & M.A. Fitzgerald (Eds.), *Educational media and technology yearbook* (23rd ed., pp. 76–93). Boulder, CO: Libraries Unlimited.

Worthy, M.J., & Bloodgood, J.W. (1992). Enhancing reading instruction through Cinderella tales. *The Reading Teacher, 46*, 290–307.

Yolen, J. (1977). America's Cinderella. *Children's Literature in Education, 8*(1), 290+.

Zipes, J.D. (1997). *Happily ever after: Fairy tales, children, and the culture industry*. New York: Routledge.

Children's Literature Cited

Buehner, C. (1996). *Fanny's dream*. Ill. M. Buehner. New York: Dial.

Haddix, M.P. (1999). *Just Ella*. New York: Simon & Schuster.

Levine, G.C. (1998). *Ella enchanted*. New York: Harper Trophy.

Meddaugh, S. (1997). *Cinderella's rat*. Boston: Houghton Mifflin.

Munsch, R.N. (1988). *The paper bag princess*. Ill. M. Martchenko. Toronto: Annick.

Scieszka, J. (1994). *The frog prince continued*. Ill. S. Johnson. New York: Puffin.

Scieszka, J. (1996). *The true story of the three little pigs! By A. Wolf*. Ill. L. Smith. New York: Puffin.

Steptoe, J. (1987). *Mufaro's beautiful daughters: An African tale*. New York: Lothrop, Lee & Shepard.

Annotated Bibliographies

Cinderella Variations

Adoff, A. (1997). *Love letters*. Ill. L. Desimini. New York: Blue Sky Press.
 In the letter format poem "Dear Prince" (pages 23–24), a young girl informs the prince that she is in no need of rescue but looks forward to him riding his blue bike down her street on

Saturday. She states that they can chase dragons together and signs the letter, "Your Potential Princess." This text stresses camaraderie and equality over passivity and rescue.

Auch, M.J. (1989). *Glass slippers give you blisters*. New York: Scholastic.

Kelly MacDonald is a sixth grader who cajoles her three best friends into auditioning for her school's production of *Cinderella*. Kelly performs poorly in her audition and the friends earn important roles. Sorely disappointed, Kelly seeks comfort from her grandmother, who encourages her to look beyond the showy front stage notoriety and participate in other ways, because not everyone can be Cinderella. Through designing sets and receiving lessons from a lighting technician, Kelly learns that her innate creativity and sense of aesthetics are valuable assets, adding just as significantly as a starring role. This book provides an interesting look at intergenerational relationships, family politics, and developing one's natural talents.

Buehner, C. (1996). *Fanny's dream*. Ill. M. Buehner. New York: Dial.

Fanny is determined to leave her life of toil. On the night of a mayor's ball, she sits on a hillside and waits for expected magical intervention. Fanny's vigil is interrupted by the kind and well-mannered Heber, who offers to wait with her. Morning comes with no sign of a fairy, but Fanny accepts Heber's proposal of marriage. The two make a good life together. Late one night, as Fanny goes out to finish chores, the tardy sprite appears and says, "You poor dear, having to wait all these years, there is still time! There is a visiting colonel at the mayor's ball tonight. Just leave everything to me!" Incredulous, Fanny turns down the offer and goes inside to report to Heber, who is reading to the children. Heber laughs at the tale and teases Fanny, saying, "Oh sure! And I am the Prince of Sahiba." Fanny winks and responds with, "Close enough." Values here include making your own happiness, self-reliance, common sense, pragmatism, and contentment.

Coville, B. (1992). *Jennifer Murdley's toad*. Ill. G.A. Lippincott. Orlando, FL: Harcourt Brace.

Jennifer is a "beauty victim" according to her father. She is obese, unpopular, and desperate to be attractive. With the intervention of a magical toad named "Buffo" from Mr. Elives's Magic Shop, Jennifer and those around her become entwined in a magical adventure. At one point, Jennifer must choose between betraying her friends or receiving what it is she desires most in life, to be "impossibly beautiful." This well-written tale examines the true nature of beauty and the role of media. Resourcefulness, integrity, inner beauty, and wit are prized over the traditional Cinderella passivity. Additional titles by Bruce Coville include *The Dragonslayers, Jeremy Thatcher, Dragon Hatcher,* and *The Skull of Truth*.

Edwards, P.D. (1999). *Dinorella: A prehistoric fairytale*. Ill. H. Cole. New York: Hyperion.

Illustrations and alliteration are charming aspects of this retelling. The dainty and dependable Dinorella is the drudge of her wicked stepfamily until her darling Fairydactyl intervenes and sends her, Sandra D. style, to Duke Dudley's Den. As it turns out, Dinorella arrives just in time to save the life of the Duke himself with some timely dirtballs and her dangling diamonds. The rest of the story unfolds, as one would expect, with plenty of clever *d* words dotting the text.

Haddix, M.P. (1999). *Just Ella*. New York: Simon & Schuster.

Princess Cynthiana Eleanora or "Ella" has spent the past 2 months living in a dream. After the "step-evils" attempt to forbid her from going to the royal ball, Ella devises a way to charm the one and only Prince Charming. As in the traditional tale, Ella loses a glass slipper, only to be packed off by the royal entourage and whisked away to the castle, where a proper spin is given to her story—complete with fairy godmother. It does not take long for Ella to see through the social and political veneer of castle life. Prince Charming is vapid and values only Ella's physical beauty. The Charming clan do not take it well when Ella decides to decline the prince's offer of marriage. Through wit, thoughtful reflection, and resourcefulness, Ella manages to escape and works toward building a satisfying, if not "happily ever after," existence for herself.

Johnston, T. (1998). *Bigfoot Cinderrrrrella*. Ill. J. Warhola. New York: Putnam.

Tall and dark as a Douglas Fir, with feet like cedar stumps, the dashing but shy Bigfoot prince is advised to throw a ball/log rolling competition to determine whom he should marry. Enter Rrrrrellla, the oddball stepdaughter who is giant, as yellow as a banana slug, hates grooming, and is the domestic servant of the family. Despite the efforts of her stepsisters and stepmother to prevent her from attending the log rolling contest, Rrrrrella's kindness to a hungry Grizzly bear is her ticket to the meeting with her "beary-godfather." With a mammoth new pair of bark clogs on her feet and her hair freshly matted, Rrrrrella runs off to steal the heart of the prince by knocking him off his log. She narrowly escapes before the magic loses effect and leaves her telltale clog behind. The prince's "Stinking Beauty" reveals herself the following day, much to the chagrin of her family, and the couple lives happily ever after deep within the old growth forest. Values here are kindness to strangers, individuality, and appreciation for difference.

Ketteman, H. (1997). *Bubba the cowboy prince: A fractured Texas tale*. Ill. J. Warhola. New York: Scholastic.

With a little help from his fairy godcow, good-hearted Bubba is given a chance to attend a ball and win the heart of Miz Lurleen, the "purtiest" and richest rancher in the county, who is aiming to find herself a feller. She finds Bubba "as cute as a cow's ear" and does not flinch when, after midnight, Bubba's trademark stench and cowboy rags are exposed. With its "good guy" male protagonist, this fun new twist on the classic Cinderella tale is sure to get a laugh from readers of all ages.

Levine, G.C. (1998). *Ella enchanted*. New York: Harper Trophy.

Ella has been given the "gift" of obedience at birth by her well-meaning fairy godmother. This is not a problem for Ella until after the arrival of the classic evil stepmother and stepsisters. Ella's unwilling obedience affords great delight to the three women until she masters her curse and defeats the magic. Complete with a "Prince Char" and glass footwear, this popular retelling of Cinderella is full of neotraditional plot twists and subtle fairy tale humor. Ella's own strengths and innate character qualities help her overcome magic to seek her own version of "happily ever after."

Meddaugh, S. (1997). *Cinderella's rat*. Boston: Houghton Mifflin.

In this fractured fairy tale, Meddaugh explores new sides of the Cinderella tale from a rat's perspective. "I was born a rat. I expected to be a rat all my days. But life is full of surprises." The main character and his sister Ruth are transformed into coachmen by Cinderella's fairy godmother only to have additional magical encounters of their own. In this story, the Cinderella motif is an amusing plot device for the telling of the rat's tale, which shows that sometimes magic backfires.

Munsch, R.N. (1988). *The paper bag princess*. Ill. M. Martchenko. Toronto: Annick.

This tale begins, "Elizabeth was a beautiful princess. She lived in a castle and had expensive princess clothes. She was going to marry a prince named Ronald." Prince Ronald is then carried away by a destructive dragon. Wearing only a paper bag, Elizabeth goes off to rescue her true love. Using great cleverness, she outwits the dragon and is told by the ungrateful prince, whom she has saved, to come back when she is dressed like a real princess. Our liberated heroine, who embodies self-determination, smartly responds, "You look like a real prince, but you are a bum." The tale is concluded with the line, "They didn't get married after all."

Perlman, J. (1995). *Cinderella penguin: Or, the little glass flipper*. New York: Puffin.

In this retelling of Cinderella, the penguin heroine bears up bravely under the cruel treatment of her step-penguin family. With some help from her Great Fairy Penguin, she steals the heart of the prince and all goes as prescribed by the tale. Cinderella ends up having her foot slammed in the cellar trapdoor to prevent her from trying on the glass flipper, only to have the greedy step-penguins send the glass footwear sailing onto the entrapped appendage. Good triumphs in this retelling, which is a pleasant addition to a Cinderella unit or a penguin theme.

Sanderson, R. (1995). *Papa Gatto: An Italian fairy tale*. Boston: Little, Brown.

Papa Gatto seeks a caretaker for his eight lively kittens and promises rich rewards for the service. When the kind and hard-working Beatrice asks her stepmother for permission to go, she is forbidden and the beautiful but wicked stepsister Sophia is sent in her place. Papa Gatto, deceived by Sophia's appearance, reaps disastrous results. Beatrice takes the job to make up for her sister's carelessness, and neither the kittens nor Beatrice have ever been so happy. Papa Gatto tells the prince of this charming young lady whose beauty shines from within and sets up a meeting. Sophia nearly succeeds in stealing Beatrice's place, only to have her ruse exposed by the romping kittens. This tale is especially interesting because Beatrice will not accept the prince's hand in marriage until she knows that he is kind and generous and grows to love him. "I would not exchange one joyless home for another," she says, and returns to her job with the kittens. The rich illustrations make this story an especially enjoyable read-aloud.

Steptoe, J. (1987). *Mufaro's beautiful daughters: An African tale*. New York: Lothrop, Lee & Shepard.

In the Zimbabwe version of Cinderella, King Mufaro is a happy man blessed with two lovely daughters. Nyasha is both kind and lovely, while Manyara is beautiful but selfish. When the two daughters are asked to meet a neighboring enchanter king, Manyara seeks to outwit her sister but fails the magical tests set before her. True to her nature, Nyasha takes the tests as opportunities to be generous and reaps the reward. The lush illustrations and excellent storytelling make this book a perennial favorite.

Wrede, P.C. (1990). *Dealing with dragons*. San Diego, CA: Harcourt Brace.

The strong-willed Princess Cimorene despises her tedious life as a "proper" princess. Following the announcement of her upcoming marriage to a neighboring prince, Cimorene runs away and seeks a dragon to capture her. Kazul, king of the dragons, is only too delighted to accept this improper princess, and the two of them form a powerful partnership that serves to stymie a plot by wizards to overthrow the dragons. This clever and well-written tale features an excellent protagonist with brains, spunk, and humor, and turns the role of "proper" princess on its ear.

(Some of the Many) Other Variations of Cinderella

Climo, S. (1989). *The Egyptian Cinderella*. Ill. R. Heller. New York: Thomas Y. Crowell.

Climo, S. (1993). *The Korean Cinderella*. Ill. R. Heller. New York: HarperCollins.

Climo, S. (1996). *The Irish Cinderlad*. Ill. L. Krupinski. New York: HarperCollins. (Male protagonist)

Climo, S. (1999). *The Persian Cinderella*. Ill. R. Florczak. New York: HarperCollins.

Coburn, J.R. (1998). *Angkat: The Cambodian Cinderella*. Ill. E. Flotte. Arcadia, CA: Shen's Books.

Coburn, J.R, with Lee, T.C. (1996). *Jouanah: A Hmong Cinderella.* Ill. A.S. O'Brien. Arcadia, CA: Shen's Books.

Cole, B. (1997). *Prince Cinders.* New York: Putnam. (Humorous contemporary male version)

Collins, S.H. (1998). *Cendrillon: A Cajun Cinderella.* Ill. P. Soper. Gretna, LA: Pelican.

de la Paz, M.J. (2001). *Abadeha: The Philippine Cinderella.* Ill. Y. Tang. Arcadia, CA: Shen's Books.

Goode, D. (2000). *Cinderella: The dog and her little glass slipper.* New York: Blue Sky Press. (Traditional European variant)

Graham, G.B. (Ed.). (1984). The jeweled slipper. In *The beggar in the blanket* (pp. 45–55). New York: Dial. (Vietnamese)

Granowsky, A. (1994). *Cinderella/That awful Cinderella.* Ill. B. Kiwak & R. Childress. Austin TX: Raintree. (In flip book fashion, offers two points of view about the Cinderella story)

Greaves, M. (2000). *Tattercoats.* Ill. M. Chamberlain. New York: Frances Lincoln. (European)

Hickox, R. (1999). *The golden sandal: A Middle Eastern Cinderella story.* Ill. W. Hillenbrand. New York: Holiday House. (Middle Eastern)

Hooks, W. (1990). *Moss gown.* Ill. D. Carrick. New York: Clarion. (Southern United States)

Huck, C. (1994). *Princess Furball.* Ill. A. Lobel. New York: Mulberry. (European)

Jackson, E. (1994). *Cinder Edna.* Ill. K. O'Malley. New York: Lothrop, Lee & Shepard. (Contemporary)

Jaffe, N. (1998). *The way meat loves salt: A Cinderella tale from the Jewish tradition.* Ill. L. August. New York: Henry Holt.

Louie, A. (1996). *Yeh-Shen: A Cinderella story from China.* Ill. E. Young. New York: Paper Star.

Martin, R. (1998). *The rough-face girl.* Ill. D. Shannon. New York: Paper Star. (Algonquin Indian)

Mayer, M. (1994). *Baba Yaga and Vasilisa the Brave.* Ill. K.Y. Craft. New York: Morrow. (Russian)

Melmed, L.K. (1994). *Prince Nautilus.* Ill. H. Sorensen. New York: Lothrop, Lee & Shepard. (Contemporary variant—heroine rewarded for bravery and resourcefulness)

Meyers, B. (1995). *Sidney Rella and the glass sneaker.* Boston: Houghton Mifflin.

Minters, F. (1994). *Cinder-Elly.* Ill. G.B. Karas. New York: Viking. (Contemporary rap version)

Perrault, C. (2000). *Cinderella: A creative tale from the collection Once Upon a Time.* Ill. R. Innocenti. New York: Creative Editions. (French)

Phelps, E.J. (Ed.). (1989). The black bull of Norroway. In *Tatterhood and other tales* (pp. 49–54). Ill. P.B. Ford. New York: Feminist Press. (Feminist; English with Norse influences)

Phumla. (1990). *Nomi and the magic fish.* Garden City, NY: Doubleday. (African-Zulu)

Pollock, P. (1996). *The turkey girl: A Zuni Cinderella.* Ill. E. Young. New York: Little, Brown.

San Souci, R.D. (1997). *Sootface: An Ojibwa Cinderella story.* Ill. D. San Souci. New York: Bantam.

San Souci, R.D. (1998). *Cendrillon: A Caribbean Cinderella.* Ill. B. Pinkney. New York: Simon & Schuster.

Schroeder, A. (1997). *Lily and the wooden bowl.* Ill. Y. Ito. New York: Bantam Doubleday Dell. (Japan)

Shorto, R. (1992). *Cinderella/The untold story of Cinderella.* Ill. T. Lewis. Secaucus, NJ: Carol Publishing Group. (Story presented from two points of view—Cinderella's and the stepsisters')

Sierra, J. (1992). *Cinderella* (Oryx Multicultural Folktale series). Ill. J. Caroselli. New York: Oryx.

Wegman, W. (1999). *Cinderella.* New York: Hyperion. (Traditional version told with dog characters)

Zipes, J. (Trans.). (1992). Cinderella. In *The complete fairy tales of the Brothers Grimm* (pp. 86–92). Ill. J.B. Gruelle. New York: Bantam. (German)

More Magical Tales

Ayres, B.H. (1992). *Matreshka*. Ill. A. Natchev. Garden City, NY: Doubleday.
Kata's kindness to a strange old woman earns her a carved and painted wooden doll that turns out to be magical. With the assistance of her small companions, Kata is able to escape from the legendary Baba Yaga, who wishes to eat her up! Kata and the Matreshka sisters are clever and daring. Children love to hear this exciting story, which is based on Russian folklore.

Banks, L.R. (1989). *The Fairy Rebel*. New York: Morrow.
Bindi is a magical baby who was borne of a wish by her mother and the indulgence of a sweet fairy named Tiki. Bindi receives a magical rose present every year from her true fairy godmother, but on Bindi's eighth birthday, the long-awaited present does not appear. A day of searching produces a dead but glowing rose that has grown from the dark holly bush in the garden. Bindi discovers too late that this is no beneficent gift but a wicked token of revenge from the evil fairy queen. The queen wishes to punish them all for Tiki's interference, but the family faces the powerful queen with bravery and a special brand of magic possessed only by Bindi.

Dahl, R. (1998). *Matilda*. Ill. Q. Blake. New York: Penguin.
The Wormwoods consider their youngest daughter a "scab" they hope to pick off and flick away as soon as possible. It is not until Matilda meets Mrs. Phelps, the city librarian, and Miss Honey, her kindergarten teacher, that her true brilliance is noticed. Living conditions at home are unbearable and school is a frightening place due to the loathsome headmistress, the Trunchbull. Matilda sharpens her keen wit and mental powers to bring about magical changes that improve life drastically for her peers, her beloved kindergarten teacher, and herself. Matilda is a learner whose spunk, cleverness, creativity, and optimism are a delight to read. This was also made into a popular children's film that is not a faithful representation of the book.

Farmer, N. (1994). *The ear, the eye and the arm*. New York: Orchard.
Rita, Kuda, and Tendai are the overprotected children of a futuristic African military dictator. Kidnapped by a series of groups, the children are exposed to extreme facets of the society in which they had lived and had never known. The element of deep magic and learned self-reliance is why this 1995 Newbery Honor Book stands out as a tale worthy of mention. Pair this with Nancy Farmer's *A Girl Named Disaster* for well-drawn, strong protagonists and a self-discovery tale couched in grand, sophisticated, and mystical adventure.

Fletcher, S. (1996). *Dragon's milk*. New York: Aladdin.
Kaeldra is an outcast in her own society. Her physical features, her uncanny ability to sense the presence of dragons, and her understandings of dragon language set her apart from others. In what begins as a quest to save the life of her sister by bringing her milk from a lactating dragon, Kaeldra embarks on a three-book adventure series blending excellent fantasy with dragon lore and adventure. Dominant values include bravery, selflessness, empathy, and courage. Other titles include *Flight of the Dragon Kyn* and *Sign of the Dove*.

Fletcher, S. (1999). *Shadow Spinner*. New York: Aladdin.
Marjan is a cripple who loves to listen to and tell stories. Marjan finds an unusual niche when she visits the harem of the much-feared Sultan. She is invited to live there and aid the heroine Shahrazad, who is responsible for saving the lives of countless young women with her storytelling. As long as Shahrazad can keep the sultan entertained, he will not seek a new

wife and murder the bride at sunrise. The tale is full of dark intrigue, danger, fascinating old tales, and details of harem life. Marjan's keen sense of observation about human nature and her bravery, loyalty, and subsequent self-discovery make a refreshingly different read.

Klause, A.C. (1995). *Alien secrets*. New York: Dell Yearling.

Robin Goodfellow, or Puck, is expelled from school and is being sent to Aurora, where her parents are working as planetary anthropologists. Puck, who is kind, strong, and brave, is thrilled with the prospect of space travel, but her insatiable curiosity leads her to an off limits/restricted area of the ship where she witnesses a vicious knife fight. Puck does not report the crime because the attacker, a fellow passenger on the voyage, is now keeping tabs on her. The story becomes rich when Puck befriends the woeful alien Hush and seeks to help him recover a prized possession. Hush is also dealing with the irony that the very ship they are on was a slave ship in the recent past and holds the tortured ghosts of his people. An exciting and dangerous mystery ensues with Puck at the center. This is an excellent introduction to the science fiction genre, with well-drawn characters and plot.

L'Engle, M. (1973). *A wrinkle in time*. New York: Dell Yearling.

The impetuous and strong-willed Meg (along with her best friend, Calvin, and enigmatic brother, Charles Wallace) is sent across the universe and time to rescue Meg's father with the help of three universal/mysterious beings. In this mystical journey, Meg must face ideas and forces in order to rescue what she loves most. A story of personal strength, integrity, and conquering the overwhelming powers of evil. A Newbery Award Book, this tale is a strange but compelling mix of metaphysics, religion, and the great power of hope, faith, love, and humility.

Lewis, C.S. (1994). *The magician's nephew*. New York: HarperCollins.

Polly and Digory set out to explore the attic passageways of the huge row houses in which they live, only to stumble into the lair of Digory's strange and frightening Uncle Andrew. The two are lured into magical worlds where they witness the birth of Narnia and unwittingly introduce evil to the land. Throughout the adventure, the two friends must struggle with issues of basic kindness, selflessness, and goodness in spite of the temptations offered them. Digory especially finds that high moral character is a valuable commodity when dealing with magic. Considered a prequel to the well-loved Chronicles of Narnia, this is the sixth book in the series.

McKinley, R. (1983). *The blue sword*. New York: Morrow.

Following the death of her father, Harry is sent to her brother in a strange outpost bordering on the Damarian Kingdom. She finds the life of being a lady tedious and longs to explore the mysterious hills where there is still said to be magic. When the King of the Hillfolk comes to ask for aid from the Outlanders in a fight against the demonic northern forces, Harry finds herself in a most unusual situation. The enigmatic king kidnaps her by walking through her wall and whisks her off to a land and a destiny she would never have believed if someone had told her of it. Harry finds that her headstrong ways and strong constitution serve her well in the desert, where a magical and nomadic horse culture dwells. She quickly learns to love her new life, but it is her uncanny skill with the legendary Blue Sword that surprises her and is the embodiment of a prophecy. Harry is a powerful female protagonist with a resolution that will have readers cheering. Courage and accepting the mantle of social responsibility are key values here.

McKinley, R. (1993). *Beauty: A retelling of the story of Beauty and the Beast*. New York: Harper Trophy.

Beauty is the intellectual, dowdy, youngest child of a merchant whose great wealth is lost. The now destitute family moves from their opulent life in the city to a remote and mysterious forest region. Rumors of recovered wealth lure Beauty's father to the city, and he is saved on his journey home by the hospitality of a magical host. The old man angers the host by plucking a rose from the garden for his youngest daughter. In order to save her father's life, Beauty volunteers to live with the beast. Magic and mystery abound in this fleshed out retelling, in which Beauty's personal integrity, courage, intellect, and humbleness earn her and those she loves a satisfying conclusion to a two-century curse.

Nesbit, E. (1996). *Five children and It*. New York: Puffin.

This wonderful story, written more than 100 years ago, is as delightful now as then. Robert, Anthea, Jane, Cyril, and "Baby" are glorying in the freedom they have by exploring the area around their seaside summer home. While digging a hole in the vast sand pits over-looking the sea, they discover an ancient *psammead*, or sand fairy. The sand fairy has tele-scopic snail's eyes, bat ears, a spider's tubby body, and thick, soft fur, while its arms and legs resemble a monkey's. The best thing of all about this creature is that it is capable of grant-ing wishes. Grand summer adventures ensue, and the children quickly realize that magic is unpredictable and the phrase "Be careful what you wish for" bears heeding. *The Story of the Amulet* is another tale featuring the children and the psammead in which they time travel, searching for an elusive and powerfully magical amulet.

Nix, G. (1997). *Sabriel*. New York: Harper Trophy.

Death and what comes after death are no mystery to Sabriel and her father the Abhorsen, both necromancers who can soothe angry or lamenting spirits. Sabriel's father has either been killed or is being held against his will in the world of the dead. It is up to Sabriel to travel to the Old Kingdom that is ruled by ancient Charter and Free Magic and seek her fa-ther. Sabriel and her companion, Touchstone, are left to defend their worlds against great evil. It is a highly dangerous journey that she must undertake with only partial training and the tools her father managed to send her via a ghoulish messenger. This is a highly exciting tale of magic, hope, strength of character, trust, and discovery of innate talent.

Pullman, P. (2001). *The golden compass*. New York: Dell Yearling.

Lyra is a child who has known only the walls of Jordan College and Oxford. Surrounded by distracted scholars and given complete freedom to roam as she wishes, Lyra stumbles into an epic political and theological battle in which she unwittingly will play a great role. Aided by her daemon, Pantalaimon, and an ancient tool called an *alehiometer*, Lyra finds herself in a life-and-death struggle involving mysterious Dust. She must attempt to save the lives of innocent children who are being sacrificed and discern what is honorable in the face of great pain, loss, deception, and evil. Mysteries abound in this fast-paced novel. The sequels, *The Subtle Knife* and *The Amber Spyglass*, continue the tale, with new companions and further sinister plots.

Quindlen, A. (1997). *Happily ever after*. Ill. J. Stevenson. New York: Viking.

Kate is a typical tomboy but has a penchant for fairy tales. One night she sighs, "I would re-ally like to try being a princess sometime." With a bit of magical intervention, Kate discov-ers she does not enjoy the life of a princess. Dangers abound in Kate's fairy tale existence but she finds she is safer without the help of her knight in shining armor—whom she must save repeatedly. During her stay at the castle, Kate takes on traditional courtly life by teach-ing all the women of the castle to love baseball. A happy ending of sorts happens when Kate is safely back home and her team wins the county baseball championship.

Rowling, J.K. (1999). *Harry Potter and the Sorcerer's Stone*. New York: Scholastic.

Following the double murder of his parents, infant Harry is left to the care of his horrendously indifferent nonmagic or *muggle* relatives, the Dursleys. At the age of 11, Harry discovers he is a natural born wizard and is invited to attend Hogwarts School of Witchcraft and Wizardry. Once at the school, there is an entire magical world to discover, complete with an aerial sport called Quidditch, magical beings, and enchanted buildings, objects, and classes. Harry meets a vast array of characters, including his best friends, Hermione and Ron, and his arch rival, Draco Malfoy—all of whom play roles in uncovering a great mystery behind the legendary philosopher's stone, which is capable of providing as much money and life as one wishes. Little does Harry know that a great destiny awaits him. With the support of his friends, Harry must keep the stone safe from evil hands and bravely face the most evil wizard of all times. Harry embodies caring for others, resourcefulness, and self-discovery. Magic, adventure, intrigue, wry humor, and varied vocabulary make this tale a must read for many children, along with subsequent books in the series.

Conclusion

Unraveling the Curriculum of Global Values

Ladislaus M. Semali

With recent school shootings in Colorado, Georgia, Arkansas, and Kentucky, family values and parental accountability are once again popular topics with politicians and talk show hosts. Politicians and pundits ponder: How could this happen in the United States at a time of economic boom? How could middle-class kids take part in such heinous acts like killing their classmates? What has happened to our family values and the global values of our nation? The authors of *Exploring Values Through Literature, Multimedia, and Literacy Events* have decided to jump into this debate to address values education. The contributors have sought to articulate the essential processes and rationales associated with the use of various forms of curriculum inquiry to teach values education.

Exploring Values Through Literature, Multimedia, and Literacy Events reinforces efforts by the Association for Supervision and Curriculum Development (ASCD), recognizing the need to teach global values in schools. In 1993, for example, ASCD devoted the entire issue of *Leadership Education* to moral and character education. The special issue concluded that a teacher cannot establish classroom rules, relate to students, or discuss a piece of literature without communicating values. The ASCD was not alone in its view. In the early 1990s, for example, I can identify several of such outcries demanding that schools take moral education more seriously. Reports such as *Why Johnny Can't Tell Right from Wrong* (Kilpatrick, 1992), *Moral Character and Civic Education in the Elementary School* (Benninga, 1991), and *Educating for Character: How Our Schools Can Teach Respect and Responsibility* (Lickona, 1991) collectively and urgently call for the return of character, moral, and citizenship education to the classroom.

Clearly, few educators worthy of their salt would deny or oppose the recommendations of these persuasive reports. However, what is often contended is how to teach these values and who will teach them. Although there is no agreement as to whether values should be taught as a separate subject or infused throughout the school curriculum, much of the literature read at school is assumed to instill character, moral, and citizenship education. Many students

211

graduate from high school after reading novels, plays, poetry, and other narratives, mistakenly confident that these books have imparted them with knowledge about how the world operates. For example, when I ask my students to tell me what values a particular novel or story imparts to the reader, they often rush to the conclusion or familiar and sometimes predictable refrain: "The moral of the story is...." Familiarity with the story is told by recalling who the protagonist and antagonist are. In other words, such exercise encourages them to look in the story for the good guys and the bad buys, separating good from evil respectively.

Encoded in such a dichotomy is a particular values system that encourages students to learn from stories written in the school canon about honesty, patriotism, individualism, decency, respect, and so forth, in order to abide by a cultural norm and accept a national culture without questioning it (Semali, 2000). In the sense here, a cultural norm is defined simply as the social practices that affirm the central values of social class in the material and symbolic wealth of society (Swanson & Lusted, 1991). Such norms form part of students' cultural knowledge—they know "what to do" with media products they encounter, and the media presentations used are as familiar to these students in their particular culture as the meanings they make.

Traditionally, as lamented by ASCD, values education has not been taken up in schools systematically. Little has been written about global values and how they became constructed, legitimized, and distributed worldwide, especially through the mass media, to manufacture the consent of people within the United States and outside. On the one hand, educators assume that global values education rests within the domain of parents. On the other hand, parents hope that schools somehow will educate and socialize their children with social values, teaching them what values they must embrace in life, what values are of most worth, and how to recognize them in texts they read in the classroom and outside of school. It is neither clear nor easy to determine how best a school curriculum can embrace the priorities or teach the wisdom of the elders of our community, wisdom that our elders have always valued as critical in bringing up children. As years pass, demographic studies tell us that our student population is becoming more diverse and our faculty members are becoming more monocultural (Cotton, 1993). Yet schools and classes of the 21st century bring together students from multiple cultures who have little understanding of each other. And to complicate matters further, you will find that whether in schools that serve populations of over 90% of students of color, or in schools that afford Caucasian students little opportunity to know and work with students of color, studies continue to show that writers of color have gained little prominent entry into secondary school reading lists (Applebome, 1995).

In such difficult circumstances, whose values must the school canon embrace? Which books on character, moral, citizenship, and values education, as demanded by the reports cited previously, must be included in the school canon and reading list? Where does one find and learn values such as dedication to excellence, faith, self-discipline, responsibility, perseverance, compassion, friendship, courage, honesty, loyalty, justice, respect for self and others, the importance of hard work, the importance of education, morals, and the ethical values of "knowing good from evil," and the commitment of service to others as the rent we all pay for living? These and other related questions, while implicitly addressed in part in some of the chapters of this book, become important questions that should be considered seriously in any discussion of values education. Clearly, values demand critical questioning to see if they stand up to reality and make explicit whose interests they legitimize.

With these thoughts in mind, it is appropriate to reflect on the significance of *Exploring Values Through Literature, Multimedia, and Literacy Events* and its contribution to literacy education. The purpose of this Conclusion is to raise some issues suggested by this volume as a whole, and to appraise the current status of values education on the basis of what has been presented here.

Viewed as a whole, the work of these writers demonstrates the extraordinary breadth and vitality of a contemporary enterprise and engagement in an important conversation about values. This book, specifically in the chapters by Baker and Schmidt, affirms that new frameworks of curriculum inquiry have entered the field of literacy education and gained legitimacy. Likewise—in chapters by Laier, Edwards, McMillon, and Turner; Xu; Kurtz; DeCorse; Pailliotet and Shaul; and Leogrande—cultural studies and critical pedagogy have begun to teach us to recognize the ubiquity of media culture in contemporary society, the growing trends toward multicultural education, and the need for media literacy that addresses the issues of multicultural and social difference (Semali & Pailliotet, 1999). The authors, especially Kurtz and Hopkinson, recognize that literature and media representations help construct our images and understanding of the world, and that education must meet the dual challenges of teaching literacy in a multicultural society while sensitizing students and the public to the inequities and injustices of a society based on gender, race, and class inequalities and discrimination. Such critical perspectives can thus help us confront some of the most serious difficulties and problems that face families, students, and teachers as we enter the 21st century.

The works presented in this book are forward looking and hopeful. They represent significant intellectual accomplishment. Clearly, they owe much of their inquiry and analytical frameworks to critical theory, cultural studies, the emerging awareness of critical stance adopted by critical pedagogy, and the perspective that critical pedagogy offers teachers and students to use in analyzing human experiences as lived members of a culture. By "critical," I mean thinking from a position that makes connections between uses of language and unequal relations of power. Like DeCorse, Xu, Pailliotet, Leogrande, and Baker, I believe the usefulness of critical pedagogy as a classroom practice lies in its ability to generate skepticism through its inquiry methods. Once we are skeptical, we can begin to investigate the questions that arise from such skepticism, the unquestioned assumptions and uncertainty of the veracity of events and ideas, or the rendering of a value-laden popular story. Such critical analysis undermines intellectual authority that tacitly dismisses some classroom practices as culturally deficient and accepts others as academically sound. It is through such analytical explorations found in Pailliotet and Shaul's chapter that we discover the origins of the myths we hold so dear to us, the stereotypes we have believed were true for so long, and the culture of denial that has become so much a part of daily routine.

In response to the new times, traditional curriculum can no longer assume that teaching the children of the 21st century will be business as usual, that knowledge is neutral and universal, and that the place called school will provide universal or global values. DeCorse emphasizes this when she assists the reader in understanding child development and relates it to learning theories. With the chipping away of the transmission model of education, the demise of the basal reader, and the ushering in of multicultural literature, teachers are left with few choices as to what to do successfully with the emerging diversity of the student body. They ask, Can schools teach values? Whose values are of most worth? Are there universal or global values that can appeal to all students regardless of race, class, or gender? What frameworks can teachers use to explore global values with students in their language arts classrooms? Xu, for example, in Chapter 3, outlines the ABCs model that aims to link teachers with students and families through classroom inquiry of deeply rooted beliefs and experiences to invoke awareness and appreciation of diversity and multicultural values. In their chapter, Laier, Edwards, McMillon, and Turner explain that providing a school environment that reflects the home cultures of its students by recognizing and appreciating the family values that students bring to the classroom is a direct response to the quest to unravel media and the textual curriculum of global values.

At this stage we can no longer ignore that curriculum, like literacy, is located in a political arena. In fact, ideology is both explicit and implicit in what is taught in the classroom. Eisner (1982) reminds us that what students learn "is not only a function of the formal and explicit content that is selected, it is also a function of the manner in which it is taught" (p. 414). In other words, the characteristics of the tasks and the tacit expectations that are a part of the structured program become themselves a part of the content. By stating this, Eisner implies that students learn from *how* they were taught as well as from *what* they were taught—from process as well as from content. This kind of process-content nexus refers to what some scholars define as the *hidden curriculum.*

According to Giroux and Purpel (1982), a hidden curriculum consists of unstated norms, values, and beliefs that are transmitted to students through the underlying rules that structure the routines and social relationships that make up school and classroom life. It is interesting to note in Leogrande's chapter how computer literacy software, for example, could account for a hidden curriculum in a school. Leogrande discusses how literacy software is rampant with values. Typical evaluations of such software focus almost exclusively on ease of use and curriculum alignment and ignore almost completely the value-laden messages that promote race, class, and gender biases; competition versus cooperation; speed; and extrinsic rewards and penalties for risk taking and mistakes as part of learning. Such hidden curricula must be exposed and constantly critically analyzed.

Any strand of hidden curriculum, whether embedded in computer software or picture books, is bound to have an influence on the academic curriculum being taught, because the norms, values, and beliefs that it represents will shape decisions about *what* will be taught and *how* it will be taught. Thus, according to Giroux and Purpel (1982), what is taught and how it is taught will then, in turn, demonstrate and convey beliefs, and it is in this way that the academic curriculum becomes an important vehicle for transmission of cultures. For example, a school board's decision to include certain books in the curriculum of a high school English class is itself a political act that may well influence the kinds of values students explore or learn in those texts. This is why critical pedagogy inquiry is so important, because all knowing can be understood as an ideological process in the context of hidden curriculum (Simon, 1983). The process of asking certain critical questions about what is taught in schools and how it is taught can help us understand the ideologies that shape particular values in a given curriculum. In essence, Eisner's (1982) comments foreshadow the expansion of curriculum inquiry to include forms of inquiry that stress the significance of creating a new language in curriculum research. Schmidt's and Baker's chapters in particular outline frameworks for what teachers can do in their classrooms to explore global values and can be seen as creating a new language in the curriculum of literacy education.

In the eyes of progressive educators, this work takes a political stance, but values education is in itself a political enterprise. The struggle or competition that rages about which values are of "most worth" becomes a contest to be engaged in by both teachers and students. How might students begin to unravel the cultural pedagogy of the hidden curriculum of values? The contributors to this book understand that students should be given opportunities to explore values through reading, writing, listening, speaking, and viewing. The Introduction emphatically states that the values of compassion, human decency, caring, sharing, cooperation, respect, and responsibility can be explored and taught through literature, multimedia, and literacy events and will facilitate the building of classroom and school communities that connect home and school for literacy learning. Xu, Laier, Edwards, McMillon, Turner, Kurtz, Pailliotet, and Shaul remind us that through literature children can discover and learn about the moral power of stories. The implication to be drawn from this book is that these trends are desirable and are to be welcomed.

Although these scholars are aware of the possibilities of curriculum inquiry in values education, they are not naive about the complexities and limitations of this enormous task. For example, they caution that cultural values do not provide the only truths, and respect for others does not mean agreement. On the basis of this perspective, I might add that we cannot overlook the dynamics of knowledge and power in the construction of global values and how such dynamics might enable or limit a successful exploration of values in a multicultural environment. A fuller explanation of this nexus might be desirable in certain cases.

First, let me begin by suggesting that a conversation about values education cannot take values (defined broadly) for granted as a good thing. From a critical standpoint, we must frequently ask, Whose values are we talking about? How did global values come about? By raising questions such as these, we problematize the suggestion that global or universal values as constructs are immune from critique. But by calling for a diagnostic critique of global values, we necessarily undermine the unintended taken-for-granted position that values are essentially a good thing. A diagnostic critique examines the insidious cultural pedagogy of U.S. media and school culture to diagnose social trends and tendencies and to read through the texts (including literature) the fantasies, fears, hopes, and desires that these texts articulate (Kellner, 1995). Such a tool would promote questioning at different levels.

Also, we must recognize the competing nature of values and the complexity of the task that lies ahead of us: the task of educating youth for a diverse and multicultural society. The chapters by Kurtz and Hopkinson give us ways to do this through the use of literature in the content areas. Davidson tackles this complex issue in his chapter concerning schoolwide values programs when he explains their creation and development. Family and community members, students, teachers, and administrators have each had a hand in the programs that thrive. Furthermore, we are reminded that the production of meaning from all forms of representations—including textbooks, multicultural literature, paintings and art in museums, mass media programs, computer software, and other school-related texts—depends on knowledge that is shared by the community (Hall, 1997). Such knowledge is shaped by the community's belief system, its worldview, its use of language, and by how one is positioned in her or his own culture in relation to other people.

One major aspect of teaching critical pedagogy to youth is to identify where that knowledge comes from and how it is constructed. Pailliotet presents a model, the "5 Ws of media literacy," for teachers and students to become the critical viewers so necessary in a society bombarded by multimedia. One might ask, How did we come to know what we know and value about certain events or groups? The common belief is that an individual's sense of self is organized according to various categories or identities such as gender, race, class, age, sexual orientation, and so on, as well as those categories encompassing different "interest groups" that include religion or political affiliation. As Leogrande explains in her chapter, the characteristics and values associated with these categories include the way we look, how we behave, the lifestyle we adopt, and even the way we buy goods and services.

As individuals or groups of people, we come to recognize how certain characteristics are considered more or less socially appropriate or acceptable. Ideas about what people are like, and how they are meant to be understood, already prevail in our culture. Leogrande, Laier, Edwards, McMillon, Turner, Pailliotet, Xu, Hopkinson, Kurtz, and Shaul explain that these ideas are embedded in mass media representations, in the textbooks our children read in schools, in myths and folklore found in the native countries from where we came or descended, from the religion we hold dear in our hearts, or from traditions we have come to love, learn, and practice. As Pailliotet and Shaul make clear, the only reason that we come to know these ideas about religion, myths, or traditions is because they are told and retold to us through media presentations, reproduced in artistic symbols and museum exhibitions, and more often, through narrative stories. For example, as Leogrande implies, media executives are in the business of reproducing a social hierarchy through such mythical stories distributed by programs, from news, soaps, and sitcoms to MTV and music. These stories allow a certain gender, race, or class to dominate or be dominated by another that claims superiority. The ideas represented in the texts children read or view give meaning to a sense of self and allow them to position themselves in relation to others. But the way representations of race, gender, class, or age are constructed is as important as the ideas and meaning they project, because they offer positions to children, through which they recognize images as similar or different from themselves and those around them. Although images and meanings change over time, we continually define ourselves in changing relations to these images and meanings. Such positioning gives us the context of meanings and strength to make the claim of who we are, what we value, or what we stand for (see Semali, 2000, Chapter 6).

Second, the important lesson to be derived from critical pedagogy is that assumptions, "common knowledge," common sense, "general" knowledge, widespread beliefs, and popular attitudes are all part of the context of meanings within which cultural norms or values are enhanced and circulated. Often overlooked in this critical perspective, however, is the fact that people construct the context of meanings out of their experiences within specific social contexts of race, gender, and class. Rather than one abstract psychological process, contexts of meanings are historically defined social practices that are subject to political, academic, and cultural hierarchies. This context and our individual ranges of knowledge, values, and attitudes are governed in turn by a system of power that offers varied "legitimacy" to these meanings, ideas, and conventions. When Leogrande and Pailliotet analyze this hierarchy, it is clear that some values or meanings come to be dominant, or acquire currency more than others do.

It is significant to note that, from this perspective, there are no absolute values of "how things are," but only many competing versions, some of which are more highly regarded in society than others and hence are circulated more widely. Ultimately, the relationship between media institutions and media audiences, between teachers and students, and between parents and children is an unequal yet contested one. Davidson's chapter on schoolwide programs addresses this relationship and sees that this inequality is not merely a question of access (e.g., Who is allowed to speak?) but, more crucially, one of language (e.g., How are they allowed to speak?). Insofar as the ability to control language—and thereby to define the terms in which the world may be talked about and represented—can be seen to reside with certain powerful (or dominant) groups in mainstream society, language may itself inevitably function to maintain existing inequalities. Therefore, in looking at multimedia texts (from literature to media to museum artifacts to computer software) as representations of people, teachers must examine global values as versions of values that have currency, the elements that are repeated across them, and the relation to common-sense definitions individuals acquire as participants of a global culture. For example, teachers must investigate the ways in which the language of the mass media or that of multicultural texts, as explained in this book, is socially and historically produced. They must examine its production, construction, and the meaning-making processes by which textual imagery and popular representation of people help shape our personal, social, and political worlds. Furthermore, the complex and contested ways in which the language of media embodies broader relationships of power, and the ways in which language users are themselves inevitably implicated in these relationships, need to be addressed carefully. Pailliotet's chapter about critical media literacy offers ways to explore some of these essential questions.

By engaging a critical examination of global values, the chapters written by Kurtz, Hopkinson, Pailliotet, and Shaul help teachers and students begin to read U.S. cultural pedagogy critically from the way values have been encoded in the daily narratives of media texts, such as television programs, newspapers, film, consumer advertising, and the school literature canon. The critical way of reading U.S. cultural pedagogy goes counter to the monoculture of objectivity often found in textbooks in today's classrooms. Schmidt clearly demonstrates in her research concerning students studying second-grade science that intellectual growth demands questions, not answers. Students will not learn to think if they approach their education as a matter of imitation or the mechanical application of rules. In this context, therefore, curriculum inquiry acquires another level of critique of the school canon that includes an analysis of the way institutions of mass culture construct, legitimize, and maintain values and ideologies in U.S. society.

Third, pedagogy has the power to oppress. It is necessary to caution here that a conversation about global values cannot assume that the text alone can teach values. Teachers and their teaching methods play a big role in how values are interpreted, reinforced, and circulated. According to Bourdieu and Passeron (1990), pedagogy becomes a form of symbolic violence in which education takes the form of imposition and inculcation, and the teacher's power is the precondition for the establishment of pedagogic communication. The contributors to this book, especially DeCorse, Schmidt, and Baker, object to this form of symbolic violence, and have worked hard to develop alternative stances and pedagogies that guide rather than control the child in his or her learning.

Bernstein (1990) would have us pay attention to visible and invisible pedagogies of values. On the one hand, "visible" pedagogies are those in which the teacher's teaching is explicit and aimed at knowledge transmission. "Invisible" pedagogies, on the other hand, are those that require the teacher to facilitate and guide the children in such a way that they appear to be learning about value without direct instruction. Cherland (1994) suggests, for example, that child-centered classrooms and whole language programs would fall into the category of invisible pedagogy, as would process-writing classrooms and readers' workshops that also involve invisible pedagogies in which the child appears to lead the way, while in fact he or she is being supported and guided by an attentive teacher. Values education as explained in the chapters of this book could be termed invisible pedagogies. Hopkinson, Kurtz, Pailliotet, and Shaul introduce historical fictional literature and picture books, including folklore, mythologies, heroes, and heroines as pedagogical sites to learn values education. Although the invisible pedagogies found in *Clara and the Freedom Quilt*, *Birdie's Lighthouse*, and *Maria's Comet* have many benefits for the individual child—including both opportunities for the child to collaborate with others in constructing knowledge and opportunities for the child to exercise agency—they also present serious problems. Their personal and private focus tends to support cultural values of individualism and personalism, and ignores the influence of the larger cultural context in people's lives (Cherland, 1994). In other words, these values are presented as though they were universal and therefore immune to critique. Such a view does not problematize the cultural context in which the cultural values of individualism and personalism are constructed, nor does it question the interests such a view might legitimate.

Perhaps what needs to be modeled for children is a critical stance that grows out of the teacher's awareness of the influence of both language and culture on our lives. This critical stance ought then to inform the study of multimedia and multicultural literature. Pailliotet and Leogrande demonstrate just how to do this with our students. The foundation of this critical stance is the teacher's realization that texts are constructed in ways that represent certain interests, and that readers are positioned, by cultural discourses of race, class, and gender, to read and respond in certain ways. Purely personal responses do not exist. Initial readings are likely to be cultural readings rather than personal, individual readings. This is because the meanings that readers assign to the texts have already been shaped for them by certain discourses before they have even begun to read (O'Neill, 1993). Children need to understand this fact in order to gain some measure of influence over their own lives. Readers are positioned to read or view a text in a certain way, and this process is neither a natural nor a neutral one. But we can at least teach our students to think critically about these cultural readings—to recognize them and analyze them, and not to pretend that they do not exist. Pailliotet and Shaul explain that teachers can also show students how the same work of literature can be interpreted in several different ways, ways that are positioned or created by particular sets of values and beliefs.

By contrast, prevalent pedagogies of knowledge transmission serve to discourage children from independent critical thought. When teachers approach the study of literature as if its first purpose were the acquisition of facts "about the text," and as if knowledge of the text were something that comes from experts outside the classroom, children end up believing that they should read only in a passive way, and that they should look to others for the meaning of what they are reading. When teachers do not value the children's own ideas, when they do not provide time for discussion, when they keep the children dependent on themselves (the teachers) for the right answers, they end up teaching them that the "learning" process amounts to the obedient absorption of information and that critical inquiry is something irrelevant (Cherland, 1994). Schmidt and Baker illustrate this critical inquiry process in their chapters. In summary, the contributions in this volume illustrate in many ways the contested nature of values education and why I insist on taking a critical stance to explore global values.

Fourth, values cannot be understood outside the realm of culture. Normative values are perpetuated by dominant culture. The contributors of this volume propose a variety of ways to relate theories of new literacy and pedagogy to practice, to actual hands-on classroom situations. They show how the concepts and methods of values education can be deployed in a variety of situations and contexts, ranging from elementary school through the higher grades. In developing values pedagogy to engage the diversity and variety of new forms of media in our always-evolving media culture, it is important to note that there is no one pedagogy that can be employed as a master method that will work in all contexts and situations. The contributors have developed frameworks that are experimental and open ended, subject to revision and development, as they are put to the test in the classroom and concrete pedagogical situations.

Fifth, it seems to me that there must be other kinds of pedagogy that implicitly teach values that teachers would like to impart. Cherland (1994), for example, suggests that it has been possible for some teachers to move from a study of "language as an individual skill and literacy as a remedial subject to language as an intersubjective experience and literacy as an investigatory subject that one learns actively and in community with others" (p. 209). Consider, for example, Hopkinson's chapter, in which the pedagogy supports both literature-response groups and literature-study groups. Literature-response groups allow children the responsibility for expressing their own individual views concerning a book that all the children in the group have read. Literature-study groups require that the children work collaboratively toward "constructing" meaning from the text that (again) they have all read, exploring possible interpretations and analyzing the author's craft (Edelsky, 1988; Peterson & Eeds, 1990). The form of pedagogy expressed in these groups assumes that knowledge is something that must be created with other people, that people should be active participants in their own education, that they learn only by thinking deeply, and that everyone can contribute something of value (Cherland, 1994). Cherland suggests the problem with this pedagogy is both that the individual responses that the children bring to the groups have already been constructed through various cultural discourses, and that the ways of analyzing text that have already been taught to the children have promoted the veneration of literature and discouraged any critical questions or challenges. In Schmidt's chapter, for example, the children still had to take a "recall test" as part of culminating inquiry.

Under these circumstances, what then must teachers do? As admitted by Cherland, there are dilemmas and contradictions that are made manifest in the transmission model of teaching that must be addressed by the teacher who takes a critical stance in his or her reflective teaching practice. Perhaps teachers can help students realize that the questions in the "recall test" were but one among many ways of assessing their mastery of the knowledge. Although some educators prefer this method of evaluation because it is easier and time-saving, they need to be aware that such transmission and rote memorization models may not provide the best opportunity for students to assume agency or engage in knowledge production. Practices that consider the acquisition of knowledge by asking critical questions about whose knowledge it is and whose interest it serves may provide students with long-lasting recall and a lifelong learning effect.

Cherland supports collaborative pedagogies. However, her caution is in order. Although collaborative pedagogies are less damaging to children than pedagogies of knowledge transmission, such pedagogies do not help children understand the wide variety of reading positions that are available to them, or foster any understanding of the various cultural discourses that produce both a body of literature and aesthetic responses to the work created. Critical pedagogy can do more to foster both an aptitude for critical thought and the development of egalitarian values. Requiring that children think critically in school would be a beginning. Thus, I concur with Cherland. I would like to see a literacy curriculum that highlights the relationship between language and power by balancing "the role of language in perpetuating or constituting systems of domination" at the center of our inquiry (Edelsky, 1988). This kind of curriculum would make it more difficult for schools to promote, and for teachers to participate in, the reproduction of social inequality. I might also add that this curriculum might alleviate some of the feelings of alienation and boredom that have plagued traditional curricula. A curriculum that highlights the relationship between language and power also exposes pockets of resistance embedded in rules, conservative mandates, and transmission methods that teachers encounter daily in their teaching practice.

Finally, in conclusion, because the studies in *Exploring Values Through Literature, Multimedia, and Literacy Events* are provisional accounts from the field, I would urge the readers of this book to apply them in a variety of actual teaching situations, and report on their successes and limitations. I encourage the reader to try out the models and adopt the concept of diagnostic critique as envisaged in critical pedagogy when engaging students in the conversation of global values. It is in such diagnostic critique that I believe educators can foster a critical mindset in our students. This means cultivating the ability to ask difficult questions and the self-confidence to reject easy answers: the two fundamental goals of critical inquiry and what it takes to be a literate person.

References

Applebome, P. (1995, March 1). Comparative literature: Times may change but the writers students read stay much the same. *The New York Times*, p. B8.

Association for Supervision and Curriculum Development. (1993). *Educational Leadership, 51*(3).

Benninga, J.S. (1991). *Moral character and civic education in the elementary school*. New York: Teachers College Press.

Bernstein, B. (1990). *Structuring of pedagogic discourse: Class, codes, and control*. London: Routledge.

Bourdieu, P., & Passeron, J. (1990). *Reproduction in education, society and culture*. London: Routledge.

Cherland, M. (1994). *Private practices: Girls reading fiction and constructing identity*. London: Taylor Francis.

Cotton, K. (1993). Fostering intercultural harmony in schools: Research finding [Online]. Topical Synthesis #7 in the School Improvement Research Series. Cited in M. Dilg, *Race and culture in the classroom: Teaching and learning through multicultural education*. New York: Teachers College Press.

Edelsky, C. (1988). Living in the author's world: Analyzing the author's craft. *The California Reader, 21*, 14–17.

Eisner, E. (1982). *Cognition and curriculum: A basis for deciding what to teach*. New York: Longman.

Giroux, H., & Purpel, D. (Eds.). (1982). *The hidden curriculum and moral education: Illusion or insight*. Berkeley, CA: McCutchan.

Hall, S. (1997). *Representation: Cultural representations and signifying practices*. London: The Open University.

Kellner, D. (1995). *Media culture: Cultural studies, identity and politics between the modern and the postmodern*. New York: Routledge.

Kilpatrick, W. (1992). *Why Johnny can't tell right from wrong: Moral illiteracy and the case for character education*. New York: Simon & Schuster.

Lickona, T. (1991). *Educating for character: How our schools can teach respect and responsibility*. New York: Bantam.

O'Neill, M. (1993). Teaching literature as cultural criticism. *English Quarterly, 25*(1), 19–25.

Peterson, R., & Eeds, M. (1990). *Grand conversations: Literature groups in action*. New York: Scholastic.

Semali, L.M. (2000). *Literacy in multimedia America: Integrating media education across the curriculum*. New York: Falmer Press.

Semali, L.M., & Pailliotet, A.W. (1999). Introduction: What is intermediality and why study it in U.S. classrooms? In L.M. Semali & A.W. Pailliotet (Eds.), *Intermediality: The teachers' handbook of critical media literacy*. Boulder, CO: Westview.

Simon, R. (1983). But who will you do it? Counter-hegemonic possibilities for work education. *Journal of Education, 165*(3), 235–256.

Swanson, G., & Lusted, D. (1991). *Representation: The media studies book*. New York: Routledge.

Author Index

Page numbers followed by *f* indicate figures.

O

OBERG, M., 66
O'BRIEN, P., 191
OGLE, D.M., 61, 128
OLLILA, L., 79
O'NEILL, M., 220
ORTONY, A., 125

P

PAILLIOTET, A.W., 4, 22, 25–26, 29, 34f, 45, 77, 79–80, 198, 213
PALMER, P., 3
PASSERON, J., 219
PBS ADULT LEARNING SERVICE, 2
PEARSON, P.D., 50, 125
PETERSON, R., 221
PIAGET, J., 11–12, 125, 140
PIKE, K., 29
PLATO, 1
PLEASANTS, H.M., 48, 64
PRESSLEY, M., 61, 68
PURPEL, D., 215

Q–R

QUESADA, A.P., 45
RAPHAEL, T.E., 72, 125
REILLY, S., 22
REINKING, D., 29
ROBINSON, M., 28
RODENBERG, R.K., 4, 22, 26, 45, 77, 80
ROSEN, E.Y., 45
ROSENBLATT, L., 25
ROUTMAN, R., 67, 70, 72
RUMELHART, D., 125
RYAN, A., 125
RYAN, K., 155, 156f–157f

S

SCHAPS, E., 147
SCHMIDT, P.R., 3–4, 27, 48–49, 125, 128
SCHWARTZ, P., 4
SELMAN, R.L., 15
SEMALI, L.M., 4, 22, 29, 45, 77, 79, 212–213
SHADE, B.J., 66
SHAUL, M., 194
SHIN, P., 15
SHOLLE, D., 22
SIMON, R., 22, 215
SIMON, S., 3
SINGER, L.A., 78
SLAVIN, R.E., 141
SOLOMON, D., 4, 147
SPINDLER, G., 49
SPINDLER, L., 49
SPRADLEY, J., 49
STEINBERG, S.R., 26, 78
STIPEK, D.J., 17
SWANSON, G., 212

T

TAYLOR, L.S., 78
TERRELL, K., 163
THOMAN, E., 24, 26, 45
TOBIN, J., 104
TYNER, K.R., 26, 34f

V

VALENZA, J.K., 79
VALMONT, W.J., 45
VYGOTSKY, L.S., 12, 126, 140

W

WASHINGTON STATE COMMISSION ON STUDENT LEARNING, 30–31

Children's Literature Author Index

Page numbers followed by *f* indicate figures.

GRAHAM, G.B., 205
GRANOWSKY, A., 205
GREAVES, M., 205
GREENFIELD, E., 73f

H

HADDIX, M.P., 193, 201
HAMANAKA, S., 152f, 175, 183
HAN, S.C., 171, 183
HAVILL, J., 73f
HEARNE, B., 110
HENKES, K., 57f
HICKOX, R., 205
HOFFMAN, M., 58f
HOOKS, W., 205
HOPKINSON, D., 102–107
HORENSTEIN, H., 174, 183
HUCK, C., 205
HUDSON, C.W., 58f

I–J

ISADORA, R., 174, 183
JACKSON, E., 205
JAFFE, N., 171, 183, 205
JAMES, J.A., 177, 183
JENNESS, A., 152f
JOHNSTON, T., 203
JOOSSE, B.M., 73f
JOSEPH, L., 110

K

KELSEY, A.G., 171, 183
KETTEMAN, H., 203
KLAUSE, A.C., 207
KNUTSON, B., 171, 183
KRAUS, R., 58f
KRUMGOLD, J., 88
KURTZ, J., 170–174, 176, 178–179, 184

L

LANKFORD, M.D., 176, 184
LEE, M., 175, 184
LEE, T.C., 205
L'ENGLE, M., 207
LEVINE, G.C., 193, 203
LEWIN, T., 175, 185
LEWIS, C.S., 207
LOUIE, A., 205
LOWRY, L., 152f

M

MACLACHLAN, P., 179, 185
MADRIGAL, A.H., 174, 185
MARTIN, B., JR., 73f
MARTIN, J.B., 110
MARTIN, R., 205
MAYER, M., 205
MCBRIER, P., 170–171, 185
MCDERMOTT, G., 172, 185
MCGILL, A., 110
MCGIRR, N., 174, 182
MCKINLEY, R., 207
MEDDAUGH, S., 196, 203
MELMED, L.K., 205
MERRILL, J., 179, 185
MEYERS, B., 205
MILLER, W., 110
MINTERS, F., 205
MOCHIZUKI, K., 177–178, 185
MOLLEL, T.M., 173–174, 185–186
MORA, P., 110
MORIN, P., 174, 186
MUNSCH, R.N., 193, 203
MUSGROVE, M.W., 177, 186

N

NATIONAL ASSOCIATION FOR THE EDUCATION OF YOUNG CHILDREN, 77, 79

NESBIT, E., 208
NIX, G., 208
NYE, N.S., 174, 186

O

OLALEYE, I., 174, 186
ONYEFULU, I., 174, 177, 186
ONYEFULU, O., 173, 186
OSOFSKY, A., 68

P

PAXTON, T., 186
PERLMAN, J., 204
PERRAULT, C., 205
PHELPS, E.J., 205
PHUMLA, 205
PINKNEY, A.D., 110
POLACCO, P., 73f, 171–172, 186
POLLOCK, P., 205
PULLMAN, P., 208

Q–R

QUINDLEN, A., 208
RINGGOLD, F., 73f
RODDY, P., 176, 186
ROSEN, M., 171, 187
ROWLING, J.K., 208
RYLANT, C., 73f

S

SANDERSON, R., 204
SAN SOUCI, R.D., 173, 187, 205

SAY, A., 178, 180, 187
SCHROEDER, A., 110, 205
SCIESZKA, J., 193, 196
SCOTT, A.H., 73f
SHORTO, R., 205
SIERRA, J., 205
SINGER, M., 178, 187
SIS, P., 111
SMITH, C.L., 174, 187
STANLEY, D., 111, 178, 187
STEPTOE, J., 73f, 173, 187, 193, 204
STRETE, C.K., 178, 187
STUVE-BODEEN, S., 174, 187

W

WALSH, E.S., 58f
WEGMAN, W., 205
WELLER, F., 111
WELLS, R., 152f
WILHELM, H., 58f
WILLIAMS, K.L., 174, 188
WILLIAMS, S.A., 178, 188
WILLIAMS, V.B., 71–72, 73f
WINTER, J., 111, 178, 188
WREDE, P.C., 204

Y–Z

YEP, L., 88
YOLEN, J., 73f, 171, 188
ZIPES, J., 206

Subject Index

Page numbers followed by *f* indicate figures.

A

B

C

CARING: beyond classroom, 161–163; ethics of, 15

CENTER FOR MEDIA LITERACY, 43

CHARACTER EDUCATION: comprehensive, 145–146, 149f; curricula for, 150–156; resurgence of interest in, 145–147. *See also* values education

CHILD DEVELOPMENT: and moral reasoning, 10–12

CHILDS, ELEANOR, 150

CHOICES: in classroom practice, 118–121

CINDERELLA STORIES, 192–193, 201–206; rationale for teaching with, 193–194

CITIZENS FOR MEDIA LITERACY, 43

CLASSROOM PRACTICES: ABCs Model in, 61–62; culturally responsive, 51; daily schedule for, 114f–115f; in sciences, 125–142; technology and, 112–124

COGNITIVE THEORIES: and moral reasoning, 10–12

COLLABORATION: on books of magical tales, 200; in classroom practice, 117–118; versus privacy, 123. *See also* interactions

COLLABORATIVE PEDAGOGIES, 222–223

COMMERCIALS: critical reading of values in, 197–198

COMMUNICATIONS: media literacy learning through, 31

COMMUNITY: and comprehensive character education, 157–161; in media, 36–37; school, 18

COMMUNITY SHARE: in Book Club, 74

COMPETITION: in software, 79, 92–93

CONCEPT MAP, 69, 70f, 127f

CONCRETE OPERATIONS STAGE, 11

CONFLICTING INFORMATION: in technology, 122–123

CONSTRUCTIVISM, 11, 221–222

CONTENT AREA CONNECTIONS, 101–142

CONVENTIONAL MORALITY, 14

COOPERATION: multicultural literature on, 170–171; in software, 92–93

COURAGE: multicultural literature on, 73f

CRITICAL MEDIA LITERACY, 197–198; definition of, 21–23

CRITICAL PEDAGOGY, 214–219, 222

CRITICAL QUESTIONING FRAMEWORKS, 33, 34f

CRITICS: students as, 39, 199

CROSS-CULTURAL ANALYSIS, 51, 53–55, 54f

CULTURAL DIFFERENCES: analysis of, 51

CULTURAL HISTORY: on magical tales, 199

CULTURAL NORMS, 212

CULTURALLY RESPONSIVE INSTRUCTION, 48–63

CULTURALLY SPECIFIC VALUES, 66

CULTURE: definition of, 66; and values, 221

CURRICULA: for character education, 150–156, 151*f*; hidden, 215; for values education, 211–224

CURRICULUM STANDARDS: for media literacy, 29–31

D

DAY, MARGE, 152

DEAR ABBY LETTERS, 199

DECISION MAKING: in magical tales, 195–196

DEEP VIEWING, 79–81; coding categories for, 80*f*, 83*f*

DEMONSTRATION: in exploring values, 68–70; in language learning, 67

DIGITAL LITERACY, 77

DIVERSITY: appreciation of, multicultural literature on, 175–176

DRAMATIC READING, 154*f*, 199

E

EDUCATIONAL VIDEO CENTER, 43

EMOTIONAL DISABILITIES, STUDENTS WITH: inquiry learning and, 129–132

ENDERS ROAD ELEMENTARY SCHOOL, 153, 159

ETHICS OF CARE, 15

EXPLORING VALUES, 4, 18*f*; activities for, 194–200; curricula for, 211–224; historical fiction and, 102–111; history of, 146–147; magical tales and, 189–209; media literacy and, 32–40; multicultural literature and, 66, 168–188; schoolwide approach to, 144–166

F

FABLES: in assessment of moral development, 13*f*

FAIRNESS: multicultural literature on, 171

FAIRY TALES, 189–209; rationale for teaching with, 193–194

FAMILY STORIES: and home-school connections, 64–75

FAMILY VALUES: concept map, 69, 70*f*; lesson framework for, 67–74; in literature, clues to, 68*f*; multicultural literature on, 66, 73*f*

FANTASY: in software, 84–86; values in, 189–209

FEEDBACK: in software, 91–92

FOCUS: inquiry learning and, 130, 132, 134–135, 137, 139

FOLKTALES, 169–179

FORMAL OPERATIONS STAGE, 11

FREYTAG'S TRIANGLE, 195–196

G

GENRES: changing, 198
GIRAFFE PROJECT, 161–162
GIRLS: software for, 95–98
GLOBAL CONNECTIONS, 167–224
GLOBAL LEARNING, 4
GRAHAM, JOHN, 161
GROUP BOOKS, 200
GROUP STORIES, 198
GUEST SPEAKERS: literary, 154f

H

HEARTWOOD ETHICS CURRICULUM, 150–151, 151f
HELPING: multicultural literature on, 73f
HERACLES, 189–190
HEROES/HEROINES: celebration of, 200; and cultural values, 189–190; identification of, 197; letters to, 196; in media, 38–39
HIDDEN CURRICULUM, 215
HISTORICAL FICTION, 102–111
HOME-SCHOOL CONNECTIONS, 47–100; literacy software and, 76–100; multicultural literature and, 64–75
HOSPITALITY: multicultural literature on, 176–177

I

IMAGINATION: multicultural literature on, 73f
INACCURACIES: in technology, 122–123
INFORMATION: conflicting, in technology, 122–123; gained and shared, inquiry learning and, 131–133, 135–136, 138–140; verification of, 123
INQUIRY: in classroom practice, 117–121; pedagogy of, 24; process of, 116f; in sciences, 125–142
INQUIRY LEARNING, 125–140
INTELLIGENCE: modes of, 16–17; in software, 90
INTERACTIONS: inquiry learning and, 130–134, 136–139. *See also* collaboration
INTERMEDIALITY, 77–78; definition of, 77
INTERNATIONAL VISUAL LITERACY ASSOCIATION, 43
INVISIBLE PEDAGOGIES, 219–220

J–K

JOURNAL ACTIVITIES, 198

KINDNESS: multicultural literature on, 171–172
KNOWLEDGE TRANSMISSION: pedagogies of, 221
K-W-L-Q PROCESS, 128, 128*f*

L

LANGUAGE LEARNING: developmental model of, 67
LANSING MIDDLE SCHOOL: values brainstorming, 147–148, 148*f*
LEARNING: Bloom's taxonomy of, 16, 17*f*
LEARNING DISABILITIES, STUDENTS WITH: inquiry learning and, 132–140
LE MOYNE COLLEGE, 154
LETTERS: advice, on magical tales, 199; to heroes/heroines, 196; to Super-Citizen, 153
LISY-MACON, LYNN, 152
LITERACY: changing nature of, 29
LITERACY LEARNING: family connections and, 158; inquiry learning and, 125–126; media literacy and, 24–26; in sciences, 125–142; technology and, 112–124; values in, teacher assistants and, 48–63
LITERATURE: promotion of, 154*f*. *See also* exploring values; multicultural literature
LOVE: multicultural literature on, 73*f*

M

MAGIC: and values, 192
MAGICAL TALES, 189–209; rationale for teaching with, 193–194
MASS MEDIA: influence of, 27–29; versus print texts, 195
McCULLOUGH, MARGIE, 162
MEANING: making, 10–19
MEDIA: increasing personal awareness of, 38; and moral development, 158–160; rewriting, 40. *See also* mass media; multimedia
MEDIA AUTOBIOGRAPHIES, 37–38
MEDIA EDUCATION FOUNDATION, 43
THE MEDIA FOUNDATION, 44
MEDIA LITERACY, 20–46, 77–78; curriculum standards for, 29–31; definition of, 20–21; instructors in, 23–24; with magical tales, 199–200; principles of, 24–25; versus print literacy, 25–26; resources on, 40, 42–46; with software, 76–100; timing of instruction in, 31–32
MEDIA WORKSHOP NEW YORK, 44
MEDLOCK, ANN, 161
MONOMYTH, 191–192
MORAL CULTURE: in schools, 150–156

MORAL DEVELOPMENT: assessment of, 13*f*–14*f*; family connections and, 158; teachers and, 17–18, 153–154, 220

MORAL DILEMMAS: in assessment of moral development, 14*f*; classroom applications of, 15*f*

MORAL REASONING: assessment of, 13*f*–14*f*; cognitive theories and, 10–12; Gilligan's model of, 15; Kohlberg's model of, 13–15; Piaget's model of, 11–12; social development theories and, 12–15

MOVIE REVIEWS, 199

MULTICULTURAL LITERATURE, 168–188; Cinderella stories in, 194–195; criteria for, 65; on family values, 73*f*; and home-school connections, 64–75; lesson framework for, 67–74; reasons for using, 64–65

MULTICULTURAL UNIT: precautions with, 179–180

MULTICULTURAL VALUES, 48–63; recommendations for promotion of, 60–62

MULTIMEDIA: precautions with, 121–122; promotion of, 154*f*

MUSIC: and magical tales, 200

N

NATIONAL TELEMEDIA COUNCIL, 44

NATIONAL VALUES, 66

NATURE: multicultural literature on, 73*f*

NEWS MEDIA: analysis of, 35–36, 36*f*

NEWSPAPER ASSOCIATION OF AMERICA NEWSPAPERS IN EDUCATION PROGRAM, 44

NEWSPAPERS: and character education, 160

NEW YORK STATE SYSTEMIC INITIATIVE PROGRAM, 126

NO PUT DOWNS PROJECT, 159

O

OBJECTIVISM, 3

OBSERVATION: in exploring values, 68–70; in language learning, 67

ODYSSEUS, 190

ORAL HISTORY: on magical tales, 199

P

PARENTS: and comprehensive character education, 157–161; and promotion of literature, 154*f*; and software evaluation, 93–98

PARTICIPATION: in exploring values, 70–72; in language learning, 67

PATIENCE: multicultural literature on, 172–173

PEDAGOGY(IES), 219–223; critical, 214–219, 222; of inquiry, 24

PERFORMANCE: in exploring values, 74; in language learning, 67

PLUS INSTITUTE, 160–161
POLITICS: and values, 214–216
POPULARITY: in software, 90
PORTISS, THOMASINA, 157
POSTCONVENTIONAL MORALITY, 14–15
PRACTICE: in exploring values, 72–74; in language learning, 67
PRECAUTIONS: with Africa unit, 179; with literacy software, 76–100; with
    multicultural unit, 179–180; with technology, 121–123
PRECONVENTIONAL MORALITY, 14
PREOPERATIONS STAGE, 11
PRIVACY: in classroom practice, technology and, 123
PUPPET SHOW, 199

R

READ-ALOUDS, 196
READING: in Book Club, 72; media literacy learning through, 29
REPRESENTATION: in media, 35
RESILIENCY/RESOURCEFULNESS: multicultural literature on, 177–179
RESPECT: in classroom practice, 117–118; multicultural literature on,
    173–175; for nature, multicultural literature on, 73f; promotion of, 148,
    149f
RESPECT PROGRAM, 155
RESPONSIBILITY: in classroom practice, 118–121; promotion of, 148, 149f
REWRITING: fairy tales, 196; media, 40
ROCK MUSIC: and magical tales, 200
ROLE-PLAYING: in exploring values, 72–74; in language learning, 67

S

SCAVENGER HUNT: supermarket/toy aisle, 38
SCHEDULE: classroom, 114f–115f
SCHEMA, 11
SCHOOL VIOLENCE, 211
SCHOOLWIDE CONNECTIONS, 143–166; strategies for, 150–163
SCIENCE, 125–142
SELF-ESTEEM: children's literature on, 57f–58f; lesson plan for, 55–57, 56f
SENSORIMOTOR STAGE, 11
SEX EDUCATION: character-based, 155–156, 156f–157f
SEXISM: in software, 79, 86–89, 95–98
SHARING: multicultural literature on, 73f
SIGHT POEMS, 197

SOCIAL ACTION: in media, 40
SOCIAL DEVELOPMENT: and moral reasoning, 12–15
SOCIAL SKILLS: in software, 92–93
SOFTWARE: bias in, 78–79; evaluation of, 78, 94–95, 95f; for girls, 95–98; selection for evaluation, 81; titles reviewed, 81f–82f; values in, 76–100
SPEED: in software, 85, 90–91
SPONGES, 198–199
SPORTS FIGURES: and character education, 160–161
STANDING TALL PROJECT, 161
STEREOTYPES: in media, 35; in software, 85–89
STUDENT RESPONSE, 10–19; to inquiry learning, 128–140
STUDENTS: as critics, 39, 199; and media, 20–46
STUDENT-TEACHER CONNECTIONS, 9–46
SUBSTANCE ABUSE: in media, 37
SUMMER READING, 154f
SUPER-CITIZEN: letters to, 153
SUPERKIDS, 78
SUSTAINED SILENT READING (SSR): schoolwide, 155

T

TABLE TALK: and moral development, 158
TEACHER ASSISTANTS: and values in literacy instruction, 48–63
TEACHERS: of media literacy, 23–24; role in moral development, 17–18, 153–154, 220; and software evaluation, 93–98
TECHNOLOGY: bias in, 78–79; challenges with, 121–123; in education, 77–79; typical classroom uses of, 113f; and values in classroom practice, 112–124
TELEVISION: and moral development, 158–160
TENNESSEAN, 160
THINK-ALOUD FORMAT, 68, 196
TOBACCO: in media, 37
TOLERANCE: children's literature on, 152f
TRADITIONAL LITERATURE, 169–179

V

VALUES: assigning, 10–19; in classroom practice, technology and, 112–124; critique of, 216–219; culturally specific, 66; culture and, 221; in Heartwood curriculum, 150; heroes/heroines and, 189–190; national, 66; selection of, 147–150, 213; in software, 76–100. *See also* exploring values
VALUES CLARIFICATION, 3

VALUES EDUCATION, 211–224; dichotomy in, 212; history of, 2–3; media literacy and, 20–46; questions on, 1; self-examination for, 18f; teacher assistants and, 48–63; timing of, 31–32; web sites for, 19
VENN DIAGRAM, 195
VERMONT HISTORICAL SOCIETY: lesson plan, 105–106
VIOLENCE: in media, 39–40; in software, 79, 92–93
VISUAL IMAGES: analysis of, 32–33, 197

W

WEB SITES: on historical fiction, 108–110; on media literacy, 33, 35, 42–43; on software evaluation, 78; on values education, 19
WELLWOOD MIDDLE SCHOOL, 155
WEST POINT ELEMENTARY SCHOOL, 162–163
WRITING: in Book Club, 73; media literacy learning through, 29